Twelve Miles
from a Lemon

A sketch of Sydney Smith by Sir Edwin Landseer

Twelve Miles from a Lemon

Selected Writings of Sydney Smith

Compiled by

Norman Taylor and Alan Hankinson

The Lutterworth Press

Cambridge

For Ruth and Joan

The Lutterworth Press
P.O. Box 60
Cambridge
CB1 2NT

British Library Cataloguing in Publication Data:
A catalogue record is available from the British Library.

ISBN 0 7188 2951 4

First Published in 1996 by The Lutterworth Press

Printed in Great Britain by Galliard (Printers) Ltd, Great Yarmouth

Contents

Acknowledgements

We are deeply indebted to Alan Bell, Librarian of the London Library and biographer of Sydney, who generously placed at our disposal typescripts of previously unpublished letters.

Our thanks, too, go to Captain and Mrs Read of the Old Rectory, Combe Florey, and to Mrs Wormald of the Old Rectory, Thornton-le-Clay, who kindly opened Sydney's homes to us; to all who provided the illustrations – Joan Alexander, the Syndics of Cambridge and Edinburgh University Libraries, the National Portrait Gallery and the British Museum; and to Mrs Spedding of Mirehouse, near Keswick, for access to the library there; and the Revd P. R. Smythe of Horningsea for the gift of the 1869 edition of Sydney's works.

Illustrations

I

Introduction

'Sydney Smith? And who was he?' is the more than likely response when Sydney's name is mentioned. Why should it be otherwise? The history books pass him by; and, if they do refer to a Sydney Smith, it is the Admiral, knighted hero of the siege of Acre during the Napoleonic Wars. By chance, in April 1825 the clergyman and the naval officer met in Paris, where the Admiral was living in retirement and Sydney a tourist. Their simultaneous presence confused Parisian society, and our Sydney invited further confusion in a letter to the Admiral from the Hotel Virginie.

> Dear Sr:
>
> I am much obligd by your kind offer of taking me to the Museum of Denon but I am unfortunately engagd to some Ladies – to see other Sights. – I think you and I should set up a Partnership – and accept invitations in common – You shall go as the Clergyman when it suits your convenience, and I will go as the hero. The Physiognomists and Craniologists will discover in you a Love of Tithes – and of conformity to [the 39] Articles – and in me a contempt of death and a Love of Glory. We shall destroy these imposters by our plan – many thanks for your politeness – I will take an early opportunity of paying my respects to you.

Already Sydney is being revealed a wit. As G.K. Chesterton wrote, 'the final and full impression is of a bubbling and boiling fountain of fancies and fun, which played day and night'. But there was much more to him than that. In 1855, ten years after Sydney's death, Abraham Hayward wrote in the *Edinburgh Review*:

> We should be guilty of an unpardonable neglect of duty were we to allow Sydney Smith to be definitively placed amongst the illustrious band of English worthies in the Temple of Fame at the risk of seeing too low a pedestal assigned to him, without urging on the attention of contemporaries, and recording for the instruction of posterity, his claims to rank as a great public benefactor, as well as his admitted superiority in what we must make bold to call his incidental and subordinate character of 'wit'. It was in this Journal that he commenced his brilliant and eminently useful career as a social, moral, and political reformer. He persevered in that career through good and evil report, with unabated vigour and vivacity, both in writing and conversation, until the

greater part of his original objects had been attained; and the simplest recapitulation of these would be sufficient to show that his countrymen have durable benefits and solid services, as well as pleasant thoughts and lively images, to thank him for.

No one man within living memory has done more to promote the improvement and well-being of mankind, by waging continual war, with pen and tongue, against ignorance and prejudice in all their modifications and varieties; nor should it be forgotten, that, although he wielded weapons very like those which had been employed in the immediately preceding age to undermine law, order, and religion, his exquisite humour was uniformly exerted on the side of justice, virtue, and rational freedom.

However, posterity has been reluctant to be instructed. 'It is remarkable how little satisfactory and sympathetic study has been made of Sydney Smith. A hundred good books ought to have been born out of that author of a thousand good things,' wrote G.K. Chesterton in 1934. Sixty years later his most recent biographer, Peter Virgin, confirms this, adding that 'his contemporaries would have been mystified by his relative obscurity', for they saw Sydney wielding the pen as mightier than the Admiral with his sword.

Our hope is that this anthology will reveal a great and good Englishman, 'the embodiment of our national genius', as Auberon Waugh described him, 'and the ideal English clergyman': one who deserves to be known, and to have a place in our history books.

Sydney fought for many causes, of many different kinds. With the help of considerable hindsight, most of us today would see them as obvious good causes, humane and sensible. In his day, however, his viewpoint was usually the minority one, unfashionable and often thoroughly unpopular. Many influential men, especially among the senior clergy of the Anglican Church, regarded him as a persistent and pestilential trouble-maker. They made sure he would never be promoted bishop. He knew this, and was regretful about it, but never deterred.

His two greatest campaigns concerned religious tolerance and political democracy. For more than 20 years he argued for the lifting of the unjust and antiquated restrictions that British law imposed on all the country's Roman Catholics. And he campaigned vigorously, in print and from public platforms, for the passing of the 1832 Reform Act to extend the parliamentary franchise to the new industrial towns and cities and to wipe away the old, corrupt 'rotten boroughs' of the shires. Both ambitions were realised in his own lifetime.

There were many more causes – against the blinkered and repressive character of English rule in Ireland; against the slave system in the United States of America; for the revision of the cruel and stupid Game Laws of

Britain; for penal reform and the removal of blatant injustices in the British legal system; for the gentler treatment of the insane; for transforming the English public school system for boys, and extending full educational opportunities to girls; against the employment of very young children as chimney sweeps; and much more besides. Beyond the age of 70 Sydney was still game for a good fight, writing to the newspapers to persuade the Great Western Railway Company to drop its policy of locking all its passengers inside their carriages when travelling between stations. He won that one too.

Chesterton proclaimed him 'one of the most remarkable of the makers of the great modern mood of liberty and liberality'.

Sydney's power as a polemicist owed much to the distinctive quality of his mind. The prevailing tone was rational and practical, coolly considered, broad-spirited and polite. The natural geniality of the man, his warm-heartedness and abiding concern for the poor and underprivileged, shines through his sentences. He used reason, but he was also a master of ridicule. He had a sharp eye for false logic and for self-seeking hypocrisy, and when he was outraged he could be scathingly ferocious and satirical. There were times, too, when his prose would take off on some high rhetorical flight, or on some wild line of fantasy and fun. He kept his readers awake and made them question the bases of their convictions. He made them laugh, as well, at the ludicrous assumptions of popular prejudices. He could charm them with the flowing cadences and the ingenuities of his argument. He often surprised them with sudden, vivid, original and apt images. The title of this book, used to convey the extreme remoteness of his new parish at Foston, twelve miles north of the city of York, is one of the best known examples of that.

Sydney lived in what the ancient Chinese would have called 'interesting times', a period of turbulence in all aspects of life – in belief and ideology, in European international relations, and in the political, economic, social and cultural life of Britain. He was not quite four years old when the rebellious American colonists set out to break away from British rule by force. He was just turned 18 when the Paris crowd stormed the prison at Bastille and launched the French Revolution in violence. The years of his 'prime of life' coincided with 20 years of almost-continuous conflict as Britain fought against the French revolutionary armies and then against the imperialistic ambitions of Napoleon, and supplied the money to keep its continental allies in the fight as well.

At home this meant new taxes and a seemingly eternal Tory government using savage and repressive laws to make sure that British society was not undermined by French revolutionary ideas. It seemed that the time of Judge Jeffreys had returned. Magistrates nominated by the government chose the juries and condemned to transportation for 14 years journalists who had attacked government policy. Habeas Corpus was suspended. Government spies, according to Macaulay, made it imprudent to talk politics in public. Those in power saw the bogey of Jacobinism everywhere, and from 1792 to 1820 all in authority – government, magistrates, officers, bishops – exercised their

power with harshness, intolerance and arrogance. Enclosures were transforming the farming countryside. The machines of the Industrial Revolution
were creating vast new factory towns and cities in the Midlands and many
parts of the North. Great wealth was generated and great poverty too. Class
divisions were intensified.

To the problems created by all these strains and stresses, Sydney brought
a mind that was fundamentally eigteenth century English – direct, practical,
calm and commonsensical, unblinkered and robust. He had an instinctive
distrust for all passionate enthusiasms. They led, as he saw all too clearly, all
around him, to intolerance and inhumanity. He had no time for the ideological
and the dogmatic and there was a lot of that about in those days, among his
fellow-churchmen and the theologians, among philosophers and political
economists, and from the poets as well, especially the new 'Romantic' school.

Sydney was born in Woodford, Essex, on 3 June, 1771, the second child of
Mr and Mrs Robert Smith. His mother was of French Huguenot extraction,
and he always said that was where his natural gaiety of spirit sprang from.
His father was very different, a grasping, mercenary and overbearing man,
constantly on the move, always trying to make his fortune by property deals
and invariably failing.

His father was a dominant and disruptive influence on Sydney's early
life. The eldest child, Robert – generally known by his nick-name 'Bobus' –
went to Eton, worked hard and made many contacts that would prove useful
in his later life. He went on to King's College, Cambridge, then studied law
and built a successful and highly lucrative career.

There was no money, so his father claimed, to give Sydney a similar start
in life. So he was sent to various prep schools, then to Winchester, which
was a particularly harsh and narrow-minded place at that time. He was unhappy at school and emerged with a firm contempt for the English public
school system, its brutality and its obsession with Latin grammar and Greek
verse. He won a scholarship to New College, Oxford, and there he was even
more unhappy, finding his tutors idle, corrupt and uninspiring. He took his
degree in 1792 and wanted to follow his brother to the bar. Once again his
father refused to find the money, which left him little alternative but to study,
without any great enthusiasm, for ordination as a priest in the Church of
England. He was ordained Deacon in 1794, and sent to be curate of the
parish of Netheravon on Salisbury Plain. He was deeply shocked by the
poverty and squalor, both physical and intellectual, of rural life. 'Poverty is
no disgrace to a man,' he said, 'but it is confoundedly inconvenient.'

But Sydney was a genuine Christian believer, with a straight-forward
and practical attitude towards his pastoral role, so that he devoted himself to
the care of his parishioners, improving their lives as best he could and endeavouring to cheer them up. He also – and this is another recurring feature
in the pattern of his life – made good friends with the local grandees, Michael
Hicks Beach and his wife.

When he could get away for a holiday break, Sydney liked to visit the fashionable spa-resort of Bath. He was there in the early winter of 1797, at the same time as a 22-year-old woman who was just beginning to try her hand as a writer of novels. David Cecil tells the story in his *Portrait of Jane Austen* (1978):

> Later in the year, by way of giving them a change, Mrs Austen took her daughters to stay with their relations at Bath. This visit is interesting in that it may have provided Jane with a model for her fiction – and a celebrated one. In the winter of that year, there was staying at Bath a young clergyman called Sydney Smith, tall, pleasant-looking and extraordinarily amusing in a vein of humour peculiarly his own. He was employed by a family called Hicks Beach as tutor to their son; the Hicks Beaches knew the Austens. A year later Jane began to write a novel later to appear as *Northanger Abbey*, in which the heroine visiting Bath meets a tall, pleasant-looking young clergyman called Henry Tilney, extraordinarily amusing and in a vein of humour very like that of Sydney Smith. Can there be any connection between these two events? Nothing, I am afraid, that can be called real evidence, no record that the two ever met – though, many years later, Sydney Smith was to profess himself an admirer of Jane Austen's novels. I fear that, in suggesting a connection, I may be yielding to a temptation that often besets biographers, namely to put forward a view on insufficient grounds just because I should like it to be true. But I cannot resist doing so. Sydney Smith was the most entertaining talker and Jane Austen the most entertaining writer of their time. Moreover their view of life at once unillusioned and good-humoured, robust and ironic, shows a close affinity of spirit. It would be delightful to think that one inspired the other.

It is even more intriguing to wonder what would have happened to their lives, and to the course of English literature, if they had fallen in love and married.

Sydney, in his new role of tutor to Michael Hicks Beach, planned to take him to Germany, but the European situation had grown too threatening and it was decided that Edinburgh would be a safer option. So Sydney went North and it proved a formative decision.

He enjoyed Edinburgh, though the Old Town of high buildings and insanitary narrow streets caused him to write, 'No smells ever equalled Scotch smells. It is the School of Physic. Walk the streets and you would imagine that every medical man had been administering cathartics to every man woman and child in the town. Yet the place is uncommonly beautiful, and I am in a constant balance between admiration and trepidation.' It was when walking down one of these streets with a friend that they came across two harridans shrieking at each other across the street from upstairs windows. 'These two women will never agree,' Sydney remarked as they walked on. 'They are arguing from different premises.' Sydney took lodgings in the New Town, still being constructed of wide straight streets and classical style houses – 'the finest street I have seen in Great Britain'.

Edinburgh was then a lively intellectual centre, 'the Athens of the North', and Sydney found it immensely stimulating. He attended lectures on anatomy and medicine, started to build a reputation as a preacher, and quickly became a member of various discussion groups and dining clubs. Although he always believed his Scottish friends took too earnest and too abstract a view of life, he enjoyed their company for the depth of their learning and the relish they had for ideas and debate. He particularly enjoyed the companionship of a group of young lawyers with radical and liberal opinions. They included Henry Brougham, Francis Jeffrey and Francis Horner who became a very close friend.

Sydney married on 2 July, 1800. The ceremony took place at Cheam in Surrey. He had been engaged for two years to Catherine Pybus, the daughter of a London banker, three years his junior. She was a woman of equable temperament, great good sense, and some money. Sydney's fortunes at this time were still very uncertain. Half a century later, in her *Memoir* of her father, their daughter Saba (later Lady Holland) wrote:

> My father's only contribution to their future ménage (save his own talents and character) were six small silver tea-spoons. . . . One day, in the madness of his joy, he came running into the room and flung them into her lap saying 'There, Kate, you lucky girl, I give you all my fortune!'

It proved to be an unusually happy marriage. The only trouble, right at the start, sprang from his father's attempts to gain access to Catherine's money, but Sydney (knowing his father all too well by this time) fought them off.

Sydney and Catherine repaired to Edinburgh, and the following year the first of their four children, Saba, was born. The year after that, Sydney fathered a different kind of off-spring, the *Edinburgh Review*.

He had already mentioned the idea to some of his Edinburgh acquaintances and received encouraging responses. On a wild evening in March 1802, in Jeffrey's top-floor flat, he and Jeffrey and Brougham were listening to the storm and discussing the repressive Tory regime of Dundas, MP for Edinburgh 'who held supreme power over the Northern division of the island', when Sydney put forward his 'bold and sagacious idea'. They should together launch a new magazine which would challenge the government's illiberal policies. Constable, a local bookseller/publisher had agreed to publish. He, Sydney, would edit the first issues. Their circle would write the articles: Horner would deal with political economy and wider moral issues; Brougham with law and history, science and mathematics; Jeffrey with literature; Sydney and other friends with a range of other subjects, topical and universal. Initially at least, they would not be paid for their contributions and they would be anonymous. They would strive to be hard-hitting, but also to keep on the safe side of the prevailing libel laws. The magazine would be issued quarterly and cost five shillings.

The first number came out in October 1802. 'No-one living at the time,' wrote Abraham Hayward, reviewing Lady Holland's *Memoir*, 'would have guessed that a group of briefless barristers, unemployed doctors, embryo statesmen, and mute inglorious orators, with the aid of an ex-curate, were about to electrify the republic of letters and inaugurate a new era in criticism.' The surprise is confirmed by Lord Cockburn in his *Memorial of his own Time*.

> The suppression of independent talent or ambition was the tendency of the times. Every Tory principle being absorbed in the horror of innovation, and that party casting all its cares upon Henry Dundas, no one could, without renouncing all his hopes, commit the treason of dreaming an independent thought. There was little genuine attraction for real talent, knowledge, or eloquence on that side; because these qualities can seldom exist in combination with abject submission.

And so,

> It is impossible for those who did not live at the time and in the heart of the scene to feel, or almost to understand, the impression made by the new luminary, or the anxieties with which its motions were observed. It was an entire and instant change of everything that the public had been accustomed to in that sort of composition. The old periodical opiates were extinguished at once.

The *Edinburgh Review* proved an immediate success, and circulation numbers quickly rose. 14,000 copies were sold of one number in 1815, and there was a steady demand for bound volumes.

> Of course [Hayward continues] the principal contributors were speedily recognised, and had a mark set against their names by the dispensers of public honours and emoluments. Their position has been thus vividly portrayed by their clerical associate: – 'From the beginning of the century to the death of Lord Liverpool was an awful period for those who had the misfortune to entertain liberal opinions, and who were too honest to sell them for the ermine of the judge or the lawn of the prelate; a long and hopeless career in your profession, – the chuckling grin of noodles, – the sarcastic leer of the genuine political rogue, – prebendaries, deans, and bishops made over your head, – reverend renegades advanced to the highest dignities of the Church for helping to rivet the fetters of Catholic and Protestant

Dissenters, and no more chance of a Whig administration than of a thaw in Zembla, – these were the penalties exacted for liberality of opinion at that period; and not only was there no pay, but there were many stripes. . . . To set on foot such a journal in such times, – to contribute towards it for many years, – to bear patiently the reproach and poverty which it caused, – and to look back and see that I have nothing to retract, and no intemperance or violence to reproach myself with, is a career of life which I must think to be extremely fortunate.'

Indeed, although Sydney soon released the editorship to Jeffrey, he continued to write, regularly and powerfully, for the magazine for the next 25 years. He covered a wide range of subjects, often very serious but always enlightened by his distinctive style – the quiet confidence of his debating tone, his elegant cadences, the practical sense of what he wrote and his wit. More than half the quotations in this anthology are taken from his articles in the *Edinburgh Review*.

In 1803, Sydney brought his tutoring duties to an end and he and his family left Edinburgh to settle in London. Something of his reputation, and several of his old Edinburgh friends, had gone before him. To live in the heart of London, he thought, was to get as close to paradise as any man could hope. He was soon involved in the city's lively club life, receiving invitations to preach and making himself ever more widely known by a series of public lectures. These were delivered at the Royal Institution in Albemarle Street. As word got around, hundreds of people converged on the hall each Saturday to hear him. His ostensible subject was moral philosophy, but he interpreted the term freely and held forth on a wide range of subjects. He described his success as 'the most perfect example of impudence recorded in history', and in a letter written 40 years later took a disparaging view of it all:

My lectures are gone to the dogs, and are utterly forgotten. I knew nothing of philosophy, but I was thoroughly aware that I wanted £200 to furnish my house. The success, however, was prodigious; all Albermarle Street blocked up with carriages, and such an uproar as I never remember to have been excited by any other literary imposture. Every week I had a new theory about conception and perception; and supported by a natural manner, a torrent of words, and an impudence scarcely credible in this prudent age. Still, in justice to myself, I must say there were some good things in them. But good and bad are all gone.

There were, in fact, many good things in the lectures, and they included one image that has given a useful phrase to the English language. He was lecturing 'On the Conduct of the Understanding':

It is a prodigious point gained if any man can find out where his powers lie, and what are his deficiences – if he can contrive to ascertain what Nature intended him for. . . . If you choose to represent the various parts in life by holes upon a table, of different shapes – some circular, some triangular, some square, some oblong – and the persons acting these parts by bits of wood of similar shapes, we shall generally find that the triangular person has got into a square hole, the oblong into the triangular, and a square person has squeezed himself into the round hole. The officer and the office, the doer and the thing done, seldom fit so exactly that we can say they were almost made for each other.

It was during these days in the heady London atmosphere, as his fame and his family increased, that he produced most of the brilliant *mots* that have made him a great favourite among the compilers of dictionaries of quotations.

The best-known of them all, perhaps, is his description of a friend's idea of heaven – 'Eating pâté de fois gras to the sound of trumpets'.

Someone mentioned that a young Scot was about to marry an Irish widow, twice his age and more than twice his size.

'Going to marry her!' cried Sydney; 'going to marry her! Impossible! You mean a part of her; he could not marry her all himself. It would be a case, not of bigamy, but trigamy; the neighbourhood or the magistrates should interfere. There is enough of her to furnish wives for a whole parish. One man marry her! – it is monstrous! You might people a colony with her; or give an assembly with her; or perhaps take your morning's walk round her, always provided there were frequent resting-places, and you were in rude health. I once was rash enough to try walking round her before breakfast, but only got half-way and gave it up exhausted. Or you might read the Riot Act and disperse her; in short, you might do anything with her but marry her.'

When he heard that his scientist friend Humphrey Davy was to marry an Edinburgh woman, famous for her attractions, he portrayed her in a letter: 'whenever she appeared at a place, though there was no garrison within 12 miles, the horizon was immediately clouded with majors'.

And he also said: 'Marriage resembles a pair of shears, so joined that they cannot be separated, often moving in opposite directions, yet punishing anyone who comes between them.'

His London career reached its triumphant apogee in the early summer of 1805 when he was invited to dine at Holland House in Kensington. Lord Holland, a leading figure in the Whig party, was a friend of Sydney's brother 'Bobus', who had recently sailed to India. Holland House was renowned for its hospitality, its role as a meeting-place for people of liberal disposition, and the glittering quality of its company. It rapidly became, as Hesketh Pearson put it, Sydney's 'spiritual home.' He loved comfortable and handsome interiors, good food and wine, and enlivening company. Before long he was a regular guest at the dinner parties, wittiest of all the company, capable of taking off into outrageous and uproarious flights of wild fantasy that reduced the room to chaos as guests and their hosts collapsed with laughter and the servants became incapable of serving. Princess Marie Lichtenstein in her *Holland House* (London, 1873) relates how Luttrell, a frequent visitor and epicure, 'once marvellous to relate let the side dishes pass by; but it was in order to contemplate a man who had failed to laugh at Sydney Smith's jokes'.

Lord and Lady Holland were to become life-long friends. In October 1805 Sydney described them in a letter to Sir James Mackintosh:

> She is very handsome, very clever, and I think very agree-able. . . . Lord Holland is quite delightful; I hardly know a talent, or virtue, that he has not little or big. The Devil could not put him out of temper. I really never saw such a man. In addition to this, think of his possessing Holland House and that he reposes every evening on that beautiful structure of flesh and blood Lady H.

Dozens of the Holland House devotees described the riotous dinner parties and paid tribute to Sydney as their presiding spirit of fun and wit. Unfortunately, they rarely made any record of exactly what he had said. There was no Boswell figure there to listen attentively and write it down, as fully as possible, as soon as he could, and so we are left with nothing more than brief and very fragmentary outlines. There were some who deplored Sydney's manner, pronouncing him smug or loud, coarse and even profligate; but the overwhelming consensus was firmly in his favour. Abraham Hayward, who was often one of the company, writes:

> He had no notion of talking for display. He talked because he could not help it: because his spirits were excited and his mind was full.
>
> Far from being jealous of competition, he was always anxious to dine in company with men who were able and entitled to hold their own; and he was never pleasanter than when some guest of congenial turn of mind assisted him to keep up the ball. On the occasion of the first attempt (at the writer's chambers in the Temple) to bring him and Theodore Hook together, Lockhart arrived with the information that Hook was priming himself (as was his wont) at the Athenæum Club, with a tumbler or two of hot punch. 'Oh,' exclaimed Sydney, 'if it comes to that, let us start fair. When Mr Hook is announced, announce Mr Smith's punch.' When they did meet they contracted a mutual liking, and Sydney ran on with his usual flow and felicity; but poor Hook had arrived at that period of his life when his wonderful powers required a greater amount of stimulants than could be decently imbibed at an ordinary London dinner with a

clergyman. He was little more than a listener, and Sydney told one of the party (the writer) that, if he had not known who Hook was, he should have taken him for a quiet, intelligent, good-natured, ordinary sort of man.

Sydney Smith almost invariably made it his special business to call out and encourage the display of any latent elements of information or agreeability in any silent, unobtrusive, or abashed member of the company. At the same time he by no means disliked mixing with what he called commonplace humdrum people, endowed with only an indistinct perception of a joke; and he rightly conceived that he had done the State good service by the invention of the 'Fool-ometer.'

At the start of 1806 Prime Minister William Pitt (the 'Younger') died, and for a brief period the Whigs were back in power, in what was called the 'Ministry of All the Talents'. Charles James Fox was Foreign Secretary, Lord Lansdowne Chancellor of the Exchequer, and Lord Holland a junior minister. Their great achievement was the abolition of the Slave Trade. Through the insistence of Lady Holland, they found a living for Sydney – the parish of Foston in North Yorkshire. It meant an extra £600 a year, when Sydney was desperately in need of a secure income. He was grateful for that, but disturbed at the prospect of having to leave London.

For a while, the danger of exile to the country was held at bay by getting a clergyman from York to look after Foston's spiritual requirements, where there had been no resident clergyman since the reign of Charles II.

The liberal-minded government did not last long. The issue of emancipating Britain's Roman Catholic population from its ancient civil disabilities had been raised. The Whigs found themselves fiercely opposed by a formidable coalition of King George III, the Tories, 99 percent of the clergymen of the Established Church, and the squirearchy of England. The government collapsed in March 1807, to be replaced by an even more dyed-in-the-wool reactionary group of Tories than Pitt had controlled, led by Sydney's bête noire Lord Eldon.

Sydney had gone on writing for the *Edinburgh Review*, but now turned his pen to a more sustained effort, a series of ten brilliant tracts arguing the case for Roman Catholic emancipation. They were called 'The Letters of Peter Plymley'. They were anonymous and for a long time Sydney disclaimed their authorship, but his style was too recognisable by this time for everyone to accept that. They proved the sensation of the 1807-8 season. A pamphlet containing all the letters ran to sixteen editions in a few months. The government was furious, but most readers were impressed and delighted and some at least were converted to the more tolerant and rational approach. This was to be Sydney's longest, most passionate and most altruistic campaign. He made many enemies by it, especially among the leading men of the Church of England. But he never stopped writing and speaking and fighting for it. The cause was finally won more than 20 years later, in 1829.

Towards the end of 1807, after the passing of the Clergy Residence Bill, the newly installed Archbishop of York, Vernon Harcourt, began to insist that Sydney should live in, or within easy reach of, his parish at Foston in Yorkshire. Sydney was dismayed and his wife Catherine devastated – there were three young children by now – but no alternative could be devised. In June 1809 the family took the coach north to start a 20-year sojourn in their remote, rural fastness. Malcolm Muggeridge in his Introduction to the Folio edition of Hesketh Pearson's *Smith of Smiths* states that Sydney's life lacked 'the Golgotha' that was needed to make it truly Christian – there was no 'bearing of the Cross'. He is, of course, quite wrong. To have possessed perhaps the ablest mind in the Church of England, and yet to have remained rector of an obscure country parish for 20 years because of his principles, after having enjoyed the delights of social success in London, especially at Holland House, and while seeing his inferiors rise to positions of power in the Church, was a cross indeed.

However, as he invariably did, Sydney set himself to make the cheerful best of things. The old rectory was derelict, so he rented a house in the village of Heslington, closer to York, and the family settled in there. The parish of Foston was also run-down, but he tackled the problems with verve, quickly making himself much more than the spiritual guide to his parishioners – friend, counsellor, doctor, apothecary, and much else besides. He became a Justice of the Peace and a turnpike trustee. He made the people behave themselves and he made them laugh. The quality and eminence of his visitors amazed them: grand carriage-folk like Lord and Lady Holland, Lord and Lady Carlisle from Castle Howard a few miles to the north, Viscount Morpeth and his wife Georgiana, Earl Grey of Howick and Lady Grey, many of the 'Edinburgh Reviewers', and many more. And he astonished them by the expert and ingenious enthusiasm with which he took up the farming of his 300-acre glebe. One of his inventions was 'The Universal Scratcher', a metal post set up in mid-field, with arms going out in all directions and at varying heights, so that all his animals, from new lambs to the cows, could happily scratch their backs. It saved him many pounds, he said, in broken gates and fence-posts.

In his letters, of course, Sydney went on deriding the tedium of life in the country, but in action he could make it exciting and joyful. There were persistent worries about money and occasional bouts of depression, but for the most part he maintained his spirit of good-will and gaiety. He kept up his friendships by correspondence, revisited Edinburgh and contrived a holiday stay in London each spring. And he built himself a splendid new rectory at Thornton le Clay, a mile from his church at Foston.

At first he commissioned an architect, but rejected his plans with the words: 'You build for glory, Sir. I for use.' So he and Catherine designed the house they wanted, and then he supervised the building of it. Work began in June 1813 and it was finished before the end of March 1814. The total cost was £4,000. 'I aimed at making it a snug parsonage,' Sydney said, 'and I think I succeeded.' In the course of all this effort and upheaval, Mrs Smith gave birth to their last child – a boy, named Wyndham, who was to give them more trouble and anxiety later on than the other three children together.

The house was big, spacious and handsome, with many out-buildings, close to the road and looking out in the other direction across his broad acres. His aims, as architect, were convenience and comfort. The rooms were large, full of light and colour, and had big fireplaces whose fires were stimulated by air-tubes from outside, another of his inventions. The family moved in and were very happy there.

The house is still there, now a private home. It was gutted by fire in 1962 so that nothing of Sydney's furniture or furnishings has survived, but it was thoughtfully restored and feels, on the inside, much as it must have done in Sydney's day – roomy, bright and cheerful. Nothing at all has changed on the outside. It looks fresh and unpretentious, with its large windows and warm, rose-coloured bricks and a roofing of red tiles.

His varied responsibilities – clerical, civic, journalistic, with his family and on the farm – kept Sydney fully occupied and happy, though a period of low prices for agricultural produce and desperately bad harvests gave him an anxious few years. Things started to look up after 1817. Then in the early 1820s a legacy from an aunt made it possible to consider holidays on the continent. In 1827 Sydney's father, who had mellowed considerably in old age, died and left them £10,000. It was the end of all financial anxieties.

Other changes were in the air. The long period of Tory rule was coming to an end at last. And so was Sydney's long exile in the North. His Whig friends back in power, he was made a prebendary of Bristol Cathedral, which meant a little more money and the chance to proclaim the virtues of religious toleration (the issue of Roman Catholic Emancipation was in the forefront once again) to the Mayor and assembled burgesses of the city. He also seized the opportunity to negotiate his transfer from Yorkshire to become Rector of Combe Florey in Somerset. In 1829 Sydney and his wife and their daughter Saba travelled south to take up residence at the Rectory.

Just before the move, what Sydney called 'the first real misfortune which ever befell me' occurred.

Their eldest surviving son Douglas, who had suffered poor health for most of his life, fell suddenly and very seriously ill with pleurisy during a visit to London with his parents. He died a week later. 'I did not know I had cared so much for anybody,' Sydney wrote three months afterwards. 'The habit of providing for human beings, and watching over them for so many years generates a fund of affection of the magnitude of which I was not aware.'

Combe Florey – 'the Valley of Flowers' – enjoys milder airs than North Yorkshire. It is a tiny, spread-out village amid hills and trees and lush vegetation. The church of St Peter and St Paul was built in the Perpendicular style, and the pulpit and pews with which it was furnished then remained for Sydney and his congregation and are still there today, though the chancel was rebuilt after his death, with the stained-glass window above the altar dedicated to his memory.

The Rectory at the end of the village was already there when Sydney became the incumbent, but it had been badly neglected, so he was able to exercise his building skills again. He extended the house into the garden by constructing two large bays, with big windows and supported by pillars, to flood with daylight the library and the upstairs drawing room. It is now the home of Captain and Mrs W.A.A. Read, who give a warm welcome to admirers of Sydney.

In December 1829 Sydney wrote to his friend Richard York, who lived at Wighill Park near Tadcaster:

You must really come down & see this country: – it is the garden of England, & our Parsonage is extremely beautiful & convenient. But the Peasantry & horses of this country are dreadfully inferior to those of the North. The former are all drunken & the latter 14 hands & [a half] high without a good point about them; in revenge the climate is very soft & mild; magnolias, hydrangeas & Myrtles live out of doors all the year, & snow seldom lies above 2 or 3 days in the winter.

Our neighbours here, are in the common line, Port & Sherry for dinner, hail rain & snow for conversation, but the best people in any place come slowly to light & lye, like Maccaroon Cakes at the bottom of an italian cream; last & best.

Sydney was delighted to be so much closer to London, especially when the railway arrived to bring London within six hours' comparatively comfortable travelling. Soon, he was actively involved in the turbulent political crisis of the time.

Violent discussion was going on, nationwide, about the need for electoral reform. Sydney's old friend Earl Grey had become Prime Minister in November 1830. His even older friend Henry Brougham, now Lord Brougham, was Lord Chancellor. The government was determined to extend the electorate and end the 'rotten boroughs'. The Tories, predominant in the House of Lords, were determined to stop them. There was rioting in the streets of some cities, and many feared revolution. In March 1831 Sydney went to Taunton to speak out powerfully in the reformist cause. Six months later he was there again to ridicule the Tory Lords by comparing them to 'Dame Partington' in the great storm (see chapter 6), who tried to mop the ocean away from her front-door on the beach. She did not succeed, he reassured his audience; and neither, in the same way, would the House of Lords. He was right. The first Reform Bill became law in June 1832.

In September 1831 Sydney was made a Canon of St Paul's, London. It was worth over £2,000 a year and meant he could spend more time in London. It also meant embarking, at the age of 60, on a new kind of career – as an administrator. He surprised many by doing the job conscientiously and efficiently, though he never learned to hold his tongue when he saw a chance of making fun of his fellow-clerics. When they were discussing the need for duck-boards around the cathedral, to save their visitors from having to wade through the mud, he dismissed the problem of finding sufficient timber with the comment: 'Let the Dean and Canons lay their heads together and the thing will be done.'

Although he was no longer writing for the *Edinburgh Review* – that came to an end in the late 1820s – he was still an active controversialist. He fought a dogged battle against changes proposed by the Ecclesiastical Commission. He argued against the idea of the secret ballot. He fought and defeated the directors of the Great Western Railway. He publicly denounced the State of Pennsylvania for ceasing to pay interest on loans it had raised a few years earlier.

Some critics have discerned a slackening in Sydney's zeal for reform in his later years, a growing reluctance to welcome change. There is evidence for the charge. It is, after all, a common enough characteristic among the ageing. But he kept a lively and cheerful outlook and, while retaining his old friends, made many new ones too. Despite his quarrel with the State of Pennsylvania, he liked the Americans he met for their 'honesty, simplicity and manliness'. Among his new English friends were the young Monckton Milnes; the emergent novelist Charles Dickens; John Ruskin, artist and art critic; and the voluble Macaulay, Edinburgh Reviewer and blossoming historian. It was Macaulay who bestowed on him the honourable and lasting title, 'The Smith of Smiths'.

Another new friend he made in the 1830s was, on the face of it, a highly unlikely one. Harriet Martineau was a very serious-minded journalist and writer. She had been brought up in a strict Nonconformist household and, though the faith had left her, retained many of its stern attitudes. Her writing was mostly about economics and social concerns, and she admitted to finding 'something very painful' in the sometimes flippant tone that Sydney used when dealing with religious matters. For all that, he contrived to charm her, so effectively that she left, in her *Autobiographical Memoir* (1877), one of the best portraits of Sydney in social action:

> In the midst of his jocose talk, Sydney Smith occasionally became suddenly serious, when some ancient topic was brought up, or some life-enduring sensibility touched; and his voice, eye and manner at such times disposed one to tears almost as much as his ordinary discourse did to laughter. Among the subjects which were thus sacred to him was that of the Anti-slavery cause. One evening, at Lord Murray's, he inquired with earnest solicitude about the truth of some news from America, during the 'reign of terror,' as we used to call the early persecution of the abolitionists. As I had received letters and newspapers just before I left home, I could tell him what he wanted to know. He expressed, with manly concern, his sorrow for the sufferings of my friends in America, and feared it must cause me terrible pain. 'Not unmixed pain,' I told him; and then I explained how well

we knew that that mighty question could be carried only by the long perseverance of the highest order of abolitionists; and that an occasional purgation of the body was necessary, to ascertain how many of even the well-disposed had soundness of principle and knowledge, as well as strength of nerve, to go through with the enterprise: so that even this cruel persecution was not a pure evil. He listened earnestly, and sympathised in my faith in my personal friends among the abolitionists; and then a merry thought came into his head, as I saw by the change in his eye. 'Now, I am surprised at you, I own,' said he. 'I am surprised at your taste, for yourself and your friends. I can fancy you enjoying a feather, (*one* feather) in your cap; but I cannot imagine you could like a bushel of them down your back with the tar.'

My first sight of Sydney Smith was when he called on me, under cover of a whimsical introduction, as he considered it. At a great music-party, where the drawing-rooms and staircases were one continuous crowd, the lady who had conveyed me fought her way to my seat, – which was, in consideration of my deafness, next to Malibran, and near the piano. My friend brought a message which Sydney Smith had passed up the staircase; – that he understood we desired one another's acquaintance, and that he was awaiting it at the bottom of the stairs. He put it to my judgment whether I, being thin, could not more easily get down to him, than he, being stout, could get up to me: and he would wait five minutes for my answer. I really could not go, under the circumstances: and it was a serious thing to give up my seat and the music; so Mr Smith sent me a good-night, and promise to call on me, claiming this negotiation as a proper introduction. He came, and sat down, broad and comfortable, in the middle of my sofa, with his hands on his stick, as if to support himself in a vast development of voice; and then he began, like the great bell of St Paul's, making me start at the first stroke. He looked with shy dislike at my trumpet, for which there was truly no occasion. I was more likely to fly to the furthest corner of the room. It was always his boast that I did not want my trumpet when he talked with me.

She also tells her 'better version' of

The story of Jeffrey and the North Pole, which appears to me strangely spoiled in the Life (Saba's *Memoir*). The incident happened while the Jeffreys were my near neighbours in London; and Mrs Sydney Smith related the incident to me at the time. Captain (afterwards Sir John) Ross had just returned from an unsuccessful polar expedition, and was bent upon going again. He used all his interest to get the government stirred up to fit out another expedition: and among others, the Lord Advocate was to be applied to, to bespeak his good offices. The mutual friend who undertook to do Captain Ross's errand to Jeffrey arrived at an unfortunate moment. Jeffrey was in delicate health, at that time, and made a great point of his daily ride; and when the applicant reached his door, he was putting his foot in the stirrup, and did not want to be detained. So he pished and pshawed, and cared nothing for the North Pole, and at length 'damned' it. The applicant spoke angrily about it to Sydney Smith, wishing that Jeffrey would take care what he was about, and use more civil language. 'What do you think he said to me?' cried the complainant. 'Why, he damned the North Pole!' 'Well, never mind! never mind!' said Sydney Smith, soothingly. 'Never mind his damning the North Pole. *I* have heard him speak disrespectfully of the equator.'

As he grew old Sydney became severely overweight and the prey to many afflictions – gout, lumbago, opthalmia, hay fever, assorted aches and agues. Some of them were painful, gout especially: 'I feel as though I were walking on my eye-balls,' he said. But in the old ebullient way, he turned it all to humour. In 1835 he wrote to his son-in-law, Dr (later Sir) Henry Holland, who had married Saba:

I am suffering from my old complaint, the Hay-fever, as it is called. My fear is of perishing by deliquescence. I melt away in Nasal and Lachrymal profluvia. . . . The membrane is so irritable that light, dust, contradiction, an absurd remark, the sight of a dissenter – anything, sets me sneezing, and if I begin sneezing at 12, I don't leave off till two o'clock, – and am heard distinctly in Taunton when the wind sets that way at a distance of 6 miles.

And in October 1844 he wrote to Lady Carlisle, who had been Lady Georgiana Morpeth:

From your ancient goodness to me, I am sure you will be glad to receive a bulletin from myself, informing you that I am making good progress; in fact, I am in a regular train of promotion: from gruel, vermicelli, and sago, I was promoted to panada, from thence to minced meat, and (such is the effect of good conduct) I was elevated to a mutton-chop. My breathlessness and giddiness are gone – chased away by the gout. If you hear of 16 or 18 pounds of human flesh, they belong to me. I look as if a curate had been taken out of me.

His general outlook remained buoyant. In June 1844 he had summed up his situation for the benefit of a French journalist who was planning to write a piece about him:

> I am 74 years of age; and being Canon of St Paul's in London, and a rector of a parish in the country, my time is divided equally between town and country. I am living amongst the best society in the Metropolis, and at ease in my circumstances; in tolerable health, a mild Whig, a tolerating Churchman, and much given to talking, laughing and noise. I dine with the rich in London, and physic the poor in the country; passing from the sauces of Dives to the sores of Lazarus. I am, upon the whole, a happy man; have found the world an entertaining world, and am thankful to Providence for the part alloted to me in it.

If his tone was milder than it had been, the wit could be as sharp as ever. In a letter to 'Bobus', contrasting their careers, he claimed that they had reversed the laws of physics: 'You have risen by your gravity. And I have sunk by my levity.'

When it became known that he was seriously ill towards the end of December 1844, the front door bell of his London home, 56 Green Street, rang constantly as friends came to enquire after him, although he was unable to see most of them. One admitted was Monckton Milnes, who asked Sydney how he had passed the previous night. 'Oh horrid, horrid, my dear fellow. I dreamt I was chained to a rock and being talked to death by Harriet Martineau and Macaulay.' In earlier years he had stood by Sir Roderick Murchison the geologist, who had angered churchfolk in the 'Moses versus Murchison' controversy, when the account of the Flood in Genesis had been called in question by his discoveries. When Sir Roderick came to see him shortly before his death, Sydney took off his nightcap and waved it above his head, crying, 'Murchison for ever' – Mr Valiant for Truth to the end.

He died peacefully on 22 February, 1845, and was buried, as he had given instructions to his old servant, Annie Kay, in the cemetery at Kensal Green, by the side of his much-loved son, Douglas.

Readers wishing to know more of Sydney's life will find one biography still in print – that of Peter Virgin, published in 1994 by HarperCollins. It is a thoroughly researched and detailed account, if sometimes unsympathetic. All the rest have to be found in second-hand book shops.

Stuart Reid wrote an affectionate account, *The Life and Times of Sydney Smith*, in 1896. He records that Foston Church was then rapidly falling into decay and had no memorial to Sydney. Happily, the situation is quite different today. Indeed it was at Foston, through the efforts of the Churchwarden, Major Peter Diggle, that the 150th Anniversary of Sydney's death was celebrated in 1995, when Lord Runcie addressed a crowded church. A consequence of this event has been the founding of the Sydney Smith Association to perpetuate his memory.

Hesketh Pearson's *The Smith of Smiths*, 'comprehensive and vivacious', was published in 1934 with a splendid Introduction by G.K. Chesterton, and again as a Penguin in 1948.

In 1980 the Clarendon Press published an excellent biography by Alan Bell.

There is far more of Sydney's writings worth the reading than this brief anthology can provides. There is a two-volume edition of his letters, edited by C. Nowell Smith and published in 1953; and a selection from these in the World's Classics Series with a delightful Introduction by Auberon Waugh, whose only fault is that he underestimates the seriousness of Sydney's Christian convictions. These, too, are out of print, but Alan Bell is intending to bring out a far more comprehensive edition of the letters at some future date.

Sydney's Collected Works, being for the most part his articles from the *Edinburgh Review*, began to be published in 1839, and ran into several editions.

The book that brings us nearest to him as a person is his daughter Saba's *Memoir* of her father, and sadly, we have only seen this in major libraries. It well deserves to be reprinted.

CAMPANERO TOLLING.

The Campanero may be heard from three miles away, 'being more powerful than the belfry of a cathedral, ringing for a new dean just appointed on
account of shabby politics, small undertsanding and good family'.

The Sloth 'which passes his life in suspense – like a young
clergyman distantly related to a bishop'

II

Travellers' Tales

Sydney was neither a compulsive nor an adventurous traveller. Most of his journeys had the simple purpose of getting him to London – from Edinburgh or his Yorkshire parish or the Rectory at Combe Florey in Somerset. He welcomed road improvements and the coming of the railways because they made his journeys speedier and more comfortable.

His trips abroad, which were rare, took him no further than Paris. He had long wished to see that city, and in 1826 a legacy from an aunt enabled him to spend three weeks there in the company of the Hollands. He met many people, among them the Machiavellian schemer and political survivor, Talleyrand. He described him forcefully as 'a pile of shit in a silk stocking'.

But he liked the city – its hotels and cuisine, the grand streets and fountains, its drawing-rooms walled by looking-glasses. Entering one such apartment, he said: 'I took it for a meeting of the clergy, and was delighted, of course.' Paris, he claimed, was 'merely an abbreviation of Paradise.'

He was back there, this time with his wife, nine years later:

Hôtel de Londres, Place Vendôme.
11th October, 1835.

Dear Mrs Austin,
We lost a day in coming from London by a refractory wheel, and another day at Dover by losing the first day. We were delighted with the Hotel of Dessein [at Calais], and admired the waiter and chambermaid as two of the best-bred people we had ever seen. The next sensation was at Rouen. Nothing (as you know) can be finer. Beautiful country, ships, trees, churches, antiquities, commerce – everything which makes life interesting and agreeable. I thank you for your advice which sent me by the Lower Road to Paris. My general plan in life has been to avoid low roads, and to walk in high places – but from Rouen to Paris is an exception.

We are well lodged in an hotel with a bad kitchen. I agree in the common praise of French living. Light wines, and meat thoroughly subdued by human skill, are more agreeable to me than the barbarous Stone-Henge masses of meat with which we feed ourselves. Paris is very full. I look at it with some attention, as I am not sure I may not end my days in it. I suspect the fifth act of life should be in great cities; it is there, in the long death of old age, that a man most forgets himself and his infirmities, receives the greatest consolation from the attentions of friends, and the greatest diversion from external circumstances.

Pray tell me how often the steamboats go from Boulogne – whether every day, or if not, what days; and when will the tides best answer so as to go from harbour to harbour in the week beginning Sunday, 25th October?: Pray excuse this trouble; I have always compunctions in asking you to do anything useful. It is as if one were to use Blonde lace for a napkin – or to drink toast and water out of a ruby cup – a clownish confusion of what is splendid and what is service-able. Love to Lucie. I remain always, dear Mrs Austin, sincerely and respectfully yours

Sydney Smith.

In the early summer of 1837 Sydney and his wife visited the Low Countries. He was not impressed:

Rotterdam May 9 1837 at the bad Hotel
of the New Bath.

My dear Lady Carlisle -

Holland and the Netherlands are not fit Countries for the habitation of man. They are usurpd from the Kingdom of Frogs, and are the proper domicile of Aquatic Reptiles. I have passd thro 300 Miles of Country compar'd to which the Country between Lobster House & York is a perfect Paradise – . The Trees are Willows, – the Water is Brackish, the roads are pavements, the people are hideous – Every thing you breathe is fog or Tobacco: it is historically wonder-ful – morally grand – physically odious -

I have seen between 7 and 800 large Women without Clothes painted by Rubens – till I positively refuse Mrs Smith to see any more – What has struck me most is their great superiority to us in Architecture – . I have made a few profound observations such as the Horses are fatter than English Horses, are more docile, have finer heads & Heels – the Soldiers are all little, there are no Birds. The Bread Butter & Cheese are better than in England – We have met with no misfortune & having gaind good intelligence before we went are profiting by it. – We shall be at Amsterdam Friday – Several persons have asked me what was thought of the War between Holland and Belgium – I tell them we lookd upon it as a quarrel between Cat & Dog – as trifling, and as foolish – they go away at this saying *Schlossen Schlassen Doshen Dashen* – the meaning of which I do not comprehend.

Through his reading and reviewing, however, Sydney travelled the world. He loved learning about strange lands – their flora and fauna, customs and beliefs and systems of government, their economies and agriculture, their explorers and colonisers. The inventiveness and variety of nature and the vagaries of human nature always fascinated him, moving him to amazement, sometimes amusement and sometimes anger.

He reviewed travel books for the *Edinburgh Review* for many years, and with a thoroughness and wealth of quotation that completely belied his claim that 'I never read a book before reviewing it; it prejudices a man so.'

He dealt with many parts of the world, usually at considerable length – Denmark, Turkey, Syria and Palestine, India and Ceylon (now Sri Lanka) – but for reasons of space we are confining our extracts to two regions, South America and Australia.

The best-known, the most entertaining and exhaustive of all Sydney's travel book reviews was published in 1826. It ran, in total, to more than 8,000 words. What follows is about a quarter of the whole.

South America

Wanderings in South America, By Charles Waterton, 'Esq., London, Mawman. 4to. 1825.

Mr Waterton is a Roman Catholic gentleman of Yorkshire, of good fortune, who, instead of passing his life at balls and assemblies, has preferred living with Indians and monkeys in the forests of Guiana. He appears in early life to have been seized with an unconquerable aversion to Piccadilly, and to that train of meteorological questions and answers, which forms the great staple of polite English conversation. From a dislike to the regular form of a journal, he throws his travels into detached pieces, which he, rather affect-edly, calls Wanderings – and of which we shall proceed to give some account.

His first Wandering was in the year 1812, through the wilds of Demerara and Essequibo, a part of *ci-devant* Dutch Guiana, in South America. The sun exhausted him by day, the musquitoes bit him by night; but on went Mr Charles Waterton!

The first thing which strikes us in this extraordinary chronicle, is the genuine zeal and inexhaustible delight with which all the barbarous countries he visits are described. He seems to love the forests, the tigers, and the apes; – to be rejoiced that he is the only man there; that he has left his species far away; and is at last in the midst of his blessed baboons! He writes with a considerable degree of force and vigour; and contrives to infuse into his reader that admir-ation of the great works, and undisturbed scenes of Nature, which animates his style, and has influenced his life and practice. There is something, too, to be highly respected and praised in the conduct of a country gentleman, who, instead of exhausting life in the chase, has dedicated a considerable portion of it to the pursuit of knowledge. There are so many temptations to complete idleness in the life of a country gentleman, so many examples of it, and so much loss to the community from it, that every exception from the practice is deserving of great praise. Some country gentlemen must remain to do the business of their countries; but, in general, there are many more than are wanted; and, generally speaking also, they are a class who should be stimulated to greater exertions. Sir Joseph Banks, a squire of large fortune in Lincolnshire, might have given up his existence to double-barrelled guns and persecutions of poachers – and all the benefits derived from his wealth, industry, and personal exertion in the cause of science, would have been lost to the community.

Mr Waterton complains, that the trees of Guiana are not more than six yards in circumference – magnitude in trees which it is not easy for a Scotch imagination to reach. Among these, pre-eminent in height rises the mora – upon whose top branches, when naked by age, or dried by accident, is perched the toucan, too high for the gun of the fowler; – around this are the green heart, famous for hardness; the tough hackea; the ducalabali, surpassing mahogany; the ebony and letter-wood, exceeding the most beautiful woods of the Old World; the locust-tree, yielding copal; and the hayawa and olou-trees, furnishing sweet-smelling resin. Upon the top of the mora grows the fig-tree. The bush-rope joins tree and tree, so as to render the forest impervious, as, descending from on high, it takes root as soon as its extremity touches the ground, and appears like shrouds and stays supporting the mainmast of a line-of-battle ship.

Demerara yields to no country in the world in her birds. The mud is flaming with the scarlet curlew. At sunset, the pelicans return from the sea to the courada trees. Among the flowers are the humming-birds. The columbine, gallinaceous, and passerine tribes people the fruit-trees. At the close of day, the vampires, or winged-bats, suck the blood of the traveller, and cool him by the flap of their wings. Nor has Nature forgotten to amuse herself here in the composition of snakes: – the camoudi has been killed from thirty to forty feet long; he does not act by venom, but by size and convolution. The Spaniards affirm that he grows to the length of eighty feet, and that he will swallow a bull; but Spaniards love the superlative. There is a *whipsnake* of a beautiful green. The labarri snake of a dirty brown, who kills you in a few minutes. Every lovely colour under heaven is lavished upon the counachouchi, the most venomous of reptiles, and known by the name of the *bush-master*. Man and beast, says Mr Waterton, fly before him, and allow him to pursue an undisputed path. . . .

One of the strange and fanciful objects of Mr Waterton's journey was, to obtain a better knowledge of the composition and nature of the *Wourali* poison, the ingredient with which the Indians poison their arrows. In the wilds of Essequibo, far away from any European settlements, there is a tribe of Indians known by the name of *Macoushi*. The *Wourali* poison is used by all the South American savages, betwixt the Amazon and the Oroonoque; but the Macoushi Indians manufacture it with the greatest skill, and of the greatest strength. A vine grows in the forest called Wourali; and from this vine, together with a good deal of nonsense and absurdity, the poison is prepared. When a native of Macoushia goes in quest of feathered game, he seldom carries his bow and arrows. It is the blow-pipe he then uses. The reed grows to an amazing length, as the part the Indians use is from 10 to 11 feet long, and no tapering can be perceived, one end being as thick as another; nor is there the slightest appearance of a knot or joint. The end which is applied to the mouth is tied round with a small silk grass cord. The arrow is from nine to ten inches long; it is made out of the leaf of a palm-tree, and pointed as sharp as a needle: about an inch of the pointed end is poisoned: the other end is burnt to make it still harder; and wild cotton is put round it for an inch and a half. The quiver holds from 500 to 600 arrows, is from 12 to 14 inches long, and in shape like a dice-box. With a quiver of these poisoned arrows over his shoulder, and his blow-pipe in his hand, the Indian stalks into the forest in quest of his feathered game. . . .

The flesh of the game is not in the slightest degree injured by the poison; nor does it appear to be corrupted sooner than that killed by the gun or knife. For the larger animals, an arrow with a poisoned spike is used. . . .

Being a *Wourali* poison fancier, Mr Waterton has recorded several instances of the power of his favourite drug. A sloth poisoned by it went gently to sleep, and died! a large ox, weighing one thousand pounds, was shot with three arrows; the poison took effect in 4 minutes, and in 25 minutes he was dead. The death seems to be very gentle; and resembles more a quiet apoplexy, brought on by hearing a long story, than any other kind of death. We have reason to congratulate ourselves, that our method of terminating disputes is by sword and pistol, and not by these medicated pins; which, we presume, will become the weapons of gentlemen in the New Republics of South America.

The *second* Journey of Mr Waterton, in the year 1816, was to Pernambucco, in the southern hemisphere, on the coast of Brazil, and from thence he proceeds to Cayenne. His plan was, to have ascended the Amazon from Para, and go into the Rio Negro, and from thence to have returned towards the source of the Essequibo, in order to examine the Crystal Mountains, and to look once more for Lake Parima, or the White Sea; but, on arriving at Cayenne, he found that to beat up the Amazon would be long and tedious; he left Cayenne, therefore, in an American ship for Paramaribo, went through the interior to Coryntin, stopped a few days at New Amsterdam, and proceeded to Demerara.

'Leave behind you' (he says to the traveller) 'your high-seasoned dishes, your wines, and your delicacies; carry nothing but what is necessary for your own comfort, and the object in view, and depend upon the skill of an Indian, or your own, for fish and game. A sheet, about twelve feet long, ten wide, painted, and with loop-holes on each side, will be of great service: in a few minutes you can suspend it betwixt two trees in the shape of a roof. Under this, in your hammock, you may defy the pelting shower, and sleep heedless of the dews of night. A hat, a shirt, and a light pair of trousers, will be all the raiment you require. Custom will soon teach you to tread lightly and barefoot on the little inequalities of the ground, and show you how to pass on, unwounded, amid the mantling briars.'

Snakes are certainly an annoyance; but the snake, though high-spirited, is not quarrelsome; he considers his fangs to be given for defence, and not for annoyance, and never inflicts a wound but to defend existence. If you tread upon him, he puts you to death for your clumsiness, merely because he does not understand what your clumsiness means; and certainly a snake, who feels fourteen or fifteen stone stamping upon his tail, has little time for reflection, and may be allowed to be poisonous and peevish. American tigers generally run away – from which several respectable gentlemen in Parliament inferred, in the American war, that American soldiers would run away also!

The description of the birds is very animated and interesting; but how far does the gentle reader imagine the campanero may be heard, whose size is that of a jay? Perhaps

300 yards. Poor innocent, ignorant reader! unconscious of what Nature has done in the forests of Cayenne, and measuring the force of tropical intonation by the sounds of a Scotch duck! The campanero may be heard three miles! – this single little bird being more powerful than the belfry of a cathedral, ringing for a new dean – just appointed on account of shabby politics, small understanding, and good family! . . .

It is impossible to contradict a gentleman who has been in the forests of Cayenne: but we are determined, as soon as a campanero is brought to England, to make him toll in a public place, and have the distance measured. The toucan has an enormous bill, makes a noise like a puppy dog, and lays his eggs in hollow trees. How astonishing are the freaks and fancies of nature! To what purpose, we say, is a bird placed in the woods of Cayenne, with a bill a yard long, making a noise like a puppy dog, and laying eggs in hollow, trees? The toucans, to be sure, might retort, to what purpose were gentlemen in Bond Street created? To what purpose were certain foolish prating Members of Parliament created? – pestering the House of Commons with their ignorance and folly, and impeding the business of the country? There is no end of such questions. So we will not enter into the metaphysics of the toucan. . . .

Just before his third journey, Mr Waterton takes leave of Sir Joseph Banks, and speaks of him with affectionate regret. 'I saw,' (says Mr W.) 'with sorrow, that death was going to rob us of him. We talked of stuffing quadrupeds; I agreed that the lips and nose ought to be cut off, and stuffed with wax.' This is the way great naturalists take an eternal farewell of each other! Upon stuffing animals, however, we have a word to say. Mr Waterton has placed at the head of his book the picture of what he is pleased to consider a nondescript species of monkey. In this exhibition our author is surely abusing his stuffing talents, and laughing at the public. It is clearly the head of a Master in Chancery – whom we have often seen backing in the House of Commons after he has delivered his message. It is foolish thus to trifle with science and natural history. Mr Waterton gives an interesting account of the sloth, an animal of which he appears to be fond, and whose habits he has studied with peculiar attention. . . .

The sloth, in its wild state, spends its life in trees, and never leaves them but from force or accident. The eagle to the sky, the mole to the ground, the sloth to the tree; but what is most extraordinary, he lives not *upon* the branches, but *under* them. He moves suspended, rests suspended, sleeps suspended, and passes his life in suspense – like a young clergyman distantly related to a bishop. Strings of ants may be observed, says our good traveller, a mile long, each carrying in its mouth a green leaf the size of a sixpence! He does not say whether this is a loyal procession, like Oak-apple Day, or for what purpose these leaves are carried; but it appears, while they are carrying the leaves, that three sorts of ant-bears are busy in eating them. . . .

Insects are the curse of tropical climates. The bête rouge lays the foundation of a tremendous ulcer. In a moment you are covered with ticks. Chigoes bury themselves in your flesh, and hatch a large colony of young chigoes in a few hours. They will not live together, but every chigoe sets up a separate ulcer, and has his own private portion of pus. Flies get entry into your mouth, into your eyes, into your nose; you eat flies, drink flies, and breathe flies.

Lizards, cockroaches, and snakes, get into the bed; ants eat up the books; scorpions sting you on the foot. Every thing bites, stings, or bruises; every second of your existence you are wounded by some piece of animal life that nobody has ever seen before, except Swammerdam and Meriam. An insect with eleven legs is swimming in your teacup, a nondescript with nine wings is struggling in the small beer, or a caterpillar with several dozen eyes in his belly is hastening over the bread and butter! All nature is alive, and seems to be gathering all her entomological hosts to eat you up, as you are standing, out of your coat, waistcoat, and breeches. Such are the tropics. All this reconciles us to our dews, fogs, vapours, and drizzle – to our apothecaries rushing about with gargles and tinctures – to our old, British, constitutional coughs, sore throats, and swelled faces. . . .

Now, what shall we say, after all, of Mr Waterton? That he has spent a great part of his life in wandering in the wild scenes he describes, and that he describes them with entertaining zeal, and real feeling. His stories draw largely sometimes on our faith; but a man who lives in the woods of Cayenne must do many odd things, and see many odd things – things utterly unknown to the dwellers in Hackney and Highgate. We do not want to rein up Mr Waterton too tightly – because we are convinced he goes best with his head free. But a little less of apostrophe, and some faint suspicion of his own powers of humour, would improve this gentleman's style. As it is, he has a considerable talent

at describing. He abounds with good feeling; and has written
a very entertaining book, which hurries the reader out of
his European parlour, into the heart of tropical forests, and
gives, over the rules and the cultivation of the civilised parts
of the earth, a momentary superiority to the freedom of the
savage, and the wild beauties of Nature. We honestly
recommend the book to our readers: it is well worth the
perusal.   *Edinburgh Review* 1826

Australia

The special and complex problems of transforming a penal colony at the
furthest end of the world into a flourishing, law-respecting land with genuine
hopes for the future was one that intrigued Sydney and formed the subject of
many of his reviews.

1. *A Statistical, Historical, and Political Description of the
Colony of New South Wales.* By W.C. Wentworth, Esq., a
Native of the Colony. Whittaker, London, 1819.

2. *Letter to Viscount Sidmouth, Secretary of State for
the Home Department, on the Transportation Laws, the
state of the Hulks, and of the Colonies in New South
Wales.* By the Hon. Henry Grey Bennet, M.P.
Ridgway, London, 1819.

3. O'Hara's *History of New South Wales.* Hatchard,
London, 1818.

This land of convicts and kangaroos is beginning to rise into
a very fine and flourishing settlement: — And great indeed
must be the natural resources, and splendid the endowments
of that land that has been able to survive the system of
neglect and oppression experienced from the mother
country, and the series of ignorant and absurd Governors
that have been selected for the administration of its affairs.
But mankind live and flourish not only in spite of storms
and tempests, but (which could not have been anticipated
previous to experience) in spite of Colonial Secretaries expressly paid to watch over their interests. The supineness
and profligacy of public officers cannot always overcome
the amazing energy with which human beings pursue their
happiness, nor the sagacity with which they determine on
the means by which that end is to be promoted. Be it our
care, however, to record, for the future inhabitants of
Australasia, the political sufferings of their larcenous forefathers; and let them appreciate, as they ought, that energy
which founded a mighty empire in spite of the afflicting
blunders and marvellous cacæconomy of their
government. . . .

In this remote part of the earth, Nature (having made horses, oxen, ducks, geese, oaks, elms, and all regular and useful productions for the rest of the world,) seems determined to have a bit of play, and to amuse herself as she pleases. Accordingly, she makes cherries with the stone on the outside; and a monstrous animal, as tall as a grenadier, with the head of a rabbit, a tail as big as a bed-post, hopping along at the rate of five hops to a mile, with three or four young kangaroos looking out of its false uterus to see what is passing. Then comes a quadruped as big as a large cat, with the eyes, colour, and skin of a mole, and the bill and web-feet of a duck – puzzling Dr Shaw, and rendering the latter half of his life miserable, from his utter inability to determine whether it was a bird or a beast. Add to this a parrot, with the legs of a sea-gull; a skate with the head of a shark; and a bird of such monstrous dimensions, that a side bone of it will dine three real carnivorous Englishmen; – together with many other productions that agitate Sir Joseph, and fill him with mingled emotions of distress and delight. . . .

The Australasians grow corn; and it is necessarily their staple. The Cape is their rival in the corn trade. The food of the inhabitants of the East Indies is rice: the voyage to Europe is too distant for so bulky an article as corn. The supply to the government stores furnished the cultivators of New South Wales with a market in the first instance, which is now become too insignificant for the great excess of the supply above the consumption. Population goes on with immense rapidity; but while so much new and fertile land is before them, the supply continues in the same proportion greater than the demand. The most obvious method of affording a market for this redundant corn is by encouraging distilleries within the colony; a measure repeatedly pressed upon the government at home, but hitherto as constantly refused. It is a measure of still greater importance to the colony, because its agriculture is subjected to the effects both of severe drought and extensive inundations, and the corn raised for the distillers would be a magazine in times of famine. A recommendation to this effect was long since made by a committee of the House of Commons; but, as it was merely a measure for the increase of human comforts, was stuffed into the improvement baskets, and forgotten. There has been in all governments a great deal of absurd canting about the consumption of spirits. We believe the best plan is to let people drink what they like, and wear what they like; to make no sumptuary laws either for the belly or the back. In the first place, laws against rum and rum water are made by men who can change a wet coat for a dry one whenever they choose, and who do not often work up to their knees in mud and water; and, in the next place, if this stimulus did all the mischief it is thought to do by the wise men of claret, its cheapness and plenty would rather lessen than increase the avidity with which it is at present sought for. . . .

It is a scandalous injustice in this colony, that persons transported for seven years, have no power of returning when that period is expired. A strong active man may sometimes work his passage home; but what is an old man or an aged female to do? Suppose a convict were to be confined in prison for seven years, and then told he might get out if he could climb over the walls, or break open the locks, what in general would be his chance of liberation? But no lock nor doors can be so secure a means of detention as the distance of Botany Bay. This is a downright trick and fraud in the administration of criminal justice. A poor wretch who is banished from his country for seven years, should be furnished with the means of returning to his country when these seven years are expired. – If it is intended he should never return, his sentence should have been banishment for life.

The most serious charge against the colony, as a place for transportation, and an experiment in criminal justice, is the extreme profligacy of manners which prevails there, and the total want of reformation among the convicts. Upon this subject, except in the regular letters, officially varnished and filled with fraudulent beatitudes for the public eye, there is, and there can be but one opinion. New South Wales is a sink of wickedness, in which the great majority of convicts of both sexes become infinitely more depraved than at the period of their arrival. How, as Mr Bennet very justly observes, can it be otherwise? The felon transported to the American plantations, became an insulated rogue among honest men. He lived for years in the family of some industrious planter, without seeing a picklock, or indulging in pleasant dialogues on the delicious burglaries of his youth. He imperceptibly glided into honest habits, and lost not only the tact for pockets, but the wish to investigate their contents. But in Botany Bay, the felon, as soon as he gets out of the ship, meets with his ancient trull, with the footpad of his heart, the convict of his affections, – the man whose hand he has often met in the same gentleman's pocket – the

being whom he would choose from the whole world to take
to the road, or to disentangle the locks of Bramah. It is impossible that vice should not become more intense in such
society. *Edinburgh Review* 1819

1. *Letter to Earl Bathurst,* by the Honourable
H. Grey Bennet, M.P.
2. *Report of the Commissioner of Inquiry into the State of
the Colony of New South Wales. Ordered by the House of
Commons to be printed, 19th June, 1822.*

Mr Bigge's Report is somewhat long, and a little clumsy;
but it is altogether the production of an honest, sensible
and respectable man, who has done his duty to the public,
and justified the expense of his mission to the fifth or pick-
pocket quarter of the globe.

What manner of man is Governor Macquarrie? – Is all
that Mr Bennet says of him in the House of Commons true?
These are the questions which Lord Bathurst sent Mr Bigge,
and very properly sent him, 28,000 miles to answer. The
answer is, that Governor Macquarrie is not a dishonest man,
nor a jobber; but arbitrary, in many things scandalously neg-
ligent, very often wrong-headed, and, upon the whole, very
deficient in that good sense, and vigorous understanding,
which his new and arduous situation so manifestly requires.

Ornamental architecture in Botany Bay! How it could
enter into the head of any human being to adorn public buildings at the Bay, or to aim at any other architectural purpose
but the exclusion of wind and rain, we are utterly at a loss
to conceive. Such an expense is not only lamentable for the
waste of property it makes in the particular instance, but
because it destroys that guarantee of sound sense which the
Government at home must require in those who preside over
distant colonies. A man who thinks of pillars and pilasters,
when half the colony are wet through for want of any covering at all, cannot be a wise or prudent person. He seems to
be ignorant, that the prevention of rheumatism in all young
colonies is a much more important object than the gratification of taste, or the display of skill. . . .

One of the great difficulties in Botany Bay is to find proper
employment for the great mass of convicts who are sent out.
Governor Macquarrie selects all the best artisans, of every
description, for the use of Government; and puts the poets,
attornies, and politicians up to auction. The evil consequences of this are manifold. In the first place, from
possessing so many of the best artificers, the Governor is

necessarily turned into a builder; and immense drafts are drawn upon the Treasury at home, for buildings better adapted for Regent Street than the Bay. In the next place, the poor settler, finding that the convict attorney is very awkward at cutting timber, or catching kangaroos, soon returns him upon the hands of Government, in a much worse plight than that in which he was received. Not only are governors thus debauched into useless and expensive builders, but the colonists, who are scheming and planning with all the activity of new settlers, cannot find workmen to execute their designs.

What two ideas are more inseparable than Beer and Britannia? – what event more awfully important to an English colony, than the erection of its first brew-house? – and that it required, in Van Diemen's Land, the greatest solicitation to the Government, and all the influence of Mr Bigge, to get it effected. The Government, having obtained possession of the best workmen, keep them; their manumission is much more infrequent than that of the useless and unprofitable convicts; in other words, one man is punished for his skill, and another rewarded for his inutility. Guilty of being a locksmith – guilty of stone masonry, or brick-making: – these are the second verdicts brought in, in New South Wales; and upon them is regulated the duration or mitigation of punishment awarded in the mother-country. At the very period when the Governor assured Lord Bathurst, in his despatches, that he kept and employed so numerous a gang of workmen, only because the inhabitants could not employ them, Mr Bigge informs us, that their services would have been most acceptable to the colonists. Most of the settlers, at the time of Mr Bigge's arrival, from repeated refusals and disappointments, had been so convinced of the impossibility of obtaining workmen, that they had ceased to make application to the Governor. . . .

Colonel Macquarrie not only dismisses honest and irreproachable men in a country where their existence is scarce, and their services inestimable, but he advances convicts to the situation and dignity of magistrates. Mr Bennet lays great stress upon this, and makes it one of his strongest charges against the Governor; and the Commissioner also takes part against it. But we confess we have great doubts on the subject; and are by no means satisfied, that the system of the Governor was not, upon the whole, the wisest and best adapted to the situation of the colony. Men are governed by words; and under the infamous term *convict*, are comprehended crimes of the most different degrees and species of guilt. One man is transported for stealing three hams and a pot of sausages; and in the next birth [sic] to him on board the transport is a young surgeon, who has been engaged in the mutiny at the Nore; the third man is for extorting money; the fourth was in a respectable situation of life at the time of the Irish Rebellion, and was so ill read in history, as to imagine that Ireland had been ill treated by England, and so bad a reasoner as to suppose, that nine Catholics ought not to pay tithes to one Protestant. Then comes a man who set his house on fire, to cheat the Phoenix Office; and, lastly, that most glaring of all human villains, a poacher, driven from Europe, wife and child, by thirty lords of manors, at the Quarter Sessions, for killing a partridge. Now, all these are crimes no doubt – particularly the last; but they are surely crimes of very different degrees of intensity, to which different degrees of contempt and horror are attached – and from which those who have committed them may, by subsequent morality, emancipate themselves, with different degrees of difficulty, and with more or less of success. A warrant granted by a reformed bacon stealer would be absurd; but there is hardly any reason why a foolish hot-brained young blockhead, who chose to favour the mutineers at the Nore, when he was sixteen years of age, may not make a very loyal subject, and a very respectable and respected magistrate when he is forty years of age, and has cast his Jacobine teeth, and fallen into the practical jobbing and loyal baseness which so commonly developes itself about that period of life. Therefore, to say that a man must be placed in no situation of trust or elevation, as a magistrate, merely because he is a convict, is to govern mankind with a dictionary, and to surrender sense and usefulness to sound.   *Edinburgh Review* 1823

The Railway

Past the age of 70, Sydney rejoiced to see the railway approaching his West Country home. In September 1842 he wrote to Lord Murray: 'We have the railroad now within five miles. Bath in two hours, London in six – in short, everywhere in no time! Every fresh accident on the railroads is an advantage and leads to an improvement. What we want is an overturn which would kill a bishop, or at least a dean. This mode of conveyance would then become perfect.'

He was engaged in one of his last campaigns. The directors of the Great Western Railway, worried at the number of their customers who contrived to fall out of moving carriages, ordered the locking of all carriage doors from the outside before the trains left each station. Sydney thought this draconian, dangerous and stupid, and his arguments were given added force by a recent accident in Paris when many passengers, locked into the carriages, were crushed and incinerated. He brought his old polemical skills to bear, with much of the old force and vivacity.

To the Editor of the *Morning Chronicle* May 21 1842

In the course of a long life I have no recollection of any accident so shocking as that on the Paris railway – a massacre so sudden, so full of torment – death at the moment of pleasure – death aggravated by all the amazement, fear, and pain which can be condensed into the last moments of existence.

Who can say that the same scene may not be acted over again on the Great Western Railroad? That in the midst of their tunnel of three miles' length the same scene of slaughter and combustion may not scatter dismay and alarm over the whole country?

It seems to me perfectly monstrous that a board of ten or twelve monopolists can read such a description, and say to the public, 'You must run your chance of being burnt or mutilated. We have arranged our plan upon the locking-in system, and we shall not incur the risk and expense of changing it.'

The plea is, that rash or drunken people will attempt to get out of the carriages which are not locked, and that this measure really originates from attention to the safety of the public; so that the lives of two hundred persons who are not drunk and are not rash, are to be endangered for the half-yearly preservation of some idiot, upon whose body the coroner is to sit, and over whom the sudden-death man is to deliver his sermon against the directors.

The very fact of locking the doors will be a frequent source of accidents. Mankind, whatever the directors may think of that process, are impatient of combustion. The Paris accident will never be forgotten. The passengers will attempt to escape through the windows, and ten times more of mischief will be done than if they had been left to escape by the doors in the usual manner.

It is not only the locking of the doors which is to be deprecated; but the effects which it has upon the imagination. Women, old people, and the sick, are all forced to travel by the railroad; and for 200 miles they live under the recollection not only of impending danger, but under the knowledge that escape is impossible – a journey comes to be contemplated with horror. Men cannot persuade the females of their family to travel by the railroad; it is inseparably connected with abominable tyranny and perilous imprisonment.

Why does the necessity of locking both doors exist only on the Great Western? Why is one of the doors left open on all other railways?

The public have a right to every advantage under permitted monopoly which they would enjoy under free competition; and they are unjust to themselves if they do not insist upon this right. If there were two parallel railways, the one locking you in, and the other not, is there the smallest doubt which would carry away all the business? Can there be any hesitation in which timid women, drunken men, sages, philosophers, bishops, and all combustible beings, would place themselves?

I very much doubt the legality of locking doors, and refusing to open them. I arrive at a station where others are admitted; but I am not suffered to get out, though perhaps at the point of death. In all other positions of life there is egress where there is ingress. Man is universally the master of his own body, except he chooses to go from Paddington to Bridgewater: there only the Habeas Corpus is refused.

Nothing, in fact, can be more utterly silly or mistaken than this over-officious care of the public; as if every man who was not a railway director was a child or a fool. But why stop here? Why are not strait-waistcoats used? Why is not the accidental traveller strapped down? Why do contusion and fracture still remain physically possible?

Is not this extreme care of the public new? When first mail coaches began to travel twelve miles an hour, the *outsides* (if I remember rightly) were never tied to the roof. In packets, landsmen are not locked into the cabin to prevent them from tumbling overboard. This affectionate nonsense prevails only on the Great Western. It is there only that men, women, and children (seeking the only mode of transit which remains) are by these tender-hearted monopolists immediately committed to their locomotive prisons. Nothing can, in fact, be so absurd as all this officious zeal. It is the duty of the directors to take all reasonable precautions to warn the public of danger – to make it clear that there is no negligence on the part of the railroad directors; and then, this done, if a fool-hardy person choose to expose himself to danger, so be it. Fools there will be on roads of iron and on roads of gravel, and they must suffer for their folly; but why are Socrates, Solon, and Solomon to be locked up?

To the Editor of the *Morning Chronicle* June 7 1842
Let the company stick up all sorts of cautions and notices
within their carriages and without; but, after that, no doors
locked. If one door is allowed to be locked, the other will
soon be so too; there is no other security to the public than
absolute prohibition of the practice. The directors and agents
of the Great Western are individually excellent men; but
the moment men meet in public boards, they cease to be
collectively excellent. The fund of morality becomes less,
as the individual contributors increase in number. I do not
accuse such respectable men of any wilful violation of truth,
but the memoirs which they are about to present will be,
without the scrupulous cross-examination of a committee
of the House of Commons, mere waste paper.

But the most absurd of all legislative enactments is this
hemiplegian law – an act of Parliament to protect one side
of the body and not the other. If the wheel comes off on the
right, the open door is uppermost, and every one is saved.
If, from any sudden avalanche on the road, the carriage is
prostrated to the left, the locked door is uppermost, all
escape is impossible, and the railroad martyrdom begins.

Leave me to escape in the best way I can, as the fire-
offices very kindly permit me to do. I know very well the
danger of getting out on the off-side; but escape is the affair
of a moment; suppose a train to have passed at that moment,
I know I am safe from any other trains for twenty minutes or
half an hour; and if I do get out on the off-side, I do not
remain in the valley of death between the two trains, but
am over to the opposite bank in an instant – only half-
roasted, or merely browned, certainly not done enough for
the Great Western directors.

On Saturday morning last, the wheel of the public
carriage, in which a friend of mine was travelling, began to
smoke, but was pacified by several buckets of water, and
proceeded. After five more miles the whole carriage was
full of smoke, the train was with difficulty stopped, and the
flagrant vehicle removed. The axle was nearly in two, and
in another mile would have been severed.

Railroad travelling is a delightful improvement of human
life. Man is become a bird; he can fly longer and quicker
than a Solan goose. The mamma rushes sixty miles in two
hours to the aching finger of her conjugating and declining
grammar boy. The early Scotchman scratches himself in the
morning mists of the North, and has his porridge in Piccadilly before the setting sun. The Puseyite priest, after a rush

of 100 miles, appears with his little volume of nonsense at the breakfast of his bookseller. Every thing is near, every thing is immediate – time, distance, and delay are abolished. But, though charming and fascinating as all this is, we must not shut our eyes to the price we shall pay for it. There will be every three or four years some dreadful massacre – whole trains will be hurled down a precipice, and 200 or 300 persons will be killed on the spot. There will be every now and then a great combustion of human bodies, as there has been at Paris; then all the newspapers up in arms – a thousand regulations, forgotten as soon as the directors dare – loud screams of the velocity whistle – monopoly locks and bolts, as before.

The locking plea of directors is philanthropy; and I admit that to guard men from the commission of moral evil is as philanthropical as to prevent physical suffering. There is, I allow, a strong propensity in mankind to travel on railroads without paying; and to lock mankind in till they have completed their share of the contract is benevolent, because it guards the species from degrading and immoral conduct, but to burn or crush a whole train merely to prevent a few immoral insides from not paying, is I hope a little more than Ripon or Gladstone will bear.

We have been, up to this point, very careless of our railway regulations. The first person of rank who is killed will put every thing in order, and produce a code of the most careful rules. I hope it will not be one of the bench of bishops; but should it be so destined, let the burnt bishop – the unwilling Latimer – remember that, however painful gradual concoction by fire may be, his death will produce unspeakable benefit to the public. Even Sodor and Man will be better than nothing. From that moment the bad effects of the monopoly are destroyed; no more fatal deference to the directors; no despotic incarceration, no barbarous inattention to the anatomy of the human body; no commitment to locomotive prisons with warrant. We shall then find it possible

'Voyager libre sans mourir.'
Sydney Smith.

III

The United States of America

Sydney was just over 30 years old when the *Edinburgh Review* was launched. The United States of America was six years younger. So the two were close contemporaries, and from time to time Sydney used the generous pages of the magazine to cast an interested and avuncular eye on the progress of the experiment in republican democracy that was going on across the Atlantic. Many British hoped the experiment would fail. But Sydney was not one of them. He liked to contrast the methods and manners of the New World with those of the Old, usually to the detriment of the Old. But he saw one great, fundamental flaw in the USA – its system of negro slavery.

1. *Travels in Canada and the United States, in 1816 and 1817.* By Lieutenant Francis Hall, 14th Light Dragoons, H.P. London. Longman & Co. 1818.

2. *Journal of Travels in the United States of North America, and in Lower Canada, performed in the Year 1817, &c. &c.* By John Palmer. London. Sherwood, Neely, & Jones. 1818.

3. *A Narrative of a Journey of Five Thousand Miles through the Eastern and Western States of America.* By Henry Bradshaw Fearon. London. Longman & Co. 1818.

4. *Travels in the Interior of America, in the Years 1809, 1818, and 1811, c.* By John Bradbury, F. L. S. Lond. 8vo. London. Sherwood, Neely, & Jones. 1817.

These four books are all very well worth reading, to any person who feels, as we do, the importance and interest of the subject of which they treat. They contain a great deal of information and amusement; and will probably decide the fate, and direct the footsteps, of many human beings, seeking a better lot than the Old World can afford them. . . .

One of the great advantages of the American government is its cheapness. The American king has about 5000l. per annum, the vice-king 1000l. They hire their Lord Liverpool at about a thousand per annum, and their Lord Sidmouth (a good bargain) at the same sum. Their Mr Crokers are inexpressibly reasonable – somewhere about the price of an English doorkeeper, or bearer of a mace. Life, however, seems to go on very well, in spite of these low salaries; and the purposes of government to be very fairly answered. Whatever may be the evils of universal suffrage in other countries, they have not yet been felt in America; and one thing, at least is established by her experience, that this institution is not necessarily followed by those tumults, the dread of which excites so much apprehension in this country. In the most democratic states, where the payment of direct taxes is the only qualification of a voter, the elections are carried on with the utmost tranquillity; and the whole business, by taking votes in each parish or section, concluded all over the state in a single day. A great deal is said by Fearon about *Caucus*, the cant word of the Americans for the committees and party meetings in which the business of elections is prepared – the influence of which he seems to consider as prejudicial. To us, however, it appears to be nothing more than the natural, fair, and unavoidable influence, which talent, popularity, and activity, always must have upon such occasions. What other influence can the leading characters of the democratic party in Congress possibly possess? Bribery is entirely out of the question – equally so is the influence of family and fortune. What then can they do, with their caucus or without it, but recommend? And what charge is it against the American government to say, that those members of whom the people have the highest opinion meet together to consult whom they shall recommend for president, and that their recommendation is successful in their different states? Could any friend to good order wish other means to be employed, or other results to follow? No statesman can wish to exclude influence, but only bad influence; – not the influence of sense and character, but the influence of money and punch.

A very disgusting feature in the character of the present English government is its extreme timidity, and the cruelty and violence to which its timidity gives birth. Some hotheaded young person, in defending the principles of liberty, and attacking those abuses to which all governments are liable, passes the bounds of reason and moderation, or is thought to have passed them by those whose interest it is to think so. What matters it whether he has or not? You are strong enough to let him alone. With such institutions as ours he can do no mischief; perhaps he may owe his celebrity to your opposition; or, if he must be opposed, write against him – set Candidus, Scrutator, Vindex, or any of the conductitious penmen of government to write him down; – any thing but the savage spectacle of a poor wretch, perhaps a very honest man, contending in vain against the weight of an immense government, pursued by a zealous attorney, and sentenced, by some candidate, perhaps, for the favour of the crown, to the long miseries of the dungeon. A still more flagrant instance may be found in our late suspensions of the Habeas Corpus act. Nothing was trusted to the voluntary activity of a brave people, thoroughly attached to their government – nothing to the good sense and prudence of the gentlemen and yeomen of the country – nothing to a little forbearance, patience, and watchfulness. There was no other security but despotism; nothing but the alienation of that right which no king nor minister can love and which no human beings but the English have had the valour to win, and the prudence to keep. . . .

The Americans, we believe, are the first persons who have discarded the tailor in the administration of justice, and his auxiliary the barber – two persons of endless importance in the codes and pandects of Europe. A judge administers justice, without a calorific wig and particoloured gown, in a coat and pantaloons. He is obeyed, however: and life and property are not badly protected in the United States. We shall be denounced by the Laureate as atheists and jacobins; but we must say, that we have doubts whether one atom of useful influence is added to men in important situations by any colour, quantity, or configuration of cloth and hair. The true progress of refinement, we conceive, is to discard all the mountebank drapery of barbarous ages. One row of gold and fur falls off after another from the robe of power, and is pick'd up and worn by the parish beadle and the exhibiter of wild beasts. Meantime, the afflicted wiseacre mourns over equality of garment; and wotteth not of two men, whose doublets have cost alike, how one shall command and the other obey.

The dress of lawyers, however, is, at all events, of less importance than their charges. Law is cheap in America: in England, it is better, in a mere pecuniary point of view, to give up forty pounds than to contend for it in a court of common law. It costs that sum in England to win a cause; and, in the court, of equity, it is better to abandon five hundred or a thousand pounds than to contend for it. We mean to say nothing disrespectful of the chancellor – who is an upright judge, a very great lawyer, and zealous to do all he can; but we believe the Court of Chancery to be in a state which imperiously requires legislative correction. We do not accuse it of any malversation, but of a complication, formality, entanglement, and delay, which the life, the wealth, and the patience of man cannot endure. How such a subject comes not to have been taken up in the House of Commons, we are wholly at a loss to conceive. We feel for climbing boys as much as anybody can do; but what is a climbing boy in a chimney to a full-grown suitor in the master's office? And whence comes it, in the midst of ten thousand compassions and charities, that no Wilberforce, or Sister Fry, has started up for the suitors in chancery? and why, in the name of these afflicted and attorney-worn people, are there united in their judge three or four offices, any one of which is sufficient to occupy the whole time of a very able and active man? . . .

Literature the Americans have none – no native literature, we mean. It is all imported. They had a Franklin, indeed; and may afford to live for half a century on his fame. There is, or was, a Mr Dwight, who wrote some poems; and his baptismal name was Timothy. There is also a small account of Virginia by Jefferson, and an epic by Joel Barlow; and some pieces of pleasantry by Mr Irving. But why should the American write books, when a six weeks' passage brings them, in their own tongue, our sense, science, and genius, in bales and hogsheads? Prairies, steamboats, grist-mills, are their natural objects for centuries to come. Then, when they have got to the Pacific Ocean – epic poems, plays, pleasures of memory, and all the elegant gratifications of an ancient people who have tamed the wild earth, and set down to amuse themselves. – This is the natural march of human affairs. . . .

The great curse of America is the institution of Slavery – of itself far more than the foulest blot upon their national character, and an evil which counterbalances all the excisemen, licensers, and tax-gatherers of England. No virtuous man ought to trust his own character, or the character of his children, to the demoralising effects produced by commanding slaves. Justice, gentleness, pity, and humility, soon give way before them. Conscience suspends its functions. The love of command – the impatience of restraint, get the better of every other feeling; and cruelty has no other limit than fear. . . . Every American who loves his country, should dedicate his whole life, and every faculty of his soul to efface this foul stain from its character. If nations rank according to their wisdom and their virtue, what right has the American, a scourger and murderer of slaves, to compare himself with the least and lowest of the European nations? – much more with this great and humane country, where the greatest lord dare not lay a finger upon the meanest peasant?

What is freedom, where all are not free? where the greatest
of God's blessings is limited, with impious caprice, to the
colour of the body? And these are the men who taunt the
English with their corrupt Parliament, with their buying and
selling votes. Let the world judge which is the most liable
to censure – we who, in the midst of our rottenness, have
torn off the manacles of slaves all over the world; – or they
who, with their idle purity, and useless perfection, have
remained mute and careless, while groans echoed and whips
clank'd round the very walls of their spotless Congress. We
wish well to America – we rejoice in her prosperity – and
are delighted to resist the absurd impertinence with which
the character of her people is often treated in this country:
but the existence of slavery in America is an atrocious crime,
with which no measures can be kept – for which her
situation affords no sort of apology – which makes liberty
itself distrusted, and the boast of it disgusting.

Edinburgh Review, 1818.

In 1820 Sydney used a review of the *Statistical Annals of the U.S.A.*, published in Philadelphia in 1818, as the launching-pad for a whole-hearted
denunciation of taxation. Addressing the American people as 'Jonathan', he
warns them against the dangers of getting into wars for no better reasons
than national pride or hopes of glory.

We can inform Jonathan what are the inevitable consequences of being too fond of glory; – TAXES upon every
article which enters into the mouth, or covers the back, or is
placed under the foot – taxes upon every thing which it is
pleasant to see, hear, feel, smell, or taste – taxes upon
warmth, light, and locomotion – taxes on every thing on
earth, and the waters under the earth – on every thing that
comes from abroad, or is grown at home – taxes on the raw
material – taxes on every fresh value that is added to it by
the industry of man – taxes on the sauce which pampers
man's appetite, and the drug that restores him to health –
on the ermine which decorates the judge, and the rope which
hangs the criminal – on the poor man's salt, and the rich
man's spice – on the brass nails of the coffin, and the ribands
of the bride – at bed or board, couchant or levant, we must
pay. – The schoolboy whips his taxed top – the beardless
youth manages his taxed horse, with a taxed bridle on a
taxed road: – and the dying Englishman, pouring his medicine, which has paid 7 per cent., into a spoon that has paid
15 per cent., – flings himself back upon his chintz bed, which
has paid 22 per cent. – and expires in the arms of an apothec-

ary who has paid a licence of a hundred pounds for the privilege of putting him to death. His whole property is then immediately taxed from 2 to 10 per cent. Besides the probate, large fees are demanded for burying him in the chancel; his virtues are handed down to posterity on taxed marble; and he is then gathered to his fathers, – to be taxed no more. In addition to all this, the habit of dealing with large sums will make the Government avaricious and profuse; and the system itself will infallibly generate the base vermin of spies and informers, and a still more pestilent race of political tools and retainers of the meanest and most odious description; – while the prodigious patronage which the collecting of this splendid revenue will throw into the hands of Government, will invest it with so vast an influence, and hold out such means and temptations to corruption, as all the virtue and public spirit, even of republicans, will be unable to resist.

Such is the land of Jonathan – and thus has it been governed. In his honest endeavours to better his situation, and in his manly purpose of resisting injury and insult, we most cordially sympathise. We hope he will always continue to watch and suspect his Government as he now does – remembering, that it is the constant tendency of those entrusted with power, to conceive that they enjoy it by their own merits, and for their own use, and not by delegation, and for the benefit of others. Thus far we are the friends and admirers of Jonathan. But he must not grow vain and ambitious; or allow himself to be dazzled by that galaxy of epithets by which his orators and newspaper scribblers endeavour to persuade their supporters that they are the greatest, the most refined, the most enlightened, and the most moral people upon earth. The effect of this is unspeakably ludicrous on this side of the Atlantic – and, even on the other, we shall imagine, must be rather humiliating to the reasonable part of the population. The Americans are a brave, industrious, and acute people; but they have hitherto given no indications of genius, and made no approaches to the heroic, either in their morality or character. They are but a recent offset indeed from England; and should make it their chief boast, for many generations to come, that they are sprung from the same race with Bacon and Shakspeare and Newton. Considering their numbers, indeed, and the favourable circumstances in which they have been placed, they have yet done marvellously little to assert the honour of such a descent, or to show that their English blood has been exalted or refined by their republican training and institutions. Their Franklins and Washingtons, and all the other sages and heroes of their revolution, were born and bred subjects of the King of England, – and not among the freest or most valued of his subjects. And, since the period of their separation, a far greater proportion of their statesmen and artists and political writers have been foreigners, than ever occurred before in the history of any civilised and educated people. During the thirty or forty years of their independence, they have done absolutely nothing for the Sciences, for the Arts, for Literature, or even for the statesman-like studies of Politics or Political Economy. Confining ourselves to our own country, and to the period that has elapsed since *they* had an independent existence, we would ask, Where are their Foxes, their Burkes, their Sheridans, their Windhams, their Horners, their Wilberforces? – where their Arkwrights, their Watts, their Davys? – their Robertsons, Blairs, Smiths, Stewarts, Paleys, and Malthuses? – their Porsons, Parrs, Burneys, or Blomfields? – their Scotts, Rogers's, Campbells, Byrons, Moores, or Crabbes? – their Siddons's, Kembles, Keans, or O'Neils? – their Wilkies, Laurences, Chantrys? – or their parallels to the hundred other names that have spread themselves over the world from our little island in the course of the last thirty years, and blest or delighted mankind by their works, inventions, or examples? In so far as we know, there is no such parallel to be produced from the whole annals of this self-adulating race. In the four quarters of the globe, who reads an American book? or goes to an American play? or looks at an American picture or statue? What does the world yet owe to American physicians or surgeons? What new substances have their chemists discovered? or what old ones have they analysed? What new constellations have been discovered by the telescopes of Americans? What have they done in the mathematics? Who drinks out of American glasses? or eats from American plates? or wears American coats or gowns? or sleeps in American blankets? Finally, under which of the old tyrannical governments of Europe is every sixth man a slave, whom his fellow-creatures may buy and sell and torture?

When these questions are fairly and favourably answered, their laudatory epithets may be allowed: but, till that can be done, we would seriously advise them to keep clear of superlatives. *Edinburgh Review* 1820

1. *Travels through Part of the United States and Canada, in 1818 and 1819.* By John M. Duncan, A.B. Glasgow, 1823.
2. *Letters from North America, written during a Tour in the United States and Canada.* By Adam Hodgson. London, 1824.
3. *An Excursion through the United States and Canada, during the Years 1822-3.* By an English Gentleman. London, 1824.

There are a set of miserable persons in England, who are dreadfully afraid of America and every thing American – whose great delight is to see that country ridiculed and vilified – and who appear to imagine that all the abuses which exist in this country acquire additional vigour and chance of duration from every book of Travels which pours forth its venom and falsehood on the United States. We shall from time to time call the attention of the public to this subject, not from any party spirit, but because we love truth, and praise excellence wherever we find it; and because we think the example of America will in many instances tend to open the eyes of Englishmen to their true interests.

The *Economy* of America is a great and important object for our imitation. The salary of Mr Bagot, our late Ambassador, was, we believe, rather higher than that of the President of the United States. The Vice-President receives rather less than the second Clerk of the House of Commons; and all salaries, civil and military, are upon the same scale; and yet no country is better served than America! Mr Hume has at last persuaded the English people to look a little into their accounts, and to see how sadly they are plundered. But we ought to suspend our contempt for America, and consider whether we have not a very momentous lesson to learn from this wise and cautious people on the subject of economy.

A lesson upon the importance of Religious Toleration, we are determined, it would seem, *not* to learn, – either from America or from any other quarter of the globe. The High Sheriff of New York, last year, was a Jew. It was with the utmost difficulty that a bill was carried this year to allow the first Duke of England to carry a gold stick before the King – because he was a Catholic! – and yet we think ourselves entitled to indulge in impertinent sneers at America, – as if civilisation did not depend more upon making wise laws for the promotion of human happiness, than in having good inns, and post-horses, and civil waiters. The circumstances of the Dissenters' marriage bill are such as would excite the contempt of a Chictaw or Cherokee, if he could be brought to understand them. A certain class of Dissenters beg they may not be compelled to say that they marry in the name of the Trinity, because they do not believe in the Trinity. Never mind, say the corruptionists, you must go on saying you marry in the name of the Trinity, whether you believe in it or not. We know that such a protestation from you will be false; but, unless you make it, your wives shall be concubines, and your children illegitimate. Is it possible to conceive a greater or more useless tyranny than this? . . .

In fact, it is hardly possible for any nation to show a greater superiority over another than the Americans, in this particular, have done over this country. They have fairly and completely, and probably for ever, extinguished that spirit of religious persecution which has been the employment and the curse of mankind for four or five centuries, – not only that persecution which imprisons and scourges for religious opinions, but the tyranny of incapacitation, which, by disqualifying from civil offices, and cutting a man off from the lawful objects of ambition, endeavours to strangle religious freedom in silence, and to enjoy all the advantages, without the blood, and noise, and fire of persecution. What passes in the mind of one mean blockhead is the general history of all persecution. 'This man pretends to know better than me – I cannot subdue him by argument; but I will take care he shall never be mayor or alderman of the town in which he lives; I will never consent to the repeal of the Test Act or to Catholic emancipation; I will teach the fellow to differ from me in religious opinions!' So says the Episcopalian to the Catholic – and so the Catholic says to the Protestant. But the wisdom of America keeps them all down – secures to them all their just rights – gives to each of them their separate pews, and bells, and steeples – makes them all aldermen in their turns – and quietly extinguishes the faggots which each is preparing for the combustion of the other. Nor is this indifference to religious subjects in the American people, but pure civilisation – a thorough comprehension of what is best calculated to secure the public happiness and peace – and a determination that this happiness and peace shall not be violated by the insolence of any human being, in the garb, and under the sanction, of religion. In this particular, the Americans are at the head of all the nations of the world: and at the same time they are, especially in the Eastern and Midland States, so far from being indifferent on subjects of religion, that they may be most

justly characterised as a very religious people: but they are
devout without being unjust (the great problem in religion);
an higher proof of civilisation than painted tea-cups, water-
proof leather, or broad cloth at two guineas a yard . . . .

The great inconvenience of American inns, however, in
the eyes of an Englishman, is one which more sociable travellers must feel less acutely – we mean the impossibility of
being alone, of having a room separate from the rest of the
company. There is nothing which an Englishman enjoys
more than the pleasure of sulkiness, – of not being forced to
hear a word from any body which may occasion to him the
necessity of replying. It is not so much that Mr Bull disdains
to talk, as that Mr Bull has nothing to say. His forefathers
have been out of spirits for six or seven hundred years, and,
seeing nothing but fog and vapour, he is out of spirits too;
and when there is no selling or buying, or no business to
settle, he prefers being alone and looking at the fire. If any
gentleman was in distress, he would willingly lend an helping hand; but he thinks it no part of neighbourhood to talk
to a person because he happens to be near him. In short,
with many excellent qualities, it must be acknowledged that
the English are the most disagreeable of all the nations of
Europe, – more surly and morose, with less disposition to
please, to exert themselves for the good of society, to make
small sacrifices, and to put themselves out of their way. They
are content with Magna Charta and Trial by Jury; and think
they are not bound to excel the rest of the world in small
behaviour, if they are superior to them in great institutions.

We are terribly afraid that some Americans spit upon the
floor, even when that floor is covered by good carpets. Now,
all claims to civilisation are suspended till this secretion is
otherwise disposed of. No English gentleman has spit upon
the floor since the Heptarchy.

The curiosity for which the Americans are so much
laughed at, is not only venial, but laudable. Where men live
in woods and forests, as is the case, of course, in remote
American settlements, it is the duty of every man to gratify
the inhabitants by telling them his name, place, age, office,
virtues, crimes, children, fortune, and remarks: and with
fellow-travellers, it seems to be almost a matter of necessity
to do so. When men ride together for 300 or 400 miles through
woods and prairies, it is of the greatest importance that they
should be able to guess at subjects most agreeable to each
other, and to multiply their common topics. Without knowing
who your companion is, it is difficult to know both what to

say and what to avoid. You may talk of honour and virtue to an attorney, or contend with a Virginia planter that men of a fair colour have no right to buy and sell men of a dusky colour.

At the end of this review Sydney summed up his views on the USA and concluded with an eloquent and prophetic denunciation of the slave system:

America seems, on the whole, to be a country possessing vast advantages, and little inconveniences; they have a cheap government, and bad roads; they pay no tithes, and have stage coaches without springs. They have no poor laws and no monopolies – but their inns are inconvenient, and travellers are teased with questions. They have no collections in the fine arts; but they have no Lord Chancellor, and they can go to law without absolute ruin. They cannot make Latin verses, but they expend immense sums in the education of the poor. In all this the balance is prodigiously in their favour: but then comes the great disgrace and danger of America – the existence of slavery, which, if not timously corrected, will one day entail (and ought to entail) a bloody servile war upon the Americans – which will separate America into slave states and states disclaiming slavery, and which remains at present as the foulest blot in the moral character of that people. An high spirited nation, who cannot endure the slightest act of foreign aggression, and who revolt at the very shadow of domestic tyranny – beat with cart-whips, and bind with chains, and murder for the merest trifles, wretched human beings who are of a more dusky colour than themselves; and have recently admitted into their Union a new State, with the express permission of ingrafting this atrocious wickedness into their constitution! No one can admire the simple wisdom and manly firmness of the Americans more than we do, or more despise the pitiful propensity which exists among Government runners to vent their small spite at their character; but on the subject of slavery, the conduct of America is, and has been, most reprehensible. It is impossible to speak of it, with too much indignation and contempt; but for it, we should look forward with unqualified pleasure to such a land of freedom, and such a magnificent spectacle of human happiness.

Edinburgh Review 1824.

In his later, more prosperous years Sydney made friends with many American visitors to Britain. A few of the more sensitive and pugnacious American journalists had fiercely resented some of his comments on American life, especially its paucity of cultural achievement. This had not worried him. To one of his young American friends, Charles Sumner, he wrote in 1838: 'I have a great admiration of America, and have met with a great number of

agreeable, enlightened Americans. There is something in the honesty, simplicity and manliness of your countrymen which pleases me very much.' He
described another friend, Daniel Webster, as 'much like a steam engine in
trousers'. He pronounced himself a 'philoyankeeist'.

In the early 1840s the happy relationship came under a cloud. Several
American states had issued bonds to finance capital projects. Sydney invested a few hundred pounds in Pennsylvania. When a period of recession
closed in a few years later, Pennsylvania was one of five states that defaulted
on repayment. The money was not of vital importance to Sydney, but he saw
it as a matter of principle and also as an opportunity to keep his polemical
skills in good fighting trim. He sent a petition to the US Congress in Washington, and made sure it got printed in the London *Morning Chronicle*.

THE HUMBLE PETITION *of the* Rev. Sydney Smith *to the*
House of Congress *at* Washington

I PETITION your honourable House to institute some
measures for the restoration of American credit, and for the
repayment of debts incurred and repudiated by several of
the States. Your Petitioner lent to the State of Pennsylvania
a sum of money, for the purpose of some public improvement. The amount, though small, is to him important, and
is a saving from a life income, made with difficulty and
privation. If their refusal to pay (from which a very large
number of English families are suffering) had been the result
of war, produced by the unjust aggression of powerful
enemies; if it had arisen from civil discord; if it had proceeded from an improvident application of means in the
first years of self-government; if it were the act of a poor
State struggling against the barrenness of nature – every
friend of America would have been contented to wait for
better times; but the fraud is committed in the profound
peace of Pennsylvania, by the richest State in the Union,
after the wise investment of the borrowed money in roads
and canals, of which the repudiators are every day reaping
the advantage. It is an act of bad faith which (all its circumstances considered) has no parallel, and no excuse.

Nor is it only the loss of property which your Petitioner
laments; he laments still more that immense power which
the bad faith of America has given to aristocratical opinions, and to the enemies of free institutions, in the old world.
It is vain any longer to appeal to history, and to point out
the wrongs which the many have received from the few.
The Americans, who boast to have improved the institutions
of the old world, have at least equalled its crimes. A great
nation, after trampling under foot all earthly tyranny, has
been guilty of a fraud as enormous as ever disgraced the

worst king of the most degraded nation of Europe.

It is most painful to your Petitioner to see that American citizens excite, wherever they may go, the recollection that they belong to a dishonest people, who pride themselves on having tricked and pillaged Europe; and this mark is fixed by their faithless legislators on some of the best and most honourable men in the world whom every Englishman has been eager to see and proud to receive.

It is a subject of serious concern to your Petitioner that you are losing all that power which the friends of freedom rejoiced that you possessed, looking upon you as the ark of human happiness, and the most splendid picture of justice and of wisdom that the world had yet seen. Little did the friends of America expect it, and sad is the spectacle to see you rejected by every State in Europe, as a nation with whom no contract can be made, because none will be kept; unstable in the very foundations of social life, deficient in the elements of good faith, men who prefer any load of infamy however great, to any pressure of taxation however light.

Nor is it only this gigantic bankruptcy for so many degrees of longitude and latitude which your Petitioner deplores, but he is alarmed also by that total want of shame with which these things have been done; the callous immorality with which Europe has been plundered, that deadness of the moral sense which seems to preclude all return to honesty, to perpetuate this new infamy, and to threaten its extension over every State of the Union.

To any man of real philanthropy, who receives pleasure from the improvements of the world, the repudiation of the public debts of America, and the shameless manner in which it has been talked of and done, is the most melancholy event which has happened during the existence of the present generation. Your Petitioner sincerely prays that the great and good men still existing among you may, by teaching to the United States the deep disgrace they have incurred in the whole world, restore them to moral health, to that high position they have lost, and which, for the happiness of mankind, it is so important they should ever maintain; for the United States are now working out the greatest of all political problems, and upon that confederacy the eyes of thinking men are intensely fixed, to see how far the mass of mankind can be trusted with the management of their own affairs, and the establishment of their own happiness.

Morning Chronicle, 18 May, 1843.

Publication of the petition brought an outburst of rage in some of the American newspapers, with much intemperate abuse. 'They call me a Minor Canon, 85 years of age, an ass, and a Xantippe, mistaking evidently the sex of that termagant person.' Among those who swelled the chorus was a General Duff Green. Sydney, at the age of 72, still relished a good public fight, and responded with two resounding letters to the *Morning Chronicle*.

To the Editor of the *Morning Chronicle* Nov. 3, 1843

I never meet a Pennsylvanian at a London dinner without feeling a disposition to seize and divide him; – to allot his beaver to one sufferer and his coat to another – to appropriate his pocket-handkerchief to the orphan, and to comfort the widow with his silver watch, Broadway rings, and the London Guide, which he always carries in his pockets. How such a man can set himself down at an English table without feeling that he owes two or three pounds to every man in company I am at a loss to conceive: he has no more right to eat with honest men than a leper has to eat with clean men. If he have a particle of honour in his composition he should shut himself up, and say, 'I cannot mingle with you, I belong to a degraded people – I must hide myself – I am a plunderer from Pennsylvania.'

Figure to yourself a Pennsylvanian receiving foreigners in his own country, walking over the public works with them, and showing them Larcenous Lake, Swindling Swamp, Crafty Canal, and Rogues' Railway, and other dishonest works. 'This swamp we gained (says the patriotic borrower) by the repudiated loan of 1828. Our canal robbery was in 1830; we pocketed your good people's money for the railroad only last year.' All this may seem very smart to the Americans; but if I had the misfortune to be born among such a people, the land of my fathers should not retain me a single moment after the act of repudiation. I would appeal from my fathers to my forefathers. I would fly to Newgate for greater purity of thought, and seek in the prisons of England for better rules of life.

To the Editor of the *Morning Chronicle*, Nov 22 1843
Sir,
Having been unwell for some days past, I have had no opportunity of paying my respects to General Duff Green, who, (whatever be his other merits,) has certainly not shown himself a Washington in defence of his country. The General demands, with a beautiful simplicity, *'Whence this morbid hatred of America?'* But this question, all-affecting as it is, is stolen from Pilpay's fables: – 'A fox,' says Pilpay, 'caught

by the leg in a trap near the farm-yard, uttered the most piercing cries of distress: forthwith all the birds of the yard gathered round him, and seemed to delight in his misfortune; hens chuckled, geese hissed, ducks quacked, and chanticleer with shrill cockadoodles rent the air. "Whence," said the fox, limping forward with infinite gravity, "whence this morbid hatred of the fox? What have I done? Whom have I injured? I am overwhelmed with astonishment at these symptoms of aversion.' " "Oh, you old villain," the poultry exclaimed, "Where are our ducklings? Where are our goslings? Did not I see you running away yesterday with my mother in your mouth? Did you not eat up all my relations last week? You ought to die the worst of deaths – to be pecked into a thousand pieces." Now hence, General Green, comes the morbid hatred of America, as you term it – because her conduct has been predatory – because she has ruined so many helpless children, so many miserable women, so many aged men – because she has disturbed the order of the world, and rifled those sacred treasures which human virtue had hoarded for human misery. Why is such hatred morbid? Why, is it not just, inevitable, innate? Why, is it not disgraceful to want it? Why, is it not honourable to feel it?

Hate America!!! I have loved and honoured America all my life; and in the *Edinburgh Review*, and at all opportunities which my trumpery sphere of action has afforded, I have never ceased to praise and defend the United States; and to every American to whom I have had the good fortune to be introduced, I have proffered all the hospitality in my power. But I cannot shut my eyes to enormous dishonesty; nor, remembering their former state, can I restrain myself from calling on them (though I copy Satan) to spring up from the gulf of infamy in which they are rolling, -

'Awake, arise, or be for ever fallen.'

I am astonished that the honest States of America do not draw a *cordon sanitaire* round their unpaying brethren – that a truly mercantile New Yorkers, and the thoroughly honest people of Massachusetts, do not in their European visits wear an uniform with 'S.S., or Solvent States,' worked in gold letters upon the coat, and receipts in full of all demands tamboured on their waistcoats, and 'our own property' figured on their pantaloons.

But the General seems shocked that I should say the Americans cannot go to war without money: but what do I mean by war? Not irruptions into Canada – not the embodying of militia in Oregon; but a long, tedious, maritime war of four or five years' duration. Is any man so foolish as to suppose that Rothschild has nothing to do with such wars as these? and that a bankrupt State, without the power of borrowing a shilling in the world, may not be crippled in such a contest? We all know that the Americans can fight. Nobody doubts their courage. I see now in my mind's eye a whole army on the plains of Pennsylvania in battle array, immense corps of insolvent light infantry, regiments of heavy horse debtors, battalions of repudiators, brigades of bank-rupts, with *Vivre sans payer, ou mourir*, on their banners, and *ære alieno* on their trumpets: all these desperate debtors would fight to the death for their country, and probably drive into the sea their invading creditors. Of their courage, I repeat again, I have no doubt. I wish I had the same confidence in their wisdom. But I believe they will become intoxicated by the flattery of unprincipled orators; and, instead of enter-ing with us into a noble competition in making calico (the great object for which the Anglo-Saxon race appears to have been created), they will waste their happiness and their money (if they can get any) in years of silly, bloody, foolish, and accursed war, to prove to the world that Perkins is a real fine gentleman, and that the carronades of the Washington steamer will carry further than those of the British Victoria, or the Robert Peel vessel of war.

I am accused of applying the epithet repudiation to States which have not repudiated. Perhaps so; but then these latter states have not paid. But what is the difference between a man who says, 'I don't owe you any thing, and will not pay you,' and another who says, 'I do owe you a sum,' and who, having admitted the debt, never pays it? There seems in the first to be some slight colour of right; but the second is broad, blazing, refulgent, meridian fraud.

It may be very true that rich and educated men in Pennsylvania wish to pay the debt, and that the real objectors are the Dutch and German agriculturists, who cannot be made to understand the effect of character upon clover. All this may be very true, but it is a domestic quarrel. Their churchwardens of reputation must make a private rate of infamy for themselves – we have nothing to do with this rate. The real quarrel is the Unpaid World *versus* the State of Pennsylvania.

And now, dear Jonathan, let me beg of you to follow the advice of a real friend, who will say to you what Wat Tyler had not the virtue to say, and what all speakers in the eleven recent Pennsylvanian elections have cautiously abstained from saying, – 'Make a great effort; book up at once, and pay.' You have no conception of the obloquy and contempt to which you are exposing yourselves all over Europe. Bull is naturally disposed to love you, but he loves nobody who does not pay him. His imaginary paradise is some planet of punctual payment, where ready money prevails, and where debt and discount are unknown.

As for me, as soon as I hear that the last farthing is paid to the last creditor, I will appear on my knees at the bar of the Pennsylvanian Senate in the plumeopicean robe of American controversy. Each Conscript Jonathan shall trickle over me a few drops of tar, and help to decorate me with those penal plumes in which the vanquished reasoner of the transatlantic world does homage to the physical superiority of his opponents. And now, having eased my soul of its indignation, and sold my stock at 40 per cent. discount, I sulkily retire from the subject, with a fixed intention of lending no more money to free and enlightened republics, but of employing my money henceforth in buying up Abyssinian bonds, and purchasing into the Turkish Fours, or the Tunis Three-and-a-half per Cent. Funds.

Sydney Smith.

Through the years, despite his criticisms and controversy, Sydney received admiring American visitors. 'If he had not been known as the wittiest man of his day, he would have been accounted one of the wisest,' wrote Mr Everett, minister of religion. Daniel Webster wrote on 8th June 1839, 'Yesterday I breakfasted with Sydney Smith, long known as the greatest wit in England. He is a clergyman of much respectability.' To Sydney he wrote, 'The pleasure of your acquaintance is one of the jewels I brought home with me. I had read *of* you and read you for 30 years. I was delighted to meet you, and to have all I knew of you refreshed and brightened by the charms of your conversation.' And when a young man called Sydney Smith arrived in New York in August 1844 he was fêted and given a public dinner – much to his confusion, for he was a cooper by trade.

Foston Rectory, the house that Sydney built and was his home 1814-29.
'You build for glory, Sir; I, for use.'

Combe Florey Rectory, which Sydney altered to let in more light. 'Never
was there a more delightful parsonage.'

IV

Town and Country

Sydney spent a large part of his life living in remote country places, longing to be in London. In one of his famous phrases he dismissed the country as a kind of healthy grave. Of London, on the other hand, he wrote: 'I believe the parallelogram between Oxford Street, Piccadilly, Regent Street and Hyde Park, encloses more intelligence and human ability, to say nothing of wealth and beauty, than the world has ever collected in such a space before.' He loved comfortable and civilised surroundings, good food and enough wine, company that was well-informed and clever, quick-witted and relaxed. It was as a regular guest at the table of Holland House in Kensington that he found his ultimate element, the ambience that inspired him to his most glorious, uproarious flights of wit and fancy. There were many times when he resented the fate which so often, and for such long periods, exiled him from these metropolitan delights.

It was the quietness, the dullness, the sheer predictability of rural living that dispirited him. 'In the country,' he said, 'I always fear that creation will expire before tea-time.' He also said: 'Whenever I enter a village, straightway I find an ass.'

He was an exact contemporary of Wordsworth and Coleridge, 'Lake Poets' and founders of the Romantic Movement in English poetry, but had none of their relish and reverence for wilderness landscapes. He was naturally suspicious of all forms of high-flown poetical effusion. His own experience and observation of country life did nothing to persuade him towards the Wordsworthian message, that daily contact with nature at its most elemental had a calming and refining and even an ennobling influence on man's character. In this respect Sydney was a true eighteenth-century Augustan, preferring landscapes that had been tamed and shaped by man and turned to good, productive use. In one of his lectures, he said:

> The sudden variation from the hill country of Gloucestershire to the Vale of Severn, as observed from Birdlip or Frowcester Hill, is strikingly sublime. You travel for twenty or five-and-twenty miles over one of the most unfortunate, desolate countries under heaven, divided by stone walls, and abandoned to screaming kites and larcenous crows: after travelling really twenty and to appearance ninety miles over this region of stone and sorrow, life begins to be a burden and you wish to perish.
>
> At the very moment when you are taking this melancholy view of human affairs, and hating the postilion, and blaming

the horses, there bursts upon your view, with all its towers, forests and streams, the deep and shaded Vale of Severn. Sterility and nakedness are thrown in the background: as far as the eye can reach, all is comfort, opulence, product and beauty: now it is an ancient city or a fair castle rising out of the forests, and now the beautiful Severn is noticed winding among the cultivated fields, and the cheerful habitations of men. The train of mournful impressions is quite effaced, and you descend rapidly into a vale of plenty, with a heart full of wonder and delight.

In one of his book reviews Sydney had a lot of fun deriding the French philosopher Jean Jacques Rousseau's claims about the beneficial effects of rural living. The book under review was *The Memoirs and Correspondence of Mme d'Epinay*, a lady who had been a great fan of Rousseau's. Sydney reported:

Mme d'Epinay was so far deluded by his declamations about the country, as to fit him up in a little hermit cottage, where there were a great many birds, and a great many plants and flowers – and where Rousseau was, as might have been expected, supremely miserable. His friends from Paris did not come to see him. The postman, the butcher, and the baker, hate romantic scenery – duchesses and marchionesses were no longer found to scramble for him. Among the real inhabitants of the country, the reputation of reading and thinking is fatal to character; and Jean Jacques cursed his own successful eloquence which had sent him from the suppers and flattery of Paris to smell the daffodils, watch sparrows, or project idle saliva into the passing stream. Very few men who have gratified, and are gratifying their vanity in a great metropolis, are qualified to quit it. Few have the plain sense to perceive that they must soon inevitably be forgotten – or the fortitude to bear it when they are.   *Edinburgh Review*, 1818

In fact, as he showed more than once in his life, Sydney did have the fortitude to withstand the pains and privations of exile from the 'great metropolis'. He made the best of his situation with his customary ebullience of spirit, but at the same time he felt free to speak his mind about it. His first clerical posting, taken up in 1794, was as curate at Netheravon near Amesbury on Salisbury Plain, a particularly depressed region. He wrote to a friend: 'Nothing can equal the profound, the immeasurable, the awful dullness of this place, in which I lie, dead and buried, in hopes of a joyful resurrection in the year 1796.'

The resurrection was delayed, but in the early summer of 1798 Sydney – appointed tutor to the son of the local squire, Mr Hicks-Beach – took up residence in the northern metropolis of Edinburgh. On their way northwards he and the adolescent, Michael, passed through the Lake District, just beginning to build its reputation as a tourist attraction. They stayed briefly in

Keswick, and Sydney decided they should honour the 'picturesque tourist' tradition and hire a guide to escort them to the summit of Skiddaw, just over 3,000 feet above sea-level. He described their adventure in a letter to Michael's parents:

Off we set, Michael the guide and myself, at one in the morning to gain the summit of Skiddaw. I, who find it rather difficult to stick upon my horse on the plainest roads, did not find that facility increased by the darkness of the morning or the precipitous paths we had to ascend.

I made no manner of doubt but that I should roll down into the town of Keswick the next morning and be picked up by the town beadle dead in a gutter; moreover I was moved a little for my reputation, for as I had a bottle of brandy in my pocket, placed there by the special exhortations of the guide and landlord, the Keswick coroner and jury would infallibly have brought me in *a Parson as died of drinking.* However, onward we moved, and arrived at the summit. The thermometer stood at 40, the wind was bitter, and the summit totally enveloped in thick clouds, which nearly wetted us through and totally cut off all view of the sun and the earth, too. Here we regaled upon biscuit and brandy, and waited for the dissipation of the vapour. The guide seemed to be about as much affected by the weather as Skiddaw itself, which mountain in height and brownness of complexion he something resembled. I was rueful enough, tho I really rejoiced in the novelty of the scene; but a more woebegone, piteous face than Michael put on you never saw – no tailor tried, cast and condemned for filching small parcels of cloth every looked so unhappy. The wind, the complaisant wind, now puffed away the vapours at intervals and gave us a hasty view on different quarters of the magnificent scene which surrounded us. When the clearance was to the east, we looked over the level country of Northumberland, and saw the light of day rising from the German Ocean. Beneath us was Keswick, all quiet, and the solemn tranquil lake of Derwent – beyond these the Westmoreland mountains began to be tinged with the golden morning, or we caught the Isle of Man, the northern coast of Ireland, the Firth of Solway, or the hills of Cheviot well known to song and history. Above us was the blue heaven, and all under were the sons of men, scattered in fair cities and upon the hills and down in the dales, and over the whole face of the earth. And so we went down – and Michael grew warm and eat a monstrous breakfast, and was right pleased with his excursion, and all was well.

Sydney spent five happy years in Edinburgh, during which he toured the Highlands, but the ride up Skiddaw was the beginning and the end of his mountaineering career.

During his twenty years at Foston, and the sixteen at Combe Florey when his duties at St. Paul's occasioned him to spend a good deal of time in London, Sydney had ample opportunity to reflect on the relative merits of town and country life. He never wrote a sustained consideration, but his letters over the years make frequent mention of the matter.

June 1801

My dear Jeffrey,
After a vertigo of one fortnight in London, I am now under-going that species of hybernation or suspended existence, called a pleasant fortnight in the country. I behave myself quietly and decently as becomes a Corpse, and hope to regain the rational and immortal part of my composition about the 20th of this month.

In the summer of 1807 he took his wife and three children for a holiday at Sonning-on-Thames, and wrote to Lady Holland:
Mrs S. is quite delighted with her Country Box – so am I. I have seen a great number of thrushes hopping before the window this Evening, but their conduct was by no means innocent or decorous.

June 24 1809

My dear Lady Holland,
This is the third day since I arrived at the village of Heslington, 200 miles from London. I missed the hackney-coaches for the first three or four days but after that prepared myself for the change from the aurelia to the grub state, and dare say I shall become fat, torpid and motionless with a very good grace.

I mean to come to town once a year, tho' of that I suppose I shall soon be weary finding my mind growing weaker and weaker and my acquaintance gradually reduced to very much neglected aunts and cousins, to whose proffered tea I shall crawl in, a penitent and Magdalene kinsman. . . .

Mrs Sydney is all rural bustle impatient for the parturition of hens and pigs; I wait patiently knowing all will come in due season.

September 9 1809

My dear Lady Holland,
I hear you laugh at me for being happy in the country, and upon this I have a few words to say. In the first place whether one lives or dies I hold and always have held to be of infi-nitely less moment than is generally supposed; but if life is the choice then it is common sense to amuse yourself with

the best you can find where you happen to be placed. I am not leading precisely the life I should chuse, but that which (all things considered, as well as I could consider them) appeared to be the most eligible. I am resolved therefore to like it and to reconcile myself to it; which is more manly than to feign myself above it, and to send up complaints by the post, of being thrown away, and being desolate and such like trash. I am prepared therefore either way. If the chances of life ever enable me to emerge, I will show you that I have not been wholly occupied by small and sordid pursuits. If (as the greater probability is) I am come to the end of my career, I give myself quietly up to horticulture, and the annual augmentation of my family. In short, if my lot be to crawl, I will crawl contentedly; if to fly, I will fly with alacrity; but as long as I can possibly avoid it I will never be unhappy.

March 1814

Dear Allen,
It is very pleasant in these deserts to see the hand writing of an old friend; it is like the print in the sand seen by Robinson Crusoe.

March 1818

My dear Lady Holland,
Nothing can exceed the evils of this spring, all agricultural operations are at least a month behindhand; and the earth that ought to be as hard as a biscuit is as soft as dough. We live here in great seclusion but happily, and comfortably. My life is cut up into little patches; I am Schoolmaster farmer doctor parson justice etc. etc.

April 20 1819

My dear Lady Holland,
I have been lame for some time by a fall from my horse. He had behaved so well and so quietly that I doubled his allowance of corn and in return he kicked me over his head in the most ignominious, and contemptuous manner. This should be a warning to you against raising servants' wages. I am recovering fast tho' sorely bruised; fifteen stone weight does not fall from, sixteen hands high with impunity.

For all his troubles and tribulations and all his jokes about life in the country, Sydney took his farming very seriously.

To William Vernon
March 29, 1818

My dear Sr -
I perfectly agree with you in the importance of agricultural Experiments but in many or most cases they are very slow

in their results, very expensive – and from the prodigious variety of circumstances very uncertain in their conclusions. – These causes explain only why they are not made so often as they ought to be – but shew more strongly the necessity that more persons should be engagd in them – You are aware perhaps that there are several Subscription Experimental farms in Ireland and England which publish the results of their Experiments – and the common practice of Agriculture involves of course a vast Mass of coarse unintentional Experiment – - – I never sow a crop without trying some experiment: for instance it is the practice of this Country to lime old ploughd Lands every fallow Year at the Expence of 48 Shillings p Acre – I always leave a part unlim'd and observe as carefully as I can the difference – -

What crops have preceded for 20 Years before? – how often ploughd? – what Substratum? – and so on – a third Infinity is the Weather – The same Gypsum may be poison if the weather is X the first 10 days in March – neutral if the Weather is Y – & a delicious pabulum if it is Z. – So that an experiment in farming is commonly a distant Approximation to the truth and proves only what was best for *that* place in *that* Year – not what will be for *another* place the *next* Year. – Still it is better than nothing – and these observations are not true of all Experiments which may be called Experiments in farming.

To *The Farmer's Magazine* August 1819

Sir,

It has been my lot to have passed the greater part of my life in cities. – About six or seven years ago, I was placed in the country, in a situation where I was under the necessity of becoming a farmer; and amongst the many expensive blunders I have made, I warn those who may find themselves in similar situations, against *Scotch Sheep* and *Oxen for ploughing*. I had heard a great deal about the fine flavour of Scotch mutton, and it was one of the great luxuries I promised myself in farming. A luxury certainly it is; but the price paid for it is such, that I would rather give up the use of animal food altogether, than obtain it by such a system of cares and anxieties. Ten times a day my men were called off from their work to hunt the Scotch sheep out of my own or my neighbour's wheat. They crawled through hedges where I should have thought a rabbit could hardly have found admission; and where crawling would not do, they had recourse to leaping. Five or six times they all assembled, and set out on their return to the North. My bailiff took a place in the mail, pursued and overtook them half way to Newcastle. Then it was quite impossible to get them fat. They consumed my turnips in winter, and my clover in the summer, without any apparent addition to their weight; 10 or 12 per cent always died of the rot: and more would have perished in the same manner, if they had not been prematurely eaten out of the way.

My ploughing oxen were an equal subject of vexation. They had a constant purging upon them, which it was impossible to stop. They ate more than twice as much as the same number of horses. They did half as much work as the same number of horses. They could not bear hot weather, nor wet weather, nor go well down hill. It took five men to shoe an ox. They ran against my gate-posts, lay down in the cart whenever they were tired, and ran away at the sight of a stranger.

I have now got into a good breed of English sheep, and useful cart-horses, and am doing very well.

May 10 1822

Dear Mrs Meynell,
I have got into all my London feelings, which come on the moment I pass Hyde Park Corner. I am languid, unfriendly, heartless, selfish, sarcastic, and insolent. Forgive me, thou inhabitant of the plains, child of nature, rural woman, agricultural female! Remember what you were in Hill-Street, and pardon the vices inevitable in the greatest of cities.

May-June ? 1825

My dear Lady Grey,
The most helpless of all beings is a poor parson, of an evening, in London in wet weather, without a carriage. The characteristic of London is that you never go where you wish, nor do what you wish, and that you always wish to be somewhere else than where you are.

June 13 1829

My dear Lady Grey,
I am extremely pleased with Combe Florey, and pronounce it to be a very pretty place in a very beautiful country. The house I shall make decently convenient. I have 60 acres of good land round it. The habit of the country is to give dinners, and not to sleep out. My neighbours look very much like other people's neighbours; their remarks are generally of a meteorological nature.

Jan. 3 1841

My dear Lady Holland,
The Hibberts are here, and the house full, light, and warm.

Time goes on well. I do all I can to love the country, and endeavour to believe those poetical lies which I read in Rogers and others, on the subject; which said deviations from truth were, by Rogers, all written in St. James's-place.

I have long since got rid of all ambition and wish for distinctions, and am much happier for it. The journey is nearly over, and I am careless and good-humoured; at least good-humoured for me, as it is not an attribute which has been largely conceded to me by Providence.

Accept my affectionate and sincere good wishes.

July 1838

My dear Georgiana,

The summer and the country, dear Georgiana, have no charms for me. I look forward anxiously to the return of bad weather, coal fires, and good society in a crowded city. I have no relish for the country; it is a kind of healthy grave. I am afraid you are not exempt from the delusions of flowers, green turf, and birds; they all afford slight gratification, but not worth an hour of rational conversation: and rational conversation in sufficient quantities is only to be had from the congregation of a million of people in one spot.

Combe Florey
Sept. 23 1842

Dearest Gee,

I am living, lively and young as I am, in the most profound solitude. I saw a crow yesterday, and had a distant view of a rabbit today. I have ceased to trouble myself about company. If anybody thinks it worth while to turn aside to the Valley of Flowers, I am most happy to see them; but I have ceased to lay plots, and to toil for visitors. I save myself by this much disappointment.

June 29 1844

Sir,

I am seventy-four years of age; and being Canon of St. Paul's in London, and a rector of a parish in the country, I am living amongst the best society in the Metropolis, and at ease in my circumstances; in tolerable health, a mild Whig, a tolerating Churchman, and much given to talking, laughing and noise. I dine with the rich in London, and physic the poor in the country; passing from the sauces of Dives to the sores of Lazarus. I am, upon the whole, a happy man; have found the world an entertaining world, and am thankful to Providence for the part allotted to me in it.

In one of his last letters, written to Lady Grey on 11 October, 1844, Sydney presented what he called the 'Combe Florey Gazette':

Mr Smith's large red Cow is expected to calve this week.
Mr Gibbs has bought Mr Smith's Lame Mare -
It rained yesterday, and a correspondent observes that it is
    not unlikely to rain today
Mr Smith is better
Mrs Smith is indisposed
A nest of black Magpies was found near this Village yesterday

In *A Memoir of the Reverend Sydney Smith* his daughter Saba recalled her
father's feelings about dining out in the country:

Though it was the general habit in Yorkshire to make visits
of two or three days at the houses in the neighbourhood, yet
not unfrequently invitations to dinner only came, and sometimes to a house at a considerable distance.

'Did you ever dine out in the country?' said my father.
'What misery human beings inflict on each other under the
name of pleasure! We went to dine last Thursday with Mr
—, a neighbouring clergyman, a haunch of venison being
the stimulus to the invitation. We set out at five o'clock;
drove in a broiling sun, on dusty roads, three miles, in our
best gowns; found Squire and parsons assembled in a small
hot room, the whole house redolent of frying; talked, as is
our wont, of roads, weather, and turnips; that done, began
to grow hungry, then serious, then impatient. At last a stripling, evidently caught up for the occasion, opened the door
and beckoned our host out of the room. After some moments
of awful suspense, he returned to us with a face of much
distress, saying, 'the woman assisting in the kitchen had
mistaken the soup for dirty water, and had thrown it away,
so we must do without it;' we all agreed it was perhaps as
well we should, under the circumstances. At last, to our
joy, dinner was announced; but oh, ye gods! as we entered
the dining-room what a gale met our nose! the venison was
high; the venison was uneatable, and was obliged to follow
the soup with all speed.

'Dinner proceeded, but our spirits flagged under these
accumulated misfortunes. There was an ominous pause
between the first and second course; we looked each other
in the face – what new disaster awaited us? The pause
became fearful. At last the door burst open, and the boy
rushed in, calling out aloud, 'Please, Sir, has Betty any right
to leather I?' What human gravity could stand this? We
roared with laughter; all took part against Betty, obtained
the second course with some difficulty, bored each other
the usual time, ordered our carriages, expecting our post-
boys to be drunk, and were grateful to Providence for not

permitting them to deposit us in a wet ditch. So much for dinners in the country!'

In the same book Saba records a moment, very late in his life, when Sydney seemed almost be be recanting his ancient anti-country opinions:

Then wandering on a little further, his black crutch-stick in his hand, and his white hairs blown about by the soft Somersetshire wind: 'It must be admitted,' said he, 'if the mind vegetates, the body rejoices, in the country. What an air this is! Our climate is so mild, that myrtles and geraniums stand out all the winter; and the effects of it on the human constitution are such, that Lady —, a model of female virtue, who never gave that excellent baronet, her husband, a moment's anxiety, declared to me with a deep sigh, after a week's residence here, that she must go, for she felt all her principles melting away under its influence. Some of my Scotch friends, it is true, complain that it is too enervating; but they are but northern barbarians, after all, and like to breathe their air raw. We civilized people of the south prefer it cooked.'

Going a few steps further: 'There, now lift your eyes, and tell me where another parsonage-house in England has such a view as that to boast of. What can Pall Mall or Piccadilly produce to rival it?'

V

Education

Sydney believed fervently in the importance of education: in elementary education for all, against which there were powerful vested interests; in the reform of the public school education which he had endured at Winchester College; and in equality of educational opportunity for women, whose conversation and correspondence he much enjoyed.

Elementary Education for All

At the beginning of Queen Victoria's reign he preached a sermon in St. Paul's Cathedral on 'The Duties of the Queen'. At this date it was estimated that about a third of working class children had no schooling at all.

First and foremost, I think, the new Queen should bend her mind to the very serious consideration of educating the people. Of the importance of this I think no reasonable doubt can exist; it does not in its effects keep pace with the exaggerated expectations of its injudicious advocates; but it presents the best chance of national improvement.

Reading and writing are mere increase of power. They may be turned, I admit, to a good or a bad purpose; but for several years of his life the child is in your hands, and you may give to that power what bias you please: thou shalt not kill – thou shalt not steal – thou shalt not bear false witness: by how many fables, by how much poetry, by how many beautiful aids of imagination, may not the fine morality of the Sacred Scriptures be engraven on the minds of the young? I believe the arm of the assassin may be often stayed by the lessons of his early life. When I see the village school, and the tattered scholars, and the aged master or mistress teaching the mechanical art of reading or writing, and thinking that they are teaching that alone, I feel that the aged instructor is protecting life, insuring property, fencing the altar, guarding the throne, giving space and liberty to all the fine powers of man, and lifting him up to his own place in the order of Creation.

There are, I am sorry to say, many countries in Europe which have taken the lead of England in the great business of education, and it is a thoroughly commendable and legitimate object of ambition in a Sovereign to overtake them. The names, too, of malefactors, and the nature of their crimes, are subjected to the Sovereign; – how is it possible that a Sovereign, with the fine feelings of youth, and with all the gentleness of her sex, should not ask herself, whether the human being whom she dooms to death, or at least does not rescue from death, has been properly warned in early youth of the horrors of that crime, for which his life is forfeited – 'Did he ever receive any education at all? – did a father and a mother watch over him? – was he brought to places of worship? – was the Word of God explained to him? – was the Book of Knowledge opened to him? – Or am I, the fountain of mercy, the nursing-mother of my people, to send a forsaken wretch from the streets to the scaffold, and to prevent by unprincipled cruelty the evils of unprincipled neglect?'

One of the vested interests opposed to universal education was the Established Church, for the imposition of universal education would necessitate state control of what was at the time, though on a much smaller scale, in its own hands. Joseph Lancaster, a Quaker, had proposed an economically viable system for elementary schooling, only to be severely criticised by a Mrs Trimmer. Sydney takes up the cudgels on behalf of Lancaster.

TRIMMER AND LANCASTER.

A Comparative View of the New Plan of Education promulgated by Mr Joseph Lancaster, in his Tracts concerning the Instruction of the Children of the Labouring Part of the Community; and of the System of Christian Education founded by our pious Forefathers for the Initiation of the Young Members of the Established Church in the Principles of the Reformed Religion.

By Mrs Trimmer. 1805.

This is a book written by a lady who has gained considerable reputation at the corner of St Paul's Churchyard; who flames in the van of Mr Newberry's shop; and is, upon the whole, dearer to mothers and aunts than any other author who pours the milk of science into the mouth of babes and sucklings. Tired at last of scribbling for children, and getting ripe in ambition, she has now written a book for grown-up people, and selected for her antagonist as stiff a controversialist as the whole field of dispute could well have supplied. Her opponent is Mr Lancaster, a Quaker, who has lately given to the world new and striking lights upon the subject of Education, and come forward to the notice of his country by spreading order, knowledge, and innocence among the lowest of mankind.

Mr Lancaster, she says, wants method in his book; and therefore her answer to him is without any arrangement. The same excuse must suffice for the desultory observations we shall make upon this lady's publication.

The first sensation of disgust we experience at Mrs Trimmer's book, was from the patronising and protecting air with which she speaks of some small part of Mr Lancaster's plan. She seems to suppose, because she has dedicated her mind to the subject, that her opinion must necessarily be valuable upon it; forgetting it to be barely possible, that her application may have made her more wrong, instead of more right. If she can make out of her case, that Mr Lancaster is doing mischief in so important a point as that of national education, she has a right, in common with every one else, to lay her complaint before the public; but a right to publish praises must be earned by something more difficult than the writing sixpenny books for children. They may be very good; though we never remember to have seen any one of them; but if they be no more remarkable for judgment and discretion than parts of the work before us, there are many thriving children quite capable of repaying the obligations they owe to their amiable instructress, and of teaching, with grateful retaliation, 'the *old* idea how to shoot.

In remarking upon the work before us, we shall exactly follow the plan of the authoress, and prefix, as she does, the titles of those subjects on which her observations are made; doing her the justice to presume, that her quotations are fairly taken from Mr Lancaster's book.

1. *Mr Lancaster's Preface.* – Mrs Trimmer here contends, in opposition to Mr Lancaster, that ever since the establishment of the Protestant Church, the education of the poor has been a national concern in this country; and the only argument she produces in support of this extravagant assertion, is an appeal to the Act of Uniformity. If there are millions of Englishmen who cannot spell their own names, or read a sign-post which bids them turn to the right or left, is it any answer to this deplorable ignorance to say, there is an Act of Parliament for public instruction? – to show the very line and chapter where the King, Lords, and Commons, in Parliament assembled, ordained the universality of reading and writing, when, centuries afterwards, the ploughman is no more capable of the one or the other than the beast which he drives? In point of fact, there is no Protestant country in the world where the education of the poor has been so grossly and infamously neglected as in England. Mr Lancaster has the very high merit of calling the public attention to this evil, and of calling it in the best way, by

new and active remedies; and this uncandid and feeble lady, instead of using the influence she has obtained over the anility of these realms, to join that useful remonstrance which Mr Lancaster has begun, pretends to deny that the evil exists; and when you ask where are the schools, rods, pedagogues, primers, histories of Jack the Giant-killer, and all the usual apparatus for education, the only things she can produce is *the Act of Uniformity and Common Prayer.*

2. *The Principles on which Mr Lancaster's Institution is conducted.* – 'Happily for mankind,' says Mr Lancaster, 'it is possible to combine precept and practice together in the education of youth: that public spirit, or general opinion, which gives such strength to vice, may be rendered serviceable to the cause of virtue; and in thus directing it, the whole secret, the beauty, and simplicity of national education consists. Suppose, for instance, it be required to train a youth to strict veracity. He has learned to read at school: he there reads the declaration of the Divine will respecting liars: he is there informed of the pernicious effects that practice produces on society at large: and he is enjoined, for the fear of God, for the approbation of his friends, and for the good of his schoolfellows, never to tell an untruth. This is a most excellent precept; but let it be taught, and yet, if the contrary practice be treated with indifference by parents, teachers, or associates, it will either weaken or destroy all the good that can be derived from it. But if the parents or teachers tenderly nip the rising shoots of vice; if the associates of youth pour contempt on the liar; he will soon hide his head with shame, and most likely leave off the practice.'

The objection which Mrs Trimmer makes to this passage is, that it is *exalting the fear of man above the fear of God.* This observation is as mischievous as it is unfounded. Undoubtedly, the fear of God ought to be the paramount principle from the very beginning of life, if it were possible to make it so; but it is a feeling which can only be built up by degrees. The awe and respect which a child entertains for its parent and instructor, is the first scaffolding upon which the sacred edifice of religion is reared. A child *begins* to pray, to act, and to abstain, not to please God, but to please the parent, who tells him that such is the will of God. The religious principle gains ground from the power of association and the improvement of reason; but without the fear of man – the desire of pleasing, and the dread of offending those with whom he lives, – it would be extremely difficulty, if not impossible, to cherish it at all in the mind of children.

If you tell (says Mr Lancaster) a child not to swear, because it is forbidden by God, and he finds every body whom he lives with addicted to that vice, the mere precept will soon be obliterated; which would acquire its just influence if aided by the effect of example. Mr Lancaster does not say that the fear of man ever *ought* to be a stronger motive than the fear of God, or that, in a thoroughly formed character, it ever *is*: he merely says, that the fear of man may be made the most powerful mean to raise up the fear of God; and nothing, in our opinion, can be more plain, more sensible, or better expressed, than his opinions upon these subjects.

Edinburgh Review, 1806.

Concerning religious education, Lady Holland recalls Sydney saying,
Of this much I am sure, that the attempt to impress notions of religion on very young children, before they are capable of thinking seriously for one moment upon anything, is to associate, for the whole of subsequent life, *ennui* and disgust with the idea of sacred reflections; and I am fully persuaded more injury is done by injudicious zeal than by neglect.'

Public Schools and Universities

Turning to public schools and universities, Sydney's review of *Essays on Professional Education* by R.L. Edgeworth, published in 1809, allowed him to express his thoughts on the classical education found there. He accepts that the study of Latin and Greek is a good mental discipline, that it helps in the acquisition of other languages, that the great classical authors are excellent examples of style:

In short, it appears to us, that there are so many excellent reasons why a certain number of scholars should be kept up in this and in every civilised country, that we should consider every system of education from which classical education was excluded, as radically erroneous, and completely absurd.

But what about the way it is taught?

That vast advantages, then, may be derived from classical learning, there can be no doubt. The advantages which are derived from classical learning by the English manner of teaching, involve another and a very different question; and we will venture to say, that there never was a more complete instance in any country of such extravagant and over-acted attachment to any branch of knowledge, as that which obtains in this country with regard to classical knowledge. A young Englishman goes to school at six or seven years old; and he remains in a course of education till twenty-three or twenty-four years of age. In all that time, his sole and exclusive occupation is learning Latin and Greek: he has scarcely a notion that there is any other kind of excellence; and the great system of facts with which he is the most perfectly acquainted, are the intrigues of the heathen Gods: with whom Pan slept? – with whom Jupiter? – whom Apollo ravished? These facts the English youth gets by heart the moment they quit the nursery; and are most sedulously and industriously instructed in them till the best and most active part of life is passed away. Now, this long career of classical learning, we may, if we please, denominate a foundation; but it is a foundation so far above ground, that there is absolutely no room to put any thing upon it. If you occupy a man with one thing till he is twenty-four years of age, you have exhausted all his leisure time: he is called into the world and compelled to act; or is surrounded with pleasures, and thinks and reads no more. If you have neglected to put other things in him, they will never get in afterwards; – if you have fed him only with words, he will remain a narrow and limited being to the end of his existence.

The bias given to men's minds is so strong, that it is no uncommon thing to meet with Englishmen, whom, but for their grey hairs and wrinkles, we might easily mistake for school-boys. Their talk is of Latin verses; and it is quite clear, if men's ages are to be dated from the state of their mental progress, that such men are eighteen years of age, and not a day older. Their minds have been so completely possessed by exaggerated notions of classical learning, that they have not been able, in the great school of the world, to form any other notion of real greatness. Attend, too, to the public feelings – look to all the terms of applause. A learned man! – a scholar! – a man of erudition! Upon whom are these epithets of approbation bestowed? Are they given to men acquainted with the science of government? thoroughly masters of the geographical and commercial relations of Europe? to men who know the properties of bodies, and their action upon each other? No: this is not learning; it is chemistry, or political economy – not learning., The distinguishing abstract term, the epithet of Scholar, is reserved for him who writes on the Æolic reduplication, and is familiar with the Sylburgian method of arranging defectives in Ω and $\mu\iota$. The picture which a young Englishman, addicted to the pursuit of knowledge, draws – his *beau idéal*, of human nature – his top and consummation of man's powers – is a knowledge of the Greek language. His object is not to reason,

to imagine, or to invent; but to conjugate, decline, and derive.
The situations of imaginary glory which he draws for himself, are the detection of an anapæst in the wrong place, or
the restoration of a dative case which Cranzius had passed
over, and the never-dying Ernesti failed to observe. If a young
classic of this kind were to meet the greatest chemist or the
greatest mechanician, or the most profound political economist of his time, in company with the greatest Greek scholar,
would the slightest comparison between them ever come
across his mind? – would he ever dream that such men as
Adam Smith and Lavoisier were equal in dignity of understanding to, or of the same utility as, Bentley and Heyne?
We are inclined to think, that the feeling excited would be a
good deal like that which was expressed by Dr George about
the praises of the great King of Prussia, who entertained
considerable doubts whether the King, with all his victo-
ries, knew how to conjugate a Greek verb in μι. . . . The
English clergy, in whose hands education entirely rests,
bring up the first young men of the country as if they were
all to keep grammar schools in little country towns; and a
nobleman, upon whose knowledge and liberality the honour
and welfare of his country may depend, is diligently worried,
for half his life, with the small pedantry of longs and shorts.
There is a timid and absurd apprehension, on the part of
ecclesiastical tutors, of letting out the minds of youth upon
difficult and important subjects. They fancy that mental
exertion must end in religious scepticism; and, to preserve
the principles of their pupils, they confine them to the safe
and elegant imbecility of classical learning. A genuine
Oxford tutor would shudder to hear his young men disputing
upon moral and political truth, forming and pulling down
theories, and indulging in all the boldness of youthful discussion. He would augur nothing from it, but impiety to
God, and treason to kings. And yet, who vilifies both more
than the holy poltroon who carefully averts from them the
searching eye of reason, and who knows no better method
of teaching the highest duties, than by extirpating the finest
qualities and habits of the mind? If our religion is a fable,
the sooner it is exploded the better. If our government is
bad, it should be amended. But we have no doubt of the
truth of the one, or of the excellence of the other; and are
convinced that both will be placed on a firmer basis, in
proportion as the minds of men are more trained to the in-
vestigation of truth. At present, we act with the minds of
our young men, as the Dutch did with their exuberant spices.

An infinite quantity of talent is annually destroyed in the Universities of England by the miserable jealousy and littleness of ecclesiastical instructors. It is in vain to say we have produced great men under this system. We have produced great men under all systems. Every Englishman must pass half his life in learning Latin and Greek; and classical learning is supposed to have produced the talents which it has not been able to extinguish. It is scarcely possible to prevent great men from rising up under any system of education, however bad. Teach men dæmonology or astrology, and you will still have a certain portion of original genius, in spite of these or any other branches of ignorance and folly. . . .

There is a delusive sort of splendour in a vast body of men pursuing one object, and thoroughly obtaining it; and yet, though it be very splendid, it is far from being useful. Classical literature is the great object at Oxford. Many minds so employed have produced many works, and much fame in that department; but if all liberal arts and science useful to human life had been taught there, – if some had dedicated themselves to chemistry, some to mathematics, some to experimental philosophy, – and if every attainment had been honoured in the mixt ratio of its difficulty and utility, – the system of such an University would have been much more valuable, but the splendour of its name something less.

When an University has been doing useless things for a long time, it appears at first degrading to them to be useful. A set of lectures upon political economy would be discouraged in Oxford, probably despised, probably not permitted. To discuss the enclosure of commons, and to dwell upon imports and exports, – to come so near to common life, would seem to be undignified and contemptible. In the same manner, the Parr, or the Bentley of his day, would be scandalised in an University to be put on a level with the discoverer of a neutral salt; and yet, what other measure is there of dignity in intellectual labour, but usefulness and difficulty? And what ought the term University to mean, but a place where every science is taught which is liberal, and at the same time useful to mankind? Nothing would so much tend to bring classical literature within proper bounds as a steady and invariable appeal to these tests in our appreciation of all human knowledge. The puffed pedant would collapse into his proper size, and the maker of verses and the rememberer of words, would soon assume that station, which is the lot of those who go up unbidden to the upper places of the feast.

In those who were destined for the Church, we would undoubtedly encourage classical learning, more than in any other body of men; but if we had to do with a young man going out into public life, we would exhort him to contemn, or at least not to affect the reputation of a great scholar, but to educate himself for the offices of civil life. He should learn what the constitution of his country really was, – how it had grown into its present state, – the perils that had threatened it, – the malignity that had attacked it – the courage that had fought for it, and the wisdom that had made it great. We would bring strongly before his mind the characters of those Englishmen who have been the steady friends of the public happiness; and, by their examples, would breathe into him a pure public taste, which should keep him untainted in all the vicissitudes of political fortune. We would teach him to burst through the well paid, and the pernicious cant of indiscriminate loyalty; and to know his Sovereign only as he discharged those duties, and displayed those qualities, for which the blood and the treasure of his people are confided to his hands. We should deem it of the utmost importance, that his attention was directed to the true principles of legislation, – what effect laws can produce upon opinions, and opinions upon laws, – what subjects are fit for legislative interference, and when men may be left to the management of their own interests. The mischief occasioned by bad laws, and the perplexity which arises from numerous laws, – the causes of national wealth, – the relations of foreign trade, – the encouragement of manufactures and agriculture, – the fictitious wealth occasioned by paper credit, – the laws of population, – the management of poverty and mendicity, – the use and abuse of monopoly, – the theory of taxation, – the consequences of the public debt. These are some of the subjects, and some of the branches of civil education, to which we would turn the minds of future judges, future senators, and future noblemen. After the first period of life had been given up to the cultivation of the classics, and the reasoning powers were now beginning to evolve themselves, these are some of the propensities in study which we would endeavour to inspire. Great knowledge at such a period of life, we could not convey; but we might fix a decided taste for its acquisition, and a strong disposition to respect it in others. The formation of some great scholars we should certainly prevent, and hinder many from learning what, in a few years, they would necessarily forget; but this loss would be well

repaid, – if we could show the future rulers of the country that
thought and labour which it requires to make a nation happy,
– or if we could inspire them with that love of public virtue,
which, after religion, we most solemnly believe to be the brightest
ornament of the mind of man.   *Edinburgh Review,* 1809
Having criticised the way in which classics were taught, in the Edinburgh
Review in 1826 Sydney enthused over the method of teaching languages
expounded by James Hamilton. Sydney's advocacy of new methods of teaching the classics might be said to have fallen on deaf ears until the Cambridge
Classics Course in the 1970s.

> 1. *The Gospel of St John, in Latin, adapted to the Hamilto-*
> *nian System, by an Analytical and Interlineary Transla-*
> *tion.* Executed under the immediate Direction of James
> Hamilton. London, 1824.
>
> 2. *The Gospel of St John, adapted to the Hamiltonian*
> *System, by an Analytical and Interlineary Translation*
> *from the Italian, with full Instructions for its use, even by*
> *those who are wholly ignorant of the Language. For the*
> *Use of Schools.* By James Hamilton, Author of the
> Hamiltonian System. London, 1825.

Literal translations are not only not used in our public
schools, but are generally discountenanced in them. A literal
translation, or any translation of a school-book, is a contraband article in English schools, which a schoolmaster would
instantly seize, as a Custom-house officer would a barrel of
gin. Mr Hamilton, on the other hand, maintains, by books
and lectures, that all boys ought to be allowed to work with
literal translations, and that it is by far the best method of
learning a language.

One of the first principles of Mr Hamilton is, to introduce
very strict literal, interlinear translations, as aids to lexicons
and dictionaries, and to make so much use of them as that the
dictionary or lexicon will be for a long time little required.

In this way Mr Hamilton contends (and appears to us to
contend justly), that the language may be acquired with
much greater ease and despatch, than by the ancient method
of beginning with grammar, and proceeding with the dictionary. . . . The interlineal translation of course spares
the trouble and time of the mechanical labour [of looking
up in dictionaries]. Immediately under the Italian word is
placed the English word. The unknown sound therefore is
instantly exchanged for one that is known. The labour here
spared is of the most irksome nature; and it is spared at a
time of life the most averse to such labour; and so painful is
this labour to many boys, that it forms an insuperable

obstacle to their progress. They prefer to be flogged, or to be sent to sea. It is useless to say of any medicine that it is valuable, if it is so nauseous that the patient flings it away. You must give me, not the best medicine you have in your shop, but the best you can get me to take.

'If you wish boys to remember any language, make the acquisition of it very tedious and disgusting.' This seems to be an odd rule; but if it be good for language, it must be good also for every species of knowledge – music, mathematics, navigation, architecture. In all these sciences aversion should be the parent of memory – impediment the cause of perfection. If difficulty is the sauce of memory, the boy who learns with the greatest difficulty will remember with the greatest tenacity; – in other words, the acquisitions of a dunce will be greater and more important than those of a clever boy. Where is the love of difficulty to end? Why not leave a boy to compose his own dictionary and grammar? It is not what is done for a boy, but what he does for himself, that is of any importance. Are there difficulties enough in the old method of acquiring languages? Would it be better if the difficulties were doubled, and thirty years given to languages, instead of fifteen? All these arguments presume the difficulty to be got over, and then the memory to be improved. But what if the difficulty is shrunk from? What if it put an end to power, instead of increasing it; and extinguish, instead of exciting, application? And when these effects are produced, you not only preclude all hopes of learning, or language, but you put an end for ever to all literary habits, and to all improvements from study. The boy who is lexicon-struck in early youth looks upon all books afterwards with horror, and goes over to the blockheads. Every boy would be pleased with books, and pleased with school, and be glad to forward the views of his parents, and obtain the praise of his master, if he found it possible to make tolerably easy progress; but he is driven to absolute despair by gerunds, and wishes himself dead! Progress is pleasure – activity is pleasure. It is impossible for a boy not to make progress, and not to be active, in the Hamiltonian method; and this pleasing state of mind we contend to be more favourable to memory, than the languid jaded spirit which much commerce with lexicons never fails to produce.

Thus, in the Hamiltonian method, a good deal of grammar necessarily impresses itself upon the mind (*chemin faisant*), as it does in the vernacular tongue, without any rule at all, and merely by habit. . . . The Hamiltonian system . . . 1.

teaches an unknown tongue by the closest interlinear translation, instead of leaving a boy to explore his way by the lexicon or dictionary. 2. It postpones the study of grammar till a considerable progress has been made in the language, and a great degree of practical grammar has been acquired. 3. It substitutes the cheerfulness and competition of the Lancasterian system for the dull solitude of the dictionary. By these means, a boy finds he is making a progress, and learning something from the very beginning. He is not overwhelmed with the first appearance of insuperable difficulties; he receives some little pay from the first moment of his apprenticeship, and is not compelled to wait for remuneration till he is out of his time. The student, having acquired the great art of understanding the sense of what is written in another tongue, may go into the study of the language as deeply and as extensively as he pleases. The old system aims at beginning with a depth and accuracy which many men never will want, which disgusts many from arriving even at moderate attainments, and is a less easy, and not more certain road to a profound skill in languages, than if attention to grammar had been deferred to a later period.

In fine, we are strongly persuaded, that the time being given, this system will make better scholars; and the degree of scholarship being given, a much shorter time will be needed. If there be any truth in this, it will make Mr Hamilton one of the most useful men of his age; for if there be any thing which fills reflecting men with melancholy and regret, it is the waste of mortal time, parental money, and puerile happiness, in the present method of pursuing Latin and Greek.

During this review Sydney pictures a father saying of his son, 'What was good enough for me is good enough for him.'

'Have I read through Lilly? – have I learnt by heart that most atrocious monument of absurdity, the Westminster Grammar? – have I been whipt for the substantives? – whipt for the verbs? – and whipt for and with the interjections? – have I picked the sense slowly, and word by word, out of Hederick? – and shall my son Daniel be exempt from all this misery? – Shall a little unknown person in Cecil Street, Strand, No. 25, pretend to tell me that all this is unnecessary? – Was it possible that I might have been spared all this? – The whole system is nonsense, and the man an imposter. If there had been any truth in it, it must have occurred to some one else before this period.' – This is a very common style of observation upon Mr Hamilton's system, and by no means an uncommon wish of the mouldering and decaying part of mankind, that the next generation should not enjoy any advantages from which they themselves have been precluded. – '*Ay, ay, it's all mighty well – but I went through this myself, and I am determined my children shall do the same.*'We are convinced that a great deal of opposition to improvement proceeds from this principle. Crabbe might make a good picture of an unbenevolent old man, slowly retiring from this sublunary scene, and lamenting that the coming race of men would be less bumped on the roads, better lighted in the streets, and less tormented with grammars and lexicons, than in the preceding age. A great deal of compliment to the wisdom of ancestors, and a great degree of alarm at the dreadful spirit of innovation, are soluble into mere jealousy and envy.   *Edinburgh Review, 1826*

Sydney repeats his mockery of this fallacy in regard to other aspects of public school life:

> *Fallacy I. – 'Because I have gone through it,*
> *my son shall go through it also.*

A man gets well pummelled at a public school; is subject to every misery and every indignity which seventeen years of age can inflict upon nine and ten; has his eye nearly knocked out, and his clothes stolen and cut to pieces; and twenty years afterwards, when he is a chrysalis, and has forgotten the miseries of his grub state, is determined to act a manly part in life, and says, 'I passed through all that myself, and I am determined my son shall pass through it as I have done;' and away goes his bleating progeny to the tyranny and servitude of the long chamber or the large dormitory. It would surely be much more rational to say, 'Because I have passed through it, I am determined my son shall not pass through it; because I was kicked for nothing, and cuffed for nothing, and fagged for everything, I will spare all these miseries to my child.' It is not for any good which may be derived from this rough usage; that has not been weighed and considered; few persons are capable of weighing its effects upon character; but there is a sort of compensatory and consolatory notion, that the present generation (whether useful or not, no matter) are not to come off scot-free, but are to have their share of ill-usage; as if the black eye and bloody nose which Master John Jackson received in 1800, are less black and bloody by the application of similar violence to similar parts of Master Thomas Jackson, the son, in 1830. This is not only sad nonsense, but cruel nonsense. The only use to be derived from the recollection of what we have suffered

in youth, is a fixed determination to screen those we educate from every evil and inconvenience, from subjection to
which there are not cogent reasons for submitting. Can anything be more stupid and preposterous than this concealed
revenge upon the rising generation, and latent envy lest they
should avail themselves of the improvements time has made,
and pass a happier youth than their fathers have done?'

Lady Holland's *Memoir*

Sydney condemned the distancing of masters from, and the power given
to prefects over, boys, and the emphasis on, and kudos given to, games. To be
a day-boy with a good home is the best fortune that can befall a boy. What
suffering would have been averted in succeeding generations had his
convictions been accepted by readers of the Review.

Remarks on the System of Education in Public Schools.
8vo. Hatchard. London, 1809.

There is a set of well-dressed, prosperous gentlemen, who
assemble daily at Mr Hatchard's shop; – clean, civil personages, well in with people in power – delighted with every
existing institution – and almost with every existing circum-
stance: – and, every now and then, one of these personages
writes a little book; – and the rest praise that little book –
expecting to be praised, in their turn, for their own little
books: – and of these little books, thus written by these clean,
civil personages, so expecting to be praised, the pamphlet
before us appears to be one.

The subject of it is the advantage of public schools; and
the author, very creditably to himself, ridicules the absurd
clamour, first set on foot by Dr Rennel, of the irreligious
tendency of public schools: he then proceeds to an invest-
igation of the effects which public schools may produce
upon the moral character; and here the subject becomes more
difficult, and the pamphlet worse.

In arguing any large or general question, it is of infinite
importance to attend to the first feelings which the mention
of the topic has a tendency to excite; and the name of a
public school brings with it immediately the idea of brilliant
classical attainments: but, upon the importance of these
studies, we are not now offering any opinion. The only
points for consideration are, whether boys are put in the
way of becoming good and wise men by these schools; and
whether they actually gather, there, those attainments, which
it pleases mankind, for the time being, to consider as
valuable, and to decorate by the name of learning.

At a public school (for such is the system established by
immemorial custom), every boy is alternately tyrant and

slave. The power which the elder part of these communities exercises over the younger, is exceedingly great – very difficult to be controlled – and accompanied, not unfrequently, with cruelty and caprice. It is the common law of the place, that the young should be implicitly obedient to the elder boys; and this obedience resembles more the submission of a slave to his master, or of sailor to his captain, than the common and natural deference which would always be shown by one boy to another a few years older than himself. Now, this system we cannot help considering as an evil, – because it inflicts upon boys, for two of three years of their lives, many painful hardships, and much unpleasant servitude. These sufferings might perhaps be of some use in military schools; but, to give to a boy the habit of enduring privations to which he will never again be called upon to submit – to enure him to pains which he will never again feel – and to subject him to the privation of comforts, with which he will always in future abound – is surely not a very useful and valuable severity in education. It is not the life in miniature which he is to lead hereafter – nor does it bear any relation to it: – he will never again be subjected to so much insolence and caprice; nor ever, in all human probability, called upon to make so many sacrifices. The servile obedience which it teaches, might be useful to a menial domestic; or the habits of enterprise which it encourages, prove of importance to a military partisan; but we cannot see what bearing it has upon the calm, regular, civil life, which the sons of gentlemen, destined to opulent idleness, or to any of the three learned professions, are destined to lead. Such a system makes many boys very miserable; and produces those bad effects upon the temper and disposition, which unjust suffering always does produce; – but what good it does, we are much at a loss to conceive. Reasonable obedience is extremely useful in forming the disposition. Submission to tyranny lays the foundation of hatred, suspicion, cunning, and a variety of odious passions. We are convinced that those young people will turn out to be the best men, who have been guarded most effectually, in their childhood, from every species of useless vexation: and experienced, in the greatest degree, the blessings of a wise and rational indulgence. But even if these effects upon future character are not produced, still, four or five years in childhood make a very considerable period of human existence: and it is by no means a trifling consideration whether they are passed happily or unhappily. The wretchedness of school tyranny is trifling enough to a man who only contemplates it, in ease of body and tranquillity of mind, through the medium of twenty intervening years; but it is as real, and quite as acute, while it lasts, as any of the sufferings of mature life: and the utility of these sufferings, or the price paid in compensation for them, should be clearly made out to a conscientious parent, before he consents to expose his children to them.

A few boys are incorrigibly idle, and a few incorrigibly eager for knowledge; but the great mass are in a state of doubt and fluctuation; and they come to school for the express purpose, not of being left to themselves – for that could be done any where – but that their wavering tastes and propensities should be decided by the intervention of a master. In a forest, or public school for oaks and elms, the trees are left to themselves; the strong plants live, and the weak ones die the towering oak that remains is admired; the saplings that perish around it are cast into the flames and forgotten. But it is not, surely, to the vegetable struggle of a forest, or the hasty glance of a forester, that a botanist would commit a favourite plant; he would naturally seek for it a situation of less hazard, and a cultivator whose limited occupations would enable him to give to it a reasonable share of his time and attention. The very meaning of education seems to us to be that the old should teach the young, and the wise direct the weak; that a man who professes to instruct, should get among his pupils, study their characters, gain their affections, and form their inclinations and aversions. In a public school, the numbers render this impossible; it is impossible that sufficient time should be found for this useful and affectionate interference. Boys, therefore, are left to their own crude conceptions and ill-formed propensities; and this neglect is called a spirited and manly education. . . .

After having said so much in opposition to the general prejudice in favour of public schools, we may be expected to state what species of school we think preferable to them; for if public schools, with all their disadvantages, are the best that can actually be found, or easily attained, the objections to them are certainly made to very little purpose.

We have no hesitation, however, in saying, that that education seems to us to be the best which mingles a domestic with a school life, and which gives to a youth the advantage which is to be derived from the learning of a master, and the emulation which results from the society of other boys, together with the affectionate vigilance which he must experience in the house of his parents.

Education for Women

The feminist movement might be said to have a 'founding father' in Sydney, who was a keen advocate of female education at a time when it was sorely neglected. In his 1810 review of *Advice to Young Ladies on the Improvement of the Mind* by Thomas Broadhurst, he writes:

> A great deal has been said of the original difference of capacity between men and women; as if women were more quick, and men more judicious – as if women were more remarkable for delicacy of association, and men for stronger powers of attention. All this, we confess, appears to us very fanciful. That there is a difference in the understandings of the men and the women we every day meet with, every body, we suppose, must perceive; but there is none surely which may not be accounted for by the difference of circumstances in which they have been placed, without referring to any conjectural difference of original conformation of mind. As long as boys and girls run about in the dirt, and trundle hoops together, they are both precisely alike. If you catch up one half of these creatures, and train them to a particular set of actions and opinions, and the other half to a perfectly opposite set, of course their understandings will differ, as one or the other sort of occupations has called this or that talent into action. There is surely no occasion to go into any deeper or more abstruse reasoning, in order to explain so very simple a phenomenon. Taking it, then, for granted, that nature has been as bountiful of understanding to one sex as the other, it is incumbent on us to consider what are the principal objections commonly made against the communication of a greater share of knowledge to women than commonly falls to their lot at present: for though it may be doubted whether women should learn all that men learn, the immense disparity which now exists between their knowledge we should hardly think could admit of any rational defence. It is not easy to imagine that there can be any just cause why a woman of forty should be more ignorant than a boy of twelve years of age. If there be any good at all in female ignorance, this (to use a very colloquial phrase) is surely too much of a good thing.
>
> We bar, in this discussion, any objection which proceeds from the mere novelty of teaching women more than they are already taught. It may be useless that their education should be improved, or it may be pernicious; and these are the fair grounds on which the question may be argued. But those who cannot bring their minds to consider such an unusual extension of knowledge, without connecting with

it some sensation of the ludicrous, should remember, that, in the progress from absolute ignorance, there is a period when cultivation of the mind is new to every rank and description of persons. A century ago, who would have believed that country gentlemen could be brought to read and spell with the ease and accuracy which we now so frequently remark, – or supposed that they could be carried up even to the elements of ancient and modern history? Nothing is more common, or more stupid, than to take the actual for the possible – to believe that all which is, is all which can be; first to laugh at every proposed deviation from practice as impossible – then, when it is carried into effect, to be astonished that it did not take place before.

Some persons are apt to contrast the acquisition of important knowledge with what they call simple pleasures; and deem it more becoming that a woman should educate flowers, make friendships with birds, and pick up plants, than enter into more difficult and fatiguing studies. If a woman have no taste and genius for higher occupations, let her engage in these, rather than remain destitute of any pursuit. But why are we necessarily to doom a girl, whatever be her taste or her capacity, to one unvaried line of petty and frivolous occupation? If she be full of strong sense and elevated curiosity, can there be any reason why she should be diluted and enfeebled down to a mere culler of simples, and fancier of birds? – why books of history and reasoning are to be torn out of her hand, and why she is to be sent, like a butterfly, to hover over the idle flowers of the field? Such amusements are innocent to those whom they can occupy; but they are not innocent to those who have too powerful understandings to be occupied by them. Light broths and fruits are innocent food only to weak or to infant stomachs; but they are poison to that organ in its perfect and mature state. But the great charm appears to be in the word *simplicity* – simple pleasure! If by a simple pleasure is meant an innocent pleasure, the observation is best answered by showing, that the pleasure which results from the acquisition of important knowledge is quite as innocent as any pleasure whatever: but if by a simple pleasure is meant one, the cause of which can be easily analysed, or which does not last long, or which in itself is very faint; then simple pleasures seem to be very nearly synonymous with small pleasures; and if the simplicity were to be a little increased, the pleasure would vanish altogether.

As it is impossible that every man should have industry

or activity sufficient to avail himself of the advantages of education, it is natural that men who are ignorant themselves, should view, with some degree of jealousy and alarm, any proposal for improving the education of women. But such men may depend upon it, however the system of female education, may be exalted, that there will never be wanting a due proportion of failures; and that after parents, guardians, and preceptors have done all in their power to make every body wise, there will still be a plentiful supply of women who have taken special care to remain otherwise; and they may rest assured, if the utter extinction of ignorance and folly be the evil they dread, that their interests will always be effectually protected, in spite of every exertion to the contrary. . . .

There are, perhaps, 50,000 females in Great Britain, who are exempted by circumstances from all necessary labour; but every human being must do something with their existence; and the pursuit of knowledge is, upon the whole, the most innocent, the most dignified, and the most useful method of filling up that idleness, of which there is always so large a portion in nations far advanced in civilisation. Let any man reflect, too, upon the solitary situation in which women are placed, – the ill treatment to which they are sometimes exposed, and which they must endure in silence, and without the power of complaining, – and he must feel convinced that the happiness of a woman will be materially increased in proportion as education has given to her the habit and the means of drawing her resources from herself. . . .

If the objections against the better education of women could be over-ruled, one of the great advantages that would ensue would be the extinction of innumerable follies. A decided and prevailing taste for one or another mode of education there must be. A century past, it was for housewifery – now it is for accomplishments. The object now is, to make women artists, – to give them an excellence in drawing, music, painting, and dancing, – of which persons who make these pursuits the occupation of their lives, and derive from them their subsistence, need not be ashamed. Now, one great evil of all this is, that it does not last. If the whole of life were an Olympic game – if we could go on feasting and dancing to the end, – this might do; but it is in truth merely a provision for the little interval between coming into life and settling in it; while it leaves a long and dreary expanse behind, devoid both of dignity and cheerfulness.

No mother, no woman who has past over the few first years of life, sings, or dances, or draws, or plays upon musical instruments. These are merely means for displaying the grace and vivacity of youth, which every woman gives up, as she gives up the dress and the manners of eighteen: she has no wish to retain them; or, if she has, she is driven out of them by diameter and derision. The system of female education, as it now stands, aims only at embellishing a few years of life, which are in themselves so full of grace and happiness, that they hardly want it; and then leaves the rest of existence a miserable prey to idle insignificance. No woman of understanding and reflection can possibly conceive she is doing justice to her children by such kind of education. The object is, to give to children resources that will endure as long as life endures – habits that time will ameliorate, not destroy, – occupations that will render sickness tolerable, solitude pleasant, age venerable, life more dignified and useful, and therefore death less terrible: and the compensation which is offered for the omission of all this, is a short-lived blaze, – a little temporary effect, which has no other consequence than to deprive the remainder of life of all taste and relish. There may be women who have a taste for the fine arts, and who evince a decided talent for drawing, or for music. In that case, there can be no objection to the cultivation of these arts; but the error is, to make such things the grand and universal object, – to insist upon it that every woman is to sing, and draw, and dance, – with nature, or against nature, – to bind her apprentice to some accomplishment, and if she cannot succeed in oil or water colours, to prefer gilding, varnishing, burnishing, box-making, to real and solid improvement in taste, knowledge, and understanding. . . .

It is of great importance to a country, that there should be as many understandings as possible actively employed within it. Mankind are much happier for the discovery of barometers, thermometers, steam-engines, and all the innumerable inventions in the arts and sciences. We are every day and every hour reaping the benefit of such talent and ingenuity. The same observation is true of such works as those of Dryden, Pope, Milton, and Shakspeare. Mankind are much happier that such individuals have lived and written; they add every day to the stock of public enjoyment – and perpetually gladden and embellish life. Now, the number of those who exercise their understandings to any good purpose, is exactly in proportion to those who exercise it at all; but, as the matter stands at present, half the talent in the universe runs to waste, and is totally unprofitable.

One of the greatest pleasures of life is conversation; – and the pleasures of conversation are of course enhanced by every increase of knowledge: not that we should meet together to talk of alkalis and angles, or to add to our stock of history and philology – though a little of these things is no bad ingredient in conversation; but let the subject be what it may, there is always a prodigious difference between the conversation of those who have been well educated and of those who have not enjoyed this advantage. Education gives fecundity of thought, copiousness of illustration, quickness, vigour, fancy, words, images, and illustrations; – it decorates every common thing, and gives the power of trifling without being undignified and absurd. The subjects themselves may not be wanted upon which the talents of an educated man have been exercised; but there is always a demand for those talents which his education has rendered strong and quick. Now, really, nothing can be further from our intention than to say any thing rude and unpleasant; but we must be excused for observing, that it is not now a very common thing to be interested by the variety and extent of female knowledge, but it is a very common thing to lament, that the finest faculties in the world have been confined to trifles utterly unworthy of their richness and their strength. . . .

In short, and to recapitulate the main points upon which we have insisted, – Why the disproportion in knowledge between the two sexes should be so great, when the inequality in natural talents is so small; or why the understanding of women should be lavished upon trifles, when nature has made it capable of better and higher things, we profess ourselves not able to understand. The affectation charged upon female knowledge is best cured by making that knowledge more general: and the economy devolved upon women is best secured by the ruin, disgrace, and inconvenience which proceeds from neglecting it. For the care of children, nature has made a direct and powerful provision; and the gentleness and elegance of women is the natural consequence of that desire to please, which is productive of the greatest part of civilisation and refinement, and which rests upon a foundation too deep to be shaken by any such modifications in education as we have proposed. If you educate women to attend to dignified and important subjects, you are multiplying, beyond measure, the chances of human improvement, by preparing and *medicating* those early impressions, which always come from the mother; and which, in a great majority of instances, are quite decisive of character and genius. Nor is it only in the business of education that women would influence the destiny of men. – If women knew more, men must learn more – for ignorance would then be shameful – and it would become the fashion to be instructed. The instruction of women improves the stock of national talents, and employs more minds for the instruction and amusement of the world; – it increases the pleasures of society, by multiplying the topics upon which the two sexes take a common interest; – and makes marriage an intercourse of understanding as well as of affection, by giving dignity and importance to the female character. The education of women favours public morals; it provides for every season of life, as well as for the brightest and the best; and leaves a woman when she is stricken by the hand of time, not as she now is, destitute of every thing, and neglected by all; but with the full power and the splendid attractions of knowledge, – diffusing the elegant pleasures of polite literature, and receiving the just homage of learned and accomplished men. *Edinburgh Review,* 1810

Lady Holland records two further pieces of advice to parents of daughters, words Jane Austen might well have borrowed to put on Mr Bennett's lips.

'Ah! what female heart can withstand a red-coat? I think this should be a part of female education; it is much neglected. As you have the rocking-horse to accustom them to ride, I would have military dolls in the nursery, to harden their hearts against officers and red-coats.'

'Never teach false morality. How exquisitely absurd to tell girls that beauty is of no value, dress of no use! Beauty is of value; her whole prospects and happiness in life may often depend upon a new gown or a becoming bonnet, and if she has five grains of common sense she will find this out. The great thing is to teach her their just value, and that there must be something better under the bonnet than a pretty face for real happiness. But never sacrifice truth.'

Lady Holland, *Memoir*

VI

Social Issues

For the greater part of his working life Sydney was a country parson and one who took his pastoral duties seriously. For much of that time he was also a Justice of the Peace, actively involved in the administration of local justice and with social problems generally. Always concerned for the poor and disadvantaged and keen to promote a more just and stable and pleasant society, he was frequently moved to use his pen to denounce and ridicule the injustices he found in a social system that was still dominated by landed interests and controlled, for the most part, by successive and highly reactionary Tory governments.

The opening decades of the nineteenth century marked a period of great change and upheaval in British economic and social life. It was also a time when the more enlightened thinkers – William Wilberforce, Robert Owen, Elizabeth Fry and many others – were campaigning for all kinds of reform. Sydney used the pages of the *Edinburgh Review* to fight for several good causes – against the exploitation of child chimney-sweeps, for the reform of prison conditions and the processes of the criminal law, the Game Laws and the Poor Law, and the treatment of the insane. Among his colleagues in the Anglican clergy, his was virtually a lone voice in all this, but that did nothing at all to deter him.

Chimney-sweeps

Today it is hard to believe that a society which considered itself civilised and Christian could have tolerated the employment of very young children, girls as well as boys, to clamber up narrow chimneys and clear them of soot and other obstructions. Their masters were often brutal. They had to climb upwards in the dark, frequently with the fire still burning, enveloped in clouds of filth, scraping the flesh off their wasted bodies. They often got stuck. Sometimes they died of suffocation, excessive heat or exhaustion.

A charitable society was formed to bring this trade to an end, and it was their evidence, submitted to both Houses of Parliament, that induced Sydney to enter the fray.

> *Account of the Proceedings of the Society for superseding the*
> *Necessity of Climbing Boys.* Baldwin, &c. London, 1816.

An excellent and well-arranged dinner is a most pleasing occurrence, and a great triumph of civilised life. It is not only the descending morsel, and the enveloping sauce – but the rank, wealth, wit, and beauty which surround the meats – the learned management of light and heat – the silent and rapid services of the attendants – the smiling and sedulous host, proffering gusts and relishes – the exotic bottles – the embossed plate – the pleasant remarks – the handsome dresses – the cunning artifices in fruit and farina! The hour of dinner, in short, includes every thing of sensual and intellectual gratification which a great nation glories in producing.

In the midst of all this, who knows that the kitchen chimney caught fire half an hour before dinner! – and that a poor little wretch, of six or seven years old, was sent up in the midst of the flames to put it out? We could not, previous to reading this evidence, have formed a conception of the miseries of these poor wretches, or that there should exist, in a civilised country, a class of human beings destined to such extreme and varied distress. We will give a short epitome of what is developed in the evidence before the, two Houses of Parliament.

Boys are made chimney sweepers at the early age of five or six.

Little boys for small flues, is a common phrase in the cards left at the door by itinerant chimney sweepers. Flues made to ovens and coppers are often less than nine inches square; and it may be easily conceived, how slender the frame of that human body must be, which can force itself through such an aperture.

What is the age of the youngest boys who have been employed in this trade, to your knowledge? About five years of age: I know one now between five and six years old, it is the man's own son in the Strand; now there is another at Somer's Town, I think, said he was between four and five, or about five; Jack Hall, a little lad, takes him about. – Did you ever know any female children employed? Yes, I know one now. About two years ago there was a woman told me she had climbed scores of times, and there is one at Paddington now whose father taught her to climb: but I have often heard talk of them when I was apprentice, in different places. – What is the smallest-sized flue you have ever met with in the course of your experience? About eight inches by nine; these they are always obliged to climb in this posture (*describing it*), keeping the arms up straight; if they slip their arms down, they get hemmed in; unless they get their arms close over their head they cannot climb.   *Lords' Minutes*, No. 1. p. 8.

We come now to burning little chimney sweepers. A large

party are invited to dinner – a great display is to be made; – and about an hour before dinner, there is an alarm that the kitchen chimney is on fire! It is impossible to put off the distinguished personages who are expected. It gets very late for the soup and fish – the cook is frantic – all eyes are turned upon the sable consolation of the master chimney sweeper – and up into the midst of the burning chimney is sent one of the miserable little infants of the brush! There is a positive prohibition of this practice, and an enactment of penalties in one of the acts of Parliament which respect chimney sweepers. But what matter acts of Parliament, when the pleasures of genteel people are concerned? Or what is a toasted child, compared to the agonies of the mistress of the house with a deranged dinner?

> Did you ever know a boy get burnt up a chimney? Yes.
> – Is that usual? Yes, I have been burnt myself, and
> have got the scars on my legs; a year ago I was up a
> chimney in Liquor Pond Street; I have been up *more
> than forty chimneys where I have been burnt.* – Did
> your master or the journeymen ever direct you to go
> up a chimney that was on fire? Yes, it is a general
> case. – Do they compel you to go up a chimney that is
> on fire? O yes, it was the general practice for two of us
> to stop at home on Sunday to be ready in case of a
> chimney being a-fire. – You say it is general to compel
> the boys to go up chimneys on fire? Yes, boys get very
> ill-treated if they do not go up.   *Lords' Minutes*, p.34.

We have been thus particular in stating the case of the chimney sweepers, and in founding it upon the basis of facts, that we may make an answer to those profligate persons who are always ready to fling an air of ridicule upon the labours of humanity, because they are desirous that what they have not virtue to do themselves, should appear to be foolish and romantic when done by others. A still higher degree of depravity than this, is to want every sort of compassion for human misery, when it is accompanied by filth, poverty, and ignorance, – to regulate humanity by the income tax, and to deem the bodily wretchedness and the dirty tears of the poor, a fit subject for pleasantry and contempt. We should have been loath to believe, that such deep-seated and disgusting immorality existed in these days; but the notice of it is forced upon us. Nor must we pass over a set of marvellously weak gentlemen, who discover democracy and revolution, in every effort to improve the condition of the lower orders, and to take off a little of the load of misery from those points where it presses the hardest. Such are the men into whose heart Mrs Fry has struck the deepest terror, – who abhor Mr Bentham and his pénitentiary; Mr Bennet and his hulks; Sir James Macintosh and his bloodless assizes; Mr Tuke and his sweeping machines, – and every other human being who is great and good enough to sacrifice his quiet to his love for his fellow-creatures. Certainly we admit that humanity is sometimes the veil of ambition or of faction; but we have no doubt that there are a great many excellent persons to whom it is misery to see misery, and pleasure to lessen it; and who by calling the public attention to the worst cases, and by giving birth to judicious legislative enactments for their improvement, have made, and are making, the world somewhat happier than they found it. Upon these principles we join hands with the friends of the chimney sweepers, and most heartily wish for the diminution of their numbers, and the limitation of their trade.

We are thoroughly convinced, there are many respectable master chimney sweepers; though we suspect their numbers have been increased by the alarm which their former tyranny excited, and by the severe laws made for their coercion: but even with good masters the trade is miserable, – with bad ones it is not to be endured; and the evidence already quoted shows us how many of that character are to be met with in the occupation of sweeping chimneys.

After all, we must own that it was quite right to throw out the bill for prohibiting the sweeping of chimneys by boys – because humanity is a modern invention; and there are many chimneys in old houses which cannot possibly be swept in any other manner. But the construction of chimneys should be attended to in some new building act; and the treatment of boys be watched over with the most severe jealousy of the law. Above all, those who have chimneys accessible to machinery, should encourage the use of machines, and not think it beneath their dignity to take a little trouble, in order to do a great deal of good. We should have been very glad to have seconded the views of the Climbing Society, and to have pleaded for the complete abolition of climbing boys, if we could conscientiously have done so. But such a measure, we are convinced from the evidence, could not be carried into execution without great injury to property, and great increased risk of fire. The Lords have investigated the matter with the greatest patience, humanity, and good sense; and they do not venture, in their Report, to recommend to the House the abolition of climbing boys. *Edinburgh Review*, 1819

The Annual Register for 1845 says that Sydney's advocacy of the chimney sweeps alleviated their miseries, but it was not until 1875 – more than half a century after the publication of this article, and more than 20 years after the further condemnation of the practice in Charles Kingsley's *The Water Babies* – that the employment of young children as chimney-sweeps was finally made illegal.

The Game Laws

Although he lived many years in the country and turned himself into a capable farmer, Sydney took no part in traditional country sports. He did not ride to hounds; he had difficulty staying on a horse's back at the best of times. He did not shoot either. Arriving to take up his parish in rural Yorkshire, he wrote to Lady Holland:

> I have laid down two rules for the country: first, not to smite the partridge; for if I fed the poor, and comforted the sick, and instructed the ignorant, yet I should do nothing worth, if I smote the partridge. If anything ever endangers the Church, it will be the strong propensity to shooting for which the clergy are remarkable. Ten thousand good shots dispersed over the country do more harm to the cause of religion than the arguments of Voltaire and Rousseau. The squire never reads, but it is not possible he can believe that religion to be genuine whose ministers destroy his game.

His second rule was to contrive a visit to London at least once every year. That letter was written in June 1809. Nearly 20 years later he wrote a light-hearted reassurance to Lady Carlisle about his attitude towards poaching:

> Pray tell the Duke that it is not my fault if there are so many poachers at Londesborough. I have preached several sermons about the Birds in the Air, and the Beasts of the Field, stating that they all belong to His Grace. I shall be under the painful necessity of mentioning the pheasants by name. I have no doubt however that with three or four sermons I can disperse the whole gang.

Poaching, however, was a serious national problem. Across the country there were large private estates, rich in pheasant, grouse, partridge, hares and other edible game; and all around them lived a vast peasant population, struggling to survive and maintain their families just above the subsistence level. Gates and fences can be climbed, and the temptation was bound to be altogether too much for many. The inevitable result was a continuous state of armed confrontation, generally at night, between the land-owners and the poachers. The land-owners employed game-keepers who set traps and snares that could break the legs of an unwary trespasser or shoot him (or her) dead. The poachers would operate in gangs. There were ambushes and pitched gun battles and people were killed. Penalties so savage were imposed on convicted poachers that juries grew reluctant to pronounce them guilty. It all made for intense antagonism between the rich and the poor, and encouraged the emergence of idle and vicious rogues.

Things were made worse by Game Laws of a fantastic absurdity – the description given by Bernard Darwin in the first volume of G.M. Young's *Early Victorian England*. Under these Game Laws, reinforced by an Act of 1818, only the wealthy, owners of land worth £100 a year or more, could carry guns and keep dogs and employ game-keepers to kill the game found on their estates. Anyone caught poaching was liable to transportation to Australia for seven years.

Most ridiculous of all, the Game Laws made all selling of game illegal. When a squire, with his keepers and guests, shot hundreds of birds – as they often did – he might eat as much as he could and give presents to his friends but the law did not allow him to sell what was left over. There was no shortage of demand. The country was full of the newly rich – factory-owners and merchants, transport magnates, financiers and professional men – who had no land themselves but a strong desire to emulate the way of life of their social superiors. Coach companies were keen to transport the game. Poulterers were eager to supply. In this way, a vast and illegal trade was encouraged, in the same manner in which the prohibition of the trade in alcohol brought about the gangsters' enormous bootlegging business in the United States in the 1920s.

Sydney deplored the social effects of this ludicrous system, and savaged the Game Laws forcefully and relentlessly in a series of articles in the *Edinburgh Review* between 1819 and 1823.

Three Letters on the Game Laws. Rest Fenner, Black and Co. London, 1818

Nothing can be more grossly absurd than the present state of the Game Laws, as far as they concern the qualification for shooting. In England, no man can possibly have a legal right to kill game, who has not 100*l.* a year in land rent. With us in Scotland, the rule is not quite so inflexible, though in principle not very different. – But we shall speak to the case which concerns by far the greatest number: and certainly it is scarcely possible to imagine a more absurd and capricious limitation. For what possible reason is a man, who has only 90*l.* per annum in land, not to kill the game which his own land nourishes? If the Legislature really conceives, as we have heard surmised by certain learned squires, that a person of such a degree of fortune should be confined to profitable pursuits, and debarred from that pernicious idleness into which he would be betrayed by field sports, it would then be expedient to make a qualification for bowls or skittles – to prevent small landowners from going to races, or following a pack of hounds – and to prohibit to men of a certain income, every other species of amusement as well as this. The only instance, however, in which this paternal care is exercised, is that in which the amusement of the smaller landowner is supposed to interfere with those of his richer neighbour. He may do what he pleases, and elect any other species of ruinous idleness but that in which the upper classes of society are his rivals.

Nay, the law is so excessively ridiculous in the case of small landed proprietors, that on a property of less than 100*l.* per annum, *no human being* has the right of shooting. It is not confined but annihilated. The Lord of the Manor may be warned off by the proprietor; and the proprietor may be informed against by any body who sees him sporting. The case is still stronger in the instance of large farms. In Northumberland, and on the borders of Scotland, there are large capitalists, who farm to the amount of two or three thousand per annum, who have the permission of their distant non-resident landlords, to do what they please with the game, and yet who dare not fire off a gun upon their own land. Can any thing be more utterly absurd and preposterous, than that the landlord and the wealthy tenant *together* cannot make up a title to the hare which is fattened upon the choicest produce of their land? That the landlord, who can let to farm the fertility of the land for growing wheat, cannot let to farm its power of growing partridges? That he may reap by deputy, but cannot on that manor shoot by deputy? Is it possible that any respectable magistrate could fine a farmer for killing a hare upon his own grounds with his landlord's consent, without feeling that he was violating every feeling of common sense and justice?

Since the enactment of the Game Laws, there has sprung up an entirely new species of property, which of course is completely overlooked by their provisions. An Englishman may possess a million of money in funds, or merchandise – may be the *Baring* or the *Hope* of Europe – provide to Government the sudden means of equipping fleets and armies, and yet be without the power of smiting a single partridge, though invited by the owner of the game to participate in his amusement. It is idle to say that the difficulty may be got over, by purchasing land: the question is, upon what principle of justice can the existence of the difficulty be defended? If the right of keeping men-servants was confined to persons who had more than 100*l.* a year in the funds, the difficulty might be got over by every man who would change his landed property to that extent. But what could justify so capricious a partiality to one species of property? There might be some apology for such laws at the time they were made; but there can be none for their not being now accommodated to the changes which time has introduced. If you choose to exclude poverty from this species of amusement, and to open it to wealth, why is it not opened to every species of wealth? What amusement can there be morally lawful to an holder of turnip land, and criminal in a possessor of Exchequer bills? What delights ought to be tolerated to Long Annuities, from which wheat and beans should be excluded? What matters whether it is scrip or short-horned cattle? . . .

We come now to the sale of game. – The foundation on which the propriety of allowing this, partly rests, is the impossibility of preventing it. There exists, and has sprung up since the Game Laws, an enormous mass of wealth, which has nothing to do with land. Do the country gentlemen imagine, that it is in the power of human laws to deprive the three per cents of pheasants? That there is upon earth, air, or sea, a single flavour (cost what crime it may to procure it), that mercantile opulence will not procure? Increase the difficulty, and you enlist vanity on the side of luxury; and make that be sought for as a display of wealth, which was before valued only for the gratification of appetite. The law may multiply penalties by reams. Squires may fret and Justices commit, and gamekeepers and poachers continue their nocturnal wars. There must be game on Lord Mayor's day, do what you will. You may multiply the crimes by which it is procured; but nothing can arrest its inevitable progress, from the wood of the esquire to the spit of the citizen. The late law for preventing the sale of game produced some little temporary difficulty in London at the beginning of the season. The poulterers were alarmed, and came to some resolutions. But the alarm soon began to subside, and the difficulties to vanish. In another season, the law will be entirely nugatory and forgotten. The experiment was tried of increased severity; and a law passed to punish poachers with transportation who were caught poaching in the night time with arms. What has the consequence been? – Not a cessation of poaching, but a succession of village guerillas; – an internecive war between the gamekeepers and marauders of game; – the whole country flung into brawls and convulsions, for the unjust and exorbitant pleasures of country gentlemen. The poacher hardly believes he is doing any wrong in taking partridges and pheasants. He would admit the justice of being transported for stealing sheep; and his

courage in such a transaction would be impaired by a consciousness he was doing wrong: but he has no such feeling
in taking game; and the preposterous punishment of transportation makes him desperate, and not timid. Single
poachers are gathered into large companies, for their mutual
protection; and go out, not only with the intention of taking
game, but of defending what they take with their lives. Such
feelings soon produce a rivalry of personal courage, and a
thirst of revenge between the villagers and the agents of
power. . . .

Poaching will exist in some degree, let the laws be what
they may; but the most certain method of checking the
poacher seems to be by underselling him. If game can be
lawfully sold, the quantity sent to market will be increased,
the price lowered, and, with that, the profits and temptations of the poacher. Not only would the prices of the
poacher be lowered, but we much doubt if he would find
any sale at all. Licenses to sell game might be confined to
real poulterers, and real occupiers of a certain portion of
land. It might be rendered penal to purchase it from any but
licensed persons; and in this way the facility of the lawful,
and the danger of the unlawful trade, would either annihilate
the poacher's trade, or reduce his prices so much, that it
would be hardly worth his while to carry it on. What poulterer in London, or in any of the large towns, would deal
with poachers, and expose himself to indictment for receiving
stolen goods, when he might supply his customers at fair
prices by dealing with the lawful proprietor of game? Opinion
is of more power than law. Such conduct would soon become infamous; and every respectable tradesman would be
shamed out of it. The consumer himself would rather buy
his game of a poulterer at an increase of price, than pick it
up clandestinely, and at a great risk, though a somewhat
smaller price, from porters and boothkeepers. Give them a
chance of getting it fairly, and they will not get in unfairly.
At present, no one has the slightest shame at violating a law
which every body feels to be absurd and unjust. . . .

It will be necessary, whenever the Game Laws are rev-
ised, that some of the worst punishments now inflicted for
an infringement of these laws should be repealed. – To transport a man for seven years, on account of partridges, and to
harass a poor wretched peasant in the Crown Office, are
very preposterous punishments for such offences: Humanity revolts against them – they are grossly tyrannical – and
it is disgraceful that they should be suffered to remain on

our statute books. But the most singular of all abuses, is the new class of punishments which the Squirarchy have themselves enacted against depredations on game. The law says, that an unqualified man who kills a pheasant, shall pay five pounds; but the Squire says he shall be shot; – and accordingly he places a spring-gun in the path of the poacher, and does all he can to take away his life. The more humane and mitigated Squire mangles him with traps; and the suprafine country gentleman only detains him in machines, which prevent his escape, but do not lacerate their captive. Of the gross illegality of such proceedings, there can be no reasonable doubt. Their immorality and cruelty are equally clear. If they are not put down by some declaratory law, it will be absolutely necessary that the Judges, in their invaluable circuits of Oyer and Terminer, should leave two or three of his Majesty's Squires to a fate too vulgar and indelicate to be alluded to in this Journal.

Men have certainly a clear right to defend their property; but then it must be by such means as the law allows: – their houses by pistols, their fields by action for trespass, their game by information. There is an end of law, if every man is to measure out his punishment for his own wrong. Nor are we able to distinguish between the guilt of two persons, – the one of whom deliberately shoots a man whom he sees in his fields – the other of whom purposely places such instruments as he knows will shoot trespassers upon his fields: Better that it should be lawful to kill a trespasser face to face, than to place engines which will kill him. The trespasser may be a child – a woman – a son or friend: – The spring-gun cannot accommodate itself to circumstances, – the Squire or the gamekeeper may.

These, then, are our opinions respecting the alterations in the Game Laws, which, as they now stand, are perhaps the only system which could possibly render the possession of game so very insecure as it now is. We would give to every man an absolute property in the Game upon his land, with full power to kill – to permit others to kill – and to sell; – we would punish any violation of that property by summary conviction, and pecuniary penalties – rising in value according to them number of offences. This would of course abolish all qualifications; and we sincerely believe it would lessen the profits of selling Game illegally, so as very materially to lessen the number of poachers. It would make Game, as an article of food, accessible to all classes, without infringing the laws. It would limit the amusements of country gentlemen within the boundaries of justice – and would enable the Magistrate cheerfully and conscientiously to execute laws, of the moderation and justice of which he must be thoroughly convinced. To this conclusion, too, we have no doubt we shall come at the last. After many years of scutigeral folly – loaded prisons – nightly battles – poachers tempted – and families ruined, these principles will finally prevail, and make law once more coincident with reason and justice.   *Edinburgh Review* 1819

It is hard to read arguments like these, so cool and cogent, humane and rational, so deeply-researched as well as deeply felt, without feeling what a loss to British jurisprudence was inflicted when Sydney's father refused to find the money for his son's legal training.

In 1831 a new Game Act was passed, permitting the public sale of legally acquired game – a *small* step in the right direction. On 11 August of that year Sydney wrote to Thomas Moore, '. . . from hence till 1st September (when men of large Fortune put men of no Fortune in prison on account of partridges). . . .'

Prisons and Prisoners' Rights

Sydney had wanted to be a lawyer and would have been a good one, and probably a very successful one, too. He did become very actively involved in the legal system when he was made a county magistrate in Yorkshire in 1814. He was proud of the English tradition of impartial justice and fought fiercely for reform when he thought it was needed.

In one of his sermons, to the Society for the Improvement of Prison Discipline, he asked questions which are as pertinent today as they were in his day: 'Are the engines of detection and punishment to be so perfect? And are we to do nothing for the prevention of crime?'

In 1819, when reform of the criminal law was under parliamentary consideration, he sent two letters of detailed advice to his influential friend Lord Lansdowne:

25 Mar 1819

Dear Lord Lansdowne,
On all such occasions there are generally too many suggestions instead of too few. The few rules I send proceed from evils I have observed. It is very singular to find the public so humane and reasonable that they will listen to these subterraneous miseries, and very good and wise in you to derive from this spirit a law of permanent humanity which will outlive it.

I remain, my dear Lord Lansdowne,
With great respect and regard, yours,
SYDNEY SMITH.
Pray do not think of answering my letter; it requires none.

PROPOSED RULES FOR PRISONS.

I.   The names of the visiting magistrates and their places of abode to be printed and stuck up in all rooms where prisoners are confined, under penalty to jailors.

II.   Names of visiting magistrates to be called over by the clerk of the peace, or clerk of assize, in open court, on the first day of any assize and quarter sessions, and the judge or chairman to ask in open court whether they have visited the prisons, and have any observation to offer upon their state and condition. Penalties to clerk of the peace and of assize.

III.   A book to be kept by the jailor, noting down the visits of magistrates to the prison, to be read in open court in the same manner.

IV.   More power to visiting magistrates to make alterations between session and session, subject to the approbation of magistrates assembled at quarter sessions or assizes.

V.   Divisions of accused and committed, young and old offenders.

VI.   Neither beer nor spirits without order of the apothecary, or permission of magistrates in writing. Heavy penalties.

VII. No Roman Catholic or Dissenter compellable to attend the prison worship if he objects to do so, and expresses himself willing to attend a clergyman of his own persuasion.

VIII. Power in two magistrates to confine for two or three days in solitary confinement any refractory prisoner.

IX.   No prisoner to be locked up in sleeping-room for more than ten hours at night. N. B. – They are now locked up in small rooms in winter from four in the evening till eight in the morning, without fire or candle, to avoid the trouble and expense of watching, lighting and warming them.

X.   No male prisoner after conviction to have less than two pounds of bread per day, if their diet is bread alone; women, a pound and a half. Prisoners before conviction to have per day not less than this, and twice a week one pound of meat each.

XI.   Money allowance to be put upon a more rational footing.

Between 1821 and 1826 Sydney wrote four long articles for the *Edinburgh Review*, dealing with conditions in the prisons and flaws in the legal system.

1. *Thoughts on the Criminal Prisons of the Country,*
occasioned by the Bill now in the House of Commons, for
Consolidating and Amending the Laws relating to Prisons.
By George Holford, Esq. M.P. Rivington. 1821.
2. *Gurney on Prisons.* Constable and Co. 1819.
3. *Report of Society for Bettering the Condition of Prisons.*
Bensley, 1820.

There are, in every county in England, large public
schools, maintained at the expense of the county, for the
encouragement of profligacy and vice, and for providing a
proper succession of housebreakers, profligates, and thieves.
They are schools, too, conducted without the smallest degree
of partiality or favour; there being no man (however mean
his birth, or obscure his situation,) who may not easily
procure admission to them. The moment any young person
evinces the slightest propensity for these pursuits, he is
provided with food, clothing, and lodging, and put to his
studies under the most accomplished thieves and cut-throats
the county can supply. There is not, to be sure, a formal
arrangement of lectures, after the manner of our Universities;
but the petty larcenous stripling, being left destitute of every
species of employment, and locked up with accomplished
villains as idle as himself, listens to their pleasant narrative
of successful crimes, and pants for the hour of freedom, that
he may begin the same bold and interesting career.

This is a perfectly true picture of the prison establishments
of many counties in England, and was so, till very lately, of
almost all; and the effects so completely answered the design,
that, in the year 1818, there were committed to the jails of the
United Kingdom more than one hundred and seven thousand
persons! a number supposed to be greater than that of all the
commitments in the other kingdoms of Europe put together.

The bodily treatment of prisoners has been greatly improved since the time of Howard. There is still, however,
much to do; and the attention of good and humane people
has been lately called to their state of moral discipline.

It is inconceivable to what a spirit of party this has given
birth; – all the fat and sleek people, – the enjoyers, – the
mumpsimus, and 'well as we are' people, are perfectly outrageous at being compelled to do their duty; and to sacrifice
time and money to the lower orders of mankind. Their first
resource was, to deny all the facts which were brought forward for the purposes of amendment; and the alderman's
sarcasm of the Turkey carpet in jails was bandied from one
hard-hearted and fat-witted gentleman to another: but the

advocates of prison-improvement are men in earnest – not playing at religion, but of deep feeling, and of indefatigable industry in charitable pursuits. Mr Buxton went in company with men of the most irreproachable veracity; and found, in the heart of the metropolis, and in a prison of which the very Turkey carpet alderman was an official visitor, scenes of horror, filth, and cruelty, which would have disgraced even the interior of a slave-ship.

This dislike of innovation proceeds sometimes from the disgust excited by false humanity, canting hypocrisy, and silly enthusiasm. It proceeds also from a stupid and indiscriminate horror of change, whether of evil for good, or good for evil. There is also much party spirit in these matters. A good deal of these humane projects and institutions originate from Dissenters. The plunderers of the public, the jobbers, and those who sell themselves to some great man, who sells himself to a greater, all scent, from afar, the danger of political change – are sensible that the correction of one abuse may lead to that of another – feel uneasy at any visible operation of public spirit and justice – hate and tremble at a man who exposes and rectifies abuses, from a sense of duty – and think, if such things are suffered to be, that their candle-ends and cheese-parings are no longer safe: and these sagacious persons, it must be said for them, are not very wrong in this feeling. Providence, which has denied to them all that is great and good, has given them a fine tact for the preservation of their plunder: their real enemy is the spirit of inquiry – the dislike of wrong – the lover of right – and the courage and diligence which are the concomitants of these virtues. When once this spirit is up, it may be as well directed to one abuse as another. To say you must not torture a prisoner with bad air and bad food, and to say you must not tax me without my consent, or that of my representative, are both emanations of the same principle, occurring to the same sort of understanding, congenial to the same disposition, published, protected, and enforced by the same qualities. This it is that really excites the horror against Mrs Fry, Mr Gurney, Mr Bennet, and Mr Buxton. Alarmists such as we have described have no particular wish that prisons should be dirty, jailors cruel, or prisoners wretched: they care little about such matters either way; but all their malice and meanness is called up into action when they see secrets brought to light, and abuses giving way before the diffusion in intelligence, and the aroused feelings of justice and compassion. As for us, we have neither love of change, nor fear of it; but a love of what is just and wise, as far as we are able to find it out. In this spirit we shall offer a few observations upon prisons, and upon the publications before us.

The new law should keep up the distinction between Jails and Houses of Correction. One of each should exist in every county, either at a distance from each other, or in such a state of juxtaposition that they might be under the same governor. To the jail should be committed all persons accused of capital offences, whose trials would come on at the Assizes; to the house of correction, all offenders whose cases would be cognizable at the Quarter-sessions. Sentence of imprisonment in the house of correction, after trial, should carry with it hard labour; sentence of imprisonment in the jail, after trial, should imply an exemption from compulsory labour. There should be no compulsory labour in jails – only in houses of correction. In using the terms *Jail* and House of Correction, we shall always attend to these distinctions. Prisoners for trial should not only not be compelled to labour, but they should have every indulgence shown to them compatible with safety. No chains – much better diet than they commonly have – all possible access to their friends and relations – and means of earning money if they choose it. The broad and obvious distinction between prisoners before and after trial should constantly be attended to; to violate it is gross tyranny and cruelty. . . .

A very great, and a very neglected object in prisons, is Diet. There should be, in every jail and house of correction, four sorts of diet; 1*st*, Bread and water; 2*dly*, Common prison diet, to be settled by the magistrates; 3*dly*, Best prison diet, to be settled by ditto; 4*thly*, Free diet, from which spirituous liquors altogether, and fermented liquors in excess, are excluded. All prisoners, before trial, should be allowed best prison diet, and be upon free diet, if they could afford it. Every sentence for imprisonment should expressly mention, to which diet the prison is confined; and no other diet should be, on any account, allowed to such prisoner after his sentence. Nothing can be so preposterous, and criminally careless, as the way in which persons confined upon sentence are suffered to live in prisons. Misdemeanants, who have money in their pockets, may be seen in many of our prisons with fish, buttered veal, rump steaks, and every kind of luxury; as the practice prevails of allowing them to purchase a pint of ale each, the rich prisoner purchases many pints of ale in the name of his poorer brethren, and drinks them himself. A jail should be a place of punishment, from which men recoil with horror – a place of real suffering, painful to the memory, terrible to the imagination; but if men can live idly, and live luxuriously, in a clean, well-aired, well-warmed, spacious habitation, is it any wonder that they set the law at defiance, and brave that magistrate who restores them to their former luxury and ease? There are a set of men well known to jailors, called *Family-men*, who are constantly returning to jail, and who may be said to spend the greater part of their life there, – up to the time when they are hanged. . . .

It is quite obvious that, if men were to appear again, six months after they were hanged, handsomer, richer, and more plump than before execution, the gallows would cease to be an object of terror. But here are men who come out of jail, and say, 'Look at us, – we can read and write, we can make baskets and shoes, and we went in ignorant of every thing: and we have learnt to do without strong liquors, and have no longer any objection to work; and we did work in the jail, and have saved money, and here it is.' What is there of terror and detriment in all this? and how are crimes to be lessened if they are thus rewarded? Of schools there cannot be too many. Penitentiaries, in the hands of wise men, may be rendered excellent institutions; but a prison must be a prison – a place of sorrow and wailing; which should be entered with horror, and quitted with earnest resolution never to return to such misery; with that deep impression, in short, of the evil, which breaks out into perpetual warning and exhortation to others. This great point effected, all other reformation must do the greatest good. . . .

In this age of charity and of prison improvement, there is one aid to prisoners which appears to be wholly overlooked; and that is, the means of regulating their defence, and providing them witnesses for their trial. A man is tried for murder, or for house-breaking or robbery, without a single shilling in his pocket. The nonsensical and capricious institutions of the English law prevent him from engaging counsel to speak in his defence, if he had the wealth of Croesus; but he has no money to employ even an attorney, or to procure a single witness, or to take out a subpoena. The Judge, we are told, is his counsel; – this is sufficiently absurd; but is it not pretended that the Judge is his witness. He solemnly declares that he has three or four witnesses who could give a completely different colour to the transaction; but they are sixty or seventy miles distant, working for their daily bread, and have no money for such a journey, nor for the expense of a residence of some days in an Assize town. They do not know even the time of the Assize, nor the modes of tendering their evidence if they could come. When every thing is so well marshalled against him on the opposite side, it would be singular if an innocent man, with such an absence of all means of defending himself, should not occasionally be hanged or transported: and accordingly we believe that such things have happened. Let any man, immediately previous to the Assizes, visit the prisoners for trial, and see the many wretches who are to answer to the most serious accusations, without one penny to defend themselves. If it appeared probable, upon inquiry, that these poor creatures had important evidence which they could not bring into Court for want of money, would it not be a wise application of compassionate funds, to give them this fair chance of establishing their innocence? It seems to us no bad *finale* of the pious labours of those who guard the poor from ill treatment during their imprisonment, to take care that they are not unjustly hanged at the expiration of the term.   *Edinburgh Review* 1821

Sydney returned to this theme the following year, and at greater length. 'This practice,' he wrote, 'is so utterly ridiculous to any body but lawyers (to whom nothing that is customary is ridiculous), that men not versant with courts of justice will not believe it.'

In 1824 he wrote, savaging the magistrates of Yorkshire North Riding, who had ruled that prisoners awaiting trial, unconvicted prisoners, if they were physically capable of work, should be forced to labour long hours on the treadmill. If they refused, they would be given nothing more than bread and water. In Sydney's eyes this was a betrayal of all the laws of common decency. It was also another blatant example of class-based injustice. The rich could buy themselves bail. The poor could not.

The Care of the Insane

In 1792 William Tuke, a Quaker, incensed by the brutal treatment meted out to a fellow Quaker at York Asylum, founded his own asylum for the mentally ill, which he called the Retreat. His grandson wrote about it, and Sydney, reading the book, was greatly impressed by the detailed evidence of the compassionate methods used at the Retreat, and their success. He quotes at length in his article in the *Edinburgh Review*, and lends his enthusiastic support to the Retreat's way of caring for the mentally ill. His article provided widespread publicity, and caused others to follow William Tuke's example.

> *Description of the Retreat, an Institution near York for Insane*
> *Persons of the Society of Friends.* By Samuel Tuke. York, 1813.
> The Retreat for insane Quakers is situated about a mile from
> the city of York, upon an eminence commanding the adja-
> cent country, and in the midst of a garden and fields be-
> longing to the institution. The great principle on which it

appears to be conducted is that of kindness to the patients. It does not appear to them, because a man is mad upon one particular subject, that he is to be considered in a state of complete mental degradation, or insensible to the feelings of kindness and gratitude. When a madman does not do what he is bid to do, the shortest method, to be sure, is to knock him down; and straps and chains, are the species of prohibitions which are the least frequently disregarded. But the Society of Friends seems rather to consult the interest of the patient than the ease of his keeper; and to aim at the government of the insane, by creating in them the kindest disposition towards those who have the command over them. Nor can any thing be more wise, humane, or interesting, than the strict attention to the feelings of their patients which seems to prevail in their institutions. . . .

Upon the whole, we have little doubt that this is the best managed asylum for the insane that has yet been established; and a part of the explanation no doubt is, that the Quakers take more pains than other people with their madmen. A mad Quaker belongs to a small and rich sect; and is, therefore, of greater importance than any other mad person of the same degree in life. After every allowance, however, which can be made for the feelings of sectaries, exercised towards their own disciples, the Quakers, it must be allowed, are a very charitable and humane people. They are always ready with their money, and, what is of far more importance, with their time and attention, for every variety of human misfortune.

They seem to set themselves down systematically before the difficulty, with the wise conviction that it is to be lessened or subdued only by great labour and thought; and that it is always increased by indolence and neglect. In this instance, they have set an example of courage, patience, and kindness, which cannot be too highly commended, or too widely diffused; and which, we are convinced, will gradually bring into repute a milder and better method of treating the insane. For the aversion to inspect places of this sort is so great, and the temptation to neglect and oppress the insane so strong, both from the love of power, and the improbability of detection, that we have no doubt of the existence of great abuses in the interior of many madhouses.

A great deal has been done for prisons; but the order of benevolence has been broken through by this preference; for the voice of misery may sooner come up from a dungeon than the oppression of a madman be healed by the hand of justice. *Edinburgh Review* 1814

Suppression of Vice

Sydney was acutely aware of the extreme class divisions in English society and the continuing tendency of the privileged to reinforce the divisions. He was delighted, and provoked to retaliation, when he detected this tendency at work in the arguments and aims of the Society for the Suppression of Vice.

Proceedings of the Society for the Suppression of Vice

Beginning with the best intentions in the world, such societies must in all probability degenerate into a receptacle
for every species of tittle-tattle, impertinence, and malice.
Men, whose trade is rat-catching, love to catch rats; the bug-
destroyer seizes on his bug with delight; and the suppressor
is gratified by finding his vice. The last soon becomes a mere
tradesman like the others; none of them moralize, or lament
that their respective evils should exist in the world. The
public feeling is swallowed up in the pursuit of a daily
occupation, and in the display of a technical skill. Here,
then, is a society of men, who invite accusation, who receive
it (almost unknown to themselves) with pleasure, and who,
if they hate dulness and inoccupation, can have very little
pleasure in the innocence of their fellow creatures. The
natural consequence of all this is, that (besides that portion
of rumour which every member contributes at the weekly
meeting) their table must be covered with anonymous lies
against the characters of individuals. Every servant discharged
from his master's service, – every villain who hates the man
he has injured, – every cowardly assassin of character, –
now knows where his accusations will be received, and
where they cannot fail to produce some portion of the mischievous effects which he wishes. The very first step of such
a Society should be, to declare, in the plainest manner, that
they would never receive any anonymous accusation. This
would be the only security to the public, that they were not
degrading themselves into a receptacle for malice and falsehood. Such a declaration would inspire some species of confidence; and make us believe that their object was neither
the love of power, nor the gratification of uncharitable feelings. The Society for the Suppression, however, have done
no such thing. They request, indeed, the signature of the
informers whom they invite; but they do not (as they ought)
make that signature an indispensable condition.

Nothing has disgusted us so much in the proceedings of
this Society, as the control which they exercise over the
amusements of the poor. One of the specious titles under
which this legal meanness is gratified is, Prevention of
Cruelty to Animals.

Of cruelty to animals, let the reader take the following specimens:-

Running an iron hook in the intestines of an animal; presenting this first animal to another as his food; and then pulling this second creature up and suspending him by the barb in his stomach.

Riding a horse till he drops, in order to see an innocent animal torn to pieces by dogs.

Keeping a poor animal upright for many weeks, to communicate a peculiar hardness to his flesh.

Making deep incisions into the flesh of another animal while living, in order to make the muscles more firm.

Immersing another animal, while living, in hot water.

Now we do fairly admit, that such abominable cruelties as these are worthy the interference of the law: and that the Society should have punished them, cannot be matter of surprise to any feeling mind. – But stop, gentle reader! these cruelties are the cruelties of the Suppressing Committee, not of the poor. You must not think of punishing these. – The first of these cruelties passes under the pretty name of *angling*; – and therefore there can be no harm in it – the more particularly as the President himself has one of the best preserved trout streams in England. – The next his *hunting*; – and as many of the Vice-Presidents and of the Committee hunt, it is not possible there can be any cruelty in hunting. The next is, a process for making *brawn* – a dish never tasted by the poor, and therefore not to be disturbed by indictment. The fourth is the mode of *crimping* cod; and the fifth, of boiling lobsters; all high-life cruelties, with which a justice of the peace has no business to meddle. The real thing which calls forth the sympathies, and harrows up the soul, is to see a number of boisterous artisans baiting a bull, or a bear; not a savage hare, or a carnivorous stag, – but a poor, innocent, timid bear; – not pursued by magistrates, and deputy lieutenants, and men of education, – but by those who must necessarily seek their relaxation in noise and tumultuous merriment, – by men whose feelings are blunted, and whose understanding is wholly devoid of refinement. The Society detail, with symptoms of great complacency, their detection of a bear-baiting in Blackboy Alley, Chick Lane, and the prosecution of the offenders before a magistrate. It appears to us, that nothing can be more partial and unjust than this kind of proceedings. A man of ten thousand a year may worry a fox as much as he pleases, – may encourage the breed of a mischievous animal on purpose to worry it; and a poor labourer is carried before a magistrate for paying sixpence to see an exhibition of courage between a dog and a bear! Any cruelty may be practised to gorge the stomachs of the rich, – none to enliven the holidays of the poor. We venerate those feelings which really protect creatures susceptible of pain, and incapable of complaint. But heaven-born pity, now-a-days, calls for the income tax, and the court guide; and ascertains the rank and fortune of the tormentor before she weeps for the pain of the sufferer. . . .

We see at the head of this Society the names of several noblemen, and of other persons moving in the fashionable world. Is it possible they can be ignorant of the innumerable offences against the law and morality which are committed by their own acquaintances and connexions? Is there one single instance where they have directed the attention of the Society to this higher species of suppression, and sacrificed men of consideration to that zeal for virtue which watches so acutely over the vices of the poor? It would give us very little pleasure to see a duchess sent to the Poultry Compter; but if we saw the Society flying at such high game, we should at least say they were honest and courageous, whatever judgment we might form of their good sense. At present they should denominate themselves a Society for suppressing the vices of persons whose income does not exceed 500*l. per annum*; and then, to put all classes upon an equal footing, there must be another society of barbers, butchers, and bakers, to return to the higher classes that moral character, by which they are so highly benefited.

Edinburgh Review 1809.

THE

EDINBURGH REVIEW,

OR

CRITICAL JOURNAL:

FOR

OCT. 1802......JAN. 1803.

TO BE CONTINUED QUARTERLY.

JUDEX DAMNATUR CUM NOCENS ABSOLVITUR.
PUBLIUS SYRUS.

VOL. I.

Edinburgh :

PRINTED BY D. WILLISON, CRAIG'S CLOSE,
FOR ARCHIBALD CONSTABLE, EDINBURGH;
AND T. N. LONGMAN & O. REES,
LONDON.

1803.

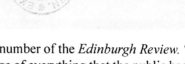

The front page of the first number of the *Edinburgh Review.* 'It was an entire and instant change of everything that the public had been accustomed to in that sort of composition.'

VII

The Arts

Sydney moved much in high society, knew many fine buildings and saw many fine works of art and craftsmanship, met countless writers and artists, and was himself (by all accounts) an accomplished and histrionic performer, from the pulpit or in the lecture hall. His writing style was very much his own – fluent and often elegant in the Augustan manner, lively with bright ideas and images, powerfully persuasive when he was arguing a case, compelling and entertaining too.

In the teeth of all this, he was also – when it came to the fine arts – something of an unashamed and unrepentant philistine.

He could listen to music, if it was melodious and not too loud and did not go on too long. The priority requirement of architecture, in his view, was to provide rooms that were warm and full of light, cheerfully furnished and encouraging to conversation and laughter. He had few comments to make on the pictorial arts but had strong views on interior decoration. His approach to art was cavalier. In her *Memoir* his daughter Saba recalled his remarks shortly after he had moved into a house near Oxford Street and Park Lane, in central London. This was in 1839.

> I hate bare walls; so I cover mine, you see, with pictures. I took the advice of two Royal Academicians, but brought their consultation to an abrupt determination by saying, Gentlemen, I forgot to mention that my highest price is five-and-thirty shillings. The public, it must be owned, treat my collection with great contempt; and even Hibbert, who has been brought up in the midst of fine pictures, and might know better, never will admire them. But look at that sea-piece, now; what would you desire more? It is true, the moon in the corner was rather dingy when I first bought it; so I had a new moon put in for half-a-crown, and now I consider it perfect.

In his own field of artistic action, that of writing, he was content to be robustly unfashionable. The emerging school of 'Romantic' poets held no appeal for him. On the whole, he thought of poets, and all those in the high-flown mystical or declamatory mode, as one of those groups – together with curates, Scottish philosophers and senior dignitaries of the Anglican Church – who were simply ludicrous.

Among the list of twenty recommendations he sent to Lady Morpeth to help her recover from low spirits was this one:

> Avoid poetry, dramatic representations (except comedy),

music, serious novels, melancholy, sentimental people, and everything likely to excite feeling or emotion, not ending in active benevolence.

He rarely commented on his own writings for the *Edinburgh Review*, but in August 1819 he wrote to his old friend Francis Jeffrey, who was editing the magazine:

You must consider that Edinburgh is a very grave place, and that you live with Philosophers – who are very intolerant of nonsense. I write for the London, not for the Scotch market, and perhaps more people read my nonsense than your sense. The complaint was loud and universal of the extreme dulness and *lengthiness* of the Edinburgh Review. Too much I admit would not do of my style; but the proportion in which it exists enlivens the Review if you appeal to the whole public, and not to the 8 or 10 grave Scotchmen with whom you live. I am a very ignorant, frivolous, half-inch person; but such as I am, I am sure I have done your Review good and *contributed* to bring it into notice. Such as I am, I shall be, and cannot promise to alter; such is my opinion of the effect of my articles.

Music

Sydney enjoyed singing, especially the songs of his Irish friend Thomas Moore. 'I am learning to sing all your songs,' he wrote to Moore. 'I have mastered "Ship Ahoy", "Love and Valour", "Dear Harp", and one or two others.'

But professional musical performances always went on far too long for him. He saw Bellini's 'I Puritani' in Paris in 1835, and found it so 'dreadfully tiresome and unintelligible' that he hoped never to see another opera. He saw to it that he did not. A few years later, when Lady Holland invited him to share their box at a performance of Rossini's 'Semiramis', he declined, politely but firmly:

My dear Lady Holland,

I have not the heart, when an amiable lady says, 'Come to 'Semiramis' in my box', to decline; but I get bolder at a distance. 'Semiramis' would be to me pure misery. I love music very little – I hate acting; I have the worst opinion of Semiramis herself, and the whole thing (I cannot help it) seems so childish and so foolish that I cannot abide it. Moreover, it would be rather out of etiquette for a Canon of St. Paul's to go to an opera; and where etiquette prevents me from doing things disagreeable to myself, I am a perfect martinet.

All these things considered, I am sure you will not be a Semiramis to me, but let me off.

He felt much the same about church music. During his time as vicar of

Foston, he saw something of the annual York Musical Festival and found it mostly ridiculous:

> Nothing can be more disgusting than an oratorio. How absurd, to see 500 people fiddling like madmen about Israelites in the Red Sea. Lord Morpeth pretends to say he was pleased, but I see a great change in him since the music-meeting. . . .
>
> The music went off very well, £20,500 was collected. I did not go once. Music for such a length of time (unless under sentence of a jury) I will not submit to. What pleasure is there in pleasure, if quantity is not attended to, as well as quality? I know nothing more agreeable than a dinner at Holland House, but it must not begin at ten in the morning and last till six.

As Canon of St. Paul's, he resisted all attempts to increase the choir. In 1841 he wrote to the Archdeacon of London:

> The whole Institution of Singing boys is a gross absurdity and instead of doubling them I should be glad to reduce them to one half.

Four years later he wrote frankly to the St. Paul's organist, who was still pressing for more choirboys:

> I think the Choir of St. Paul's as good as any in England. We have gone on with it for two hundred years; why not be content? You talk of competing with other cathedrals, but cathedrals are not to consider themselves rival opera houses. We shall come by and by to act anthems. It is enough if your music is decent, and does not put us to shame. It is a matter of perfect indifference to me whether Westminster bawls louder than St. Paul's. We are there to pray, and the singing is a very subordinate consideration.

But Sydney was susceptible to the charms of music. In the summer of 1844 he wrote to Lady Grey from Combe Florey:

> There is an excellent musical family living in London; and finding them all ill, and singing flat, I brought them down here for three weeks, where they have grown extremely corpulent. . . . Their singing is certainly very remarkable, and the little boy, at the age of seven, composes hymns; I mean sets them to music. I have always said that if I were to begin life again I would dedicate it to music; it is the only cheap and unpunished rapture upon earth.

Theatre

Sydney had no more interest in theatre than he had in opera. The period he lived in was one of outstanding actors – Kemble and Mrs Siddons, Edmund Kean and Macready – and outstanding writing about stage performances

from critics like William Hazlitt and Charles Lamb, but he was not attracted.
From Edinburgh in 1799 he wrote to Mrs Hicks Beach:

> Kemble the player is come down here and these wicked
> people are employing Passion Week in going to tragedies
> and comedies. It is I am told extremely ludicrous to see him
> on the Stage; half his time is employed in prompting the
> other actors and correcting their motions. The other evening
> he was stabbed, and he was forced to put his assassin in
> mind that it was time to stab him; which you will allow
> was rather an awkward circumstance. I sent Michael once,
> but had not myself the curiosity to go. . . . I should not be
> much disquieted if I never saw him again.

Many years later he wrote to Mrs Grote:

> You cannot excite my envy by all the descriptions of your
> dramas and melodrama; you may as well paint the luxuries
> of barley-meal to a tiger, or turn a leopard into a field of
> clover. All this class of pleasures inspires me with the same
> nausea as I feel at the sight of a rich plum-cake or sweet-
> meats; I prefer the dryest bread of common life.

In the last year of his life Sydney wrote to Alfred Novello:

> Sir,
>
> There are in all Countries fixd and regular absurdities which
> it is almost atheistical to call in question. Such is the admir-
> ation of Shakespere in England. To be well read in
> Shakespere is Literature, to quote from Shakespere is wit,
> to be acquainted with every word he uses is learning. Of the
> beauties of Shakespere I am deeply sensible, but I am equally
> sensible that there is in his plays an incredible heap of the
> worst trash and nonsense. I wish him to be more forgotten
> and less considered.

Writing

Sydney was widely read in many fields – in modern novels as well as travel
books, memoirs and history, the plays and poetry and stories of the past,
sermons and the Bible, in English and French, Latin and Greek. In 1820,
when his son Douglas was a scholar at Westminster College, he sent him this
reading advice:

> In the time you can give to English reading you should
> consider what it is most needful to have, what it is most
> shameful to want – shirts and stockings, before frills and
> collars. Such is the history of your own country, to be studied
> in Hume, then in Rapin's History of England, with Tindal's
> Continuation. Hume takes you to the end of James the
> Second, Rapin and Tindal will carry you to the end of Anne.
> Then, Coxe's 'Life of Sir Robert Walpole', and the 'Duke of

Marlborough'; and these read with attention to dates and geography. Then, the history of the other three or four enlightened nations in Europe. For the English poets, I will let you off at present with Milton, Dryden, Pope, and Shakespeare; and remember, always in books keep the best company. Don't read a line of Ovid till you have mastered Virgil; nor of Massinger, till you are familiar with Shakespeare.

When it came to reading for pleasure, Sydney believed there was only one, over-riding rule of judgement. He stated it in his review of a three-volume novel called *Granby*:

The main question as to a novel is – did it amuse? were you surprised at dinner coming so soon? did you mistake eleven for ten, and twelve for eleven? were you too late to dress? and did you sit up beyond the usual hour? If a novel produces these effects, it is good; if it does not – story, language, love, scandal itself cannot save it. It is only meant to please; it must do that, or it does nothing.

Edinburgh Review 1826

He was an avid reader of novels, especially those of Walter Scott. They had known and enjoyed each other's company and admired each other's writing since Sydney's early days in Edinburgh. In 1819, writing to thank Constable for sending him *The Bride of Lammermoor*, he said:

It would be profanation to call him Mr Walter Scott. I should as soon say Mr Shakespeare or Mr Fielding. Sir William and Lady Ashton are excellent, and highly dramatic. Drumthwacket is very well done; parts of Caleb are excellent. . . . When I get hold of one of these novels, turnips, sermons, and justice-business are all forgotten.

More than once he complained that Scott frequently portrayed virtually the same characters in succeeding stories. 'Meg Merrilies', he said, 'appears afresh in every novel.' When *The Fortunes of Nigel* came out in 1822, he wrote to Constable:

Many thanks for Nigel; a far better novel than The Pirate though not of the highest order of Scott's novels. It is the first novel in which there is no Meg Merrilies. There is, however, a Dominie Sampson in the horologer. The first volume is admirable. The miser's daughter is very good; so is the murder. The story execrable; the gentlemanlike, light, witty conversation always (as in all his novels) very bad. Horrors or humour are his forte. He must avoid running into length – great part of the second volume very long and tiresome; but upon the whole the novel will do – keeps up the reputation of the author; and does not impair the very noble and honourable estate which he has in his brains.

In the late 1830s, when the early works of the young Charles Dickens were exploding onto the literary scene, Sydney was at first put off by the pen-name 'Boz'. But he was soon won over. To a friend he wrote:

> Read Boz's Sketches, if you have not already read them. I think them written with great power, and that the soul of Hogarth has migrated into the body of Mr Dickens. I had long heard of them but was deterred by the vulgarity of the name.

A year later he was saying: 'Nickleby is very good. I stood out against Mr Dickens as long as I could, but he has conquered me.'

The two men met in June 1839 and took to each other immediately. In January 1843, when the first episode of *Martin Chuzzlewitt* appeared, Sydney wrote to Dickens:

> You have been so used to these sort of impertinences that I believe you will excuse me for saying how very much I am pleased with the first number of your new work. Pecksniff and his daughters and Pinch are admirable – quite first-rate painting, such as no one buy yourself can execute. . . . I am impatient for the next number. P.S. Chuffey is admirable. I never read a finer piece of writing; it is deeply pathetic and affecting.

In July the same year, when the American chapters appeared, he wrote again:

> Excellent! nothing can be better! You must settle it with the Americans as you can, but I have nothing to do with that. I have only to certify that the number is full of wit, humour, and power of description.

By this time Dickens was dedicated to his writing career, which was something that Sydney, in theory at least, did not approve of. He wrote to Lady Carlisle in September 1843: 'But wretched is the man who lives by literature – better to live by restoring the daily polish to the polluted shoe – or by guiding from street to street the conductitious vehicles of the metropolis.'

Sydney took a fiercely moral line against all kinds of writing that sought to put sin, especially sexual adventurism, in a glamorous light. His review of Mme de Stael's novel *Delphine* opened with the words 'This dismal trash. . .', savaged the book and its translation, and then delivered a general condemnation:

> The immorality of any book (in our estimation) is to be determined by the general impressions it leaves on those minds, whose principles, not yet *ossified*, are capable of affording a less powerful defence to its influence. The most dangerous effect that any fictitious character can produce, is when two or three of its popular vices are varnished over with every thing that is captivating and gracious in the exterior, and ennobled by association with splendid virtues: this apology will be more sure of its effect, if the faults are not against nature, but against society. The aversion to murder and

cruelty could not perhaps be so overcome; but a regard to the sanctity of marriage vows, to the sacred and sensitive delicacy of the female character, and to numberless restrictions important to the well-being of our species, may easily be relaxed by this subtle and voluptuous confusion of good and evil. It is in vain to say the fable evinces, in the last act, that vice is productive of misery. We may decorate a villain with graces and felicities for nine volumes, and hang him in the last page. This is not teaching virtue, but gilding the gallows, and raising up splendid associations in favour of being hanged. In such an union of the *amiable* and the vicious, (especially if the vices are such, to the commission of which there is no want of natural disposition,) the vice will not degrade the man, but the man will ennoble the vice. We shall wish to be him we admire, *in spite* of his vices, and, if the novel be well written, even *in consequence* of his vice. There exists, through the whole of this novel, a show of exquisite sensibility to the evils which individuals suffer by the inflexible rules of virtue prescribed by society, and an eager disposition to apologise for particular transgressions. Such doctrine is not confined to Madame de Staël; an Arcadian cant is gaining fast upon Spartan gravity; and the happiness diffused, and the beautiful order established in society, by this unbending discipline, is wholly swallowed up in compassion for the unfortunate and interesting individual. Either the exceptions or the rule must be given up: every highwayman who thrusts his pistol into a chaise window has met with *unforeseen misfortunes*; and every loose matron who flies into the arms of her *Greville* was compelled to marry an old man whom she detested, by an avaricious and unfeeling father. The passions want not accelerating, but retarding machinery. This fatal and foolish sophistry has power enough over every heart, not to need the aid of fine composition, and well-contrived incident – auxiliaries which Madame de Staël intended to bring forward in the cause, though she has fortunately not succeeded. . . .

The morality of all this is the old morality of Farquhar, Vanburgh, and Congreve – that every witty man may transgress the seventh commandment, which was never meant for the protection of husbands who labour under the incapacity of making repartees.

To conclude – Our general opinion of this book is, that it is calculated to shed a mild lustre over adultery; by gentle and convenient gradation, to destroy the modesty and the caution of women; to facilitate the acquisition of easy vices, and encumber the difficulty of virtue. What a wretched qualification of this censure to add, that the badness of the principles is alone corrected by the badness of the style, and that this celebrated lady would have been very guilty, is she had not been very dull!   *Edinburgh Review* 1803

Sydney's own sphere of writing was the polemical, cogently arguing a case, ridiculing the follies and abuses and injustices of his time. His foremost aim was to persuade, and to that end he made himself a master of a most effective style – coolly rational in tone, fluent and elegant in manner, serious for the greater part but seasoned with wit and good humour. In a letter he wrote to Lady Holland in October 1818, he criticised his friend Henry Brougham's pamphleteering style:

> Brougham's pamphlet accidentally happens to be very dull. It is not of much importance but there was no absolute necessity for its being so. Wit and declamation would be misplaced, but a clever man may be bright and flowing while he is argumentative and prudent.

Sydney had a natural grace in his writing style. He liked to surprise his reader with sudden, unexpected jokes and sallies, odd words of his own coining, and images that were original and vivid and very apt. He also had a natural feeling for the flow and balance of a sentence. He refers to this, in a characteristic way, in a previously unpublished letter that he wrote to Georgiana, Lady Morpeth, in July 1842:

> What a pretty name is Georgiana: many people would say What a pretty name Georgiana is, but this would be inelegant – and it is more tolerable to be slovenly in dress than in style. Dress covers only the mortal body and adorns it but style is the vehicle of the spirit.

Poetry

Sydney was a prose writer. He wrote very little verse, which is a shame because, when he did attempt it, his carefully crafted rhyming couplets were reminiscent of those of Alexander Pope himself, the most accomplished of all the English versifiers.

But Sydney found most poetical forms and styles altogether too overblown and misguided for his taste. He wrote to Lady Dacre in 1837:

> Many thanks, dear Lady Dacre, for your beautiful translations in your beautiful book -
> I read forthwith several beautiful sonnets upon Love, which paint with great fidelity some of the worst symptoms of that terrible disorder, than which none destroys more completely the happiness of common existence, and substitutes for the activity which Life demands a long and sickly dream with moments of pleasure and days of intolerable pain. The Poets are full of false views: they make mankind

believe that happiness consists in falling in love, and living in the country – I say: live in London; like many people, fall in love, with nobody. To these rules of life I add: read Lady Dacre's Translations, and attend her Monday evening parties.

One of his London friends, Samuel Rogers, was a popular poet, so highly regarded that he was offered the Laureateship when Wordsworth died in 1850. Sydney, although fond of the man, could not take his poetry seriously. Hesketh Pearson tells this story in *The Smith of Smiths*:

'How is Rogers?' asked someone.

'He is not very well,' replied Sydney.

'Why, what is the matter?'

'Oh, don't you know he has produced a couplet? When he is delivered of a couplet, with infinite labour and pain, he takes to his bed, has straw laid down, the knocker tied up, expects his friends to call and make inquiries, and the answer at the door invariably is 'Mr Rogers and his little couplet are as well as can be expected'. When he produces an Alexandrine he keeps his bed a day longer.'

He was an exact contemporary of Wordsworth and Coleridge, but in no way moved by their poetry or impressed by the Romantic Movement which they inaugurated. In 1814, when Francis Jeffrey published his famous review of Wordsworth's 'The Excursion' which opened with the words 'This will never do. . .', Sydney remonstrated with him:

I have not read the review of Wordsworth, because the subject is to me so very uninteresting; but may I ask was it worth while to take any more notice of a man respecting whom the public opinion is completely made up? and do not such repeated attacks upon the man wear in some little degree the shape of persecution?

Sydney's view of Wordsworth is one of the few examples of his getting things entirely wrong. Just a few years after he wrote those lines, Wordsworth's reputation began to soar, to the point where he became a revered national figure and one of the founders of the Victorian world-view.

DAME PARTINGTON and the OCEAN (OF REFORM)
Published by Thos McLean, 26 Haymarket, Oct 19th 1831.

After Sydney's speech at Taunton (p.130) on 1 March, 1831, prints appeared of Dame Partington, with a face remarkably like that of the Duke of Wellington.

VIII

Politics

Sydney was deeply concerned about politics, national and international, all his adult life. He hated war and had to live through two decades of it. He hated repression and vindictiveness and lived under more than two decades of that. He hated stupidity, too, and saw plenty of that throughout his life. Although the great majority of his friends were active on the liberal Whig side of the great political divide of the time, he was too independent of mind and spirit ever to become a rigid party man himself. But there was never any doubt where he stood on the key issues. Towards the end of 1819, when many feared that Britain was heading for revolution and terror, he summed up his attitudes in a letter to Lord Grey:

> What I want to see the State do is to lessen in these sad times some of their numerous enemies. Why not do something for the Catholics and scratch them off the list? Then come the Protestant Dissenters. Then of measures, – a mitigation of the game-laws – commutation of tithes – granting to such towns as Birmingham and Manchester the seats in Parliament taken from the rottenness of Cornwall – revision of the Penal Code – sale of the Crown lands – sacrifice of the Droits of Admiralty against a new war; – anything that would show the Government to the people in some other attitude than that of taxing, punishing, and restraining. I believe what Tierney said to be strictly true that the House of Commons is falling into contempt with the people. Democracy has many more friends among tradesmen and persons of that class of life than is known or supposed commonly. I believe the feeling is most rapidly increasing and that Parliament in two or three years' time will meet under much greater circumstances of terror than those under which it is at present assembled.

That was written a few weeks after what was called 'the massacre of Peterloo'. A mass meeting had been held at St Peter's Field in Manchester to demand electoral reform. So many people turned up that the magistrates lost their nerve, ordered the arrest of the leading speaker, and sent a troop of Hussars, armed with sabres, into the crowd. Eleven people were killed and about 400 were wounded. On 3 January, 1820, Sydney wrote to Edward Davenport:

> My opinion is the same as yours upon the Peterloo Business:
> I have no doubt but that every thing would have ended at

Manchester as it did at Leeds had there been the same forbearance on the part of the Magistrates – either they lost (no
great Loss) their heads – or the Devils of local Spite and
malice had enter'd into them: or the Nostrils of the Clerical
magistrates Smelt preferment & Court favor – but let it have
been what it will the effects have been most deplorable.

There was a national outcry, but the government responded by rushing
through more restrictions on public gatherings. For a while, uncharacteristic-
ally, Sydney was close to despair. In February 1821 he wrote to Lady Grey:

There is an end for ever of all idea of Whigs coming into
power; the Kingdom is in the hands of an Oligarchy, who
see what a good thing they have got of it, and are too cunning,
and too well aware of the Tameability of Mankind to give it
up. Lord Castlereagh smiles when Tierney prophecies resist-
ance; his Lordship knows very well that he has got the people
under, for ninety nine purposes out of an hundred, and that
he can keep them where he has got them – Of all ingenious
instruments of despotism I must commend a popular
Assembly, where the majority are paid and hired, and a few
bold and able men by their brave Speeches make other
people believe they are free.

Three days later, in another letter, he was saying:

I agree with you that there is an end for ever of the Whigs
coming into power. The country belongs to the Duke of
Rutland, Lord Lonsdale, the Duke of Newcastle, and about
twenty other holders of boroughs. They are our masters! If
any little opportunity presents itself, we will hang them,
but most probably there will be no such opportunity; it always is twenty to one against the people. There is nothing
(if you will believe the Opposition) so difficult as to bully a
whole people; whereas, in fact, there is nothing so easy, as
that great artist Lord Castlereagh so well knows.

He held all the Tory grandees of those long repressive years in contempt,
but reserved his fiercest venom for Lord Eldon, who was Lord Chancellor
for 25 years between 1801 and 1827. After Eldon's death, a biography was
published. Sydney read it and commented in a letter to Lady Grey:

He seems to have been a cunning canting old Rogue whose
object was to make all the money he could by office at any
expense to the public happiness. In addition he was the
bigotted Enemy of every sort of improvement and retarded
by his influence for more than 25 years those changes which
the State of the Country absolutely required. I know where
he is now – in that particular part of certain regions which
are set apart for Canting and Hypocrisy.

When Tory rule finally began to crumble in the late 1820s, the first great issue was Roman Catholic Emancipation. This was won in 1829. The next great issue was electoral reform and in this, too, Sydney played a powerfully influential role.

The first version of the proposed Reform Bill was introduced into Parliament by the Whig government on 1 March, 1831. Sydney was immediately fighting in the front line. On 9 March he addressed a public meeting in Taunton, making effective mock of those who were suggesting that the men who controlled the rotten boroughs ought to be financially compensated for their impending losses:

> When I was a young man, the place in England I remember as the most notorious for highwaymen and their exploits was Finchley Common, near the metropolis; but Finchley Common, gentlemen, in the progress of improvement, came to be enclosed, and the highwaymen lost by these means the opportunity of exercising their gallant vocation. I remember a friend of mine proposed to draw up for them a petition to the House of Commons for compensation, which ran in this manner – 'We, your loyal highwaymen of Finchley Common and its neighbourhood, having, at great expense, laid in a stock of blunder busses, pistols, and other instruments for plundering the public, and finding ourselves impeded in the exercise of our calling by the said enclosure of the said Common of Finchley, humbly petition your Honourable House will be pleased to assign to us such compensation as your Honourable House in its wisdom and justice may think fit.' Gentlemen, I must leave the application to you.

A long and ferocious battle ensued. The government changed hands briefly, then the Whigs were back in power, with Lord Grey at the helm and several of Sydney's old friends in the Cabinet: Lord Brougham, Lord Holland, Lord Lansdowne and the Earl of Carlisle. Another Reform Bill was approved by the House of Commons, then rejected by the House of Lords. Three days after the Lords voted, there was another public meeting in Taunton, in the Castle Hall because so many people wanted to attend. Once again Sydney spoke, this time to make the House of Lords look ridiculous with a brilliant and astonishing image:

> Mr Bailiff, I have spoken so often on this subject, that I am sure both you and the gentlemen here present will be obliged to me for saying but little, and that favour I am as willing to confer, as you can be to receive it. I feel most deeply the event which has taken place, because, by putting the two Houses of Parliament in collision with each other, it will impede the public business, and diminish the public prosperity. I feel it as a churchman, because I cannot but blush to see to many dignitaries of the Church arrayed against the

wishes and happiness of the people. I feel it more than all, because I believe it will sow the seeds of deadly hatred between the aristocracy and the great mass of the people. The loss of the bill I do not feel, and for the best of all possible reasons – because I have not the slightest idea that it *is* lost. I have no more doubt, before the expiration of the winter, that this bill will pass, than I have that the annual tax bills will pass, and greater certainty than this no man can have, for Franklin tells us, there are but two things certain in this world – death and taxes. As for the possibility of the House of Lords preventing ere long a reform of Parliament, I hold it to be the most absurd notion that ever entered into human imagination. I do not mean to be disrespectful, but the attempt of the Lords to stop the progress of reform, reminds me very forcibly of the great storm of Sidmouth, and of the conduct of the excellent Mrs Partington on that occasion. In the winter of 1824, there set in a great flood upon that town – the tide rose to an incredible height – the waves rushed in upon the houses, and everything was threatened with destruction. In the midst of this sublime and terrible storm, Dame Partington, who lived upon the beach, was seen at the door of her house with mop and pattens, trundling her mop, squeezing out the sea-water, and vigorously pushing away the Atlantic Ocean. The Atlantic was roused. Mrs Partington's spirit was up; but I need not tell you that the contest was unequal. The Atlantic Ocean beat Mrs Partington. She was excellent at a slop, or a puddle, but she should not have meddled with a tempest. Gentlemen, be at your ease – be quiet and steady. You will beat Mrs Partington.

The gathering dissolved in laughter. Sydney had illustrated his story by miming the old lady's efforts with her mop. Soon the whole country was laughing, and prints were on sale depicting 'Dame Partington', with a face remarkably like that of the Tory leader, the Duke of Wellington, in action against the Atlantic Ocean. The Reform Bill passed into law on June 4 1832.

In later years Sydney rather regretted that he had not spoken out in the pages of the *Edinburgh Review*, more frequently and forcefully, against war, its horrors, expense and folly. In 1839, when he was putting together the three-volume collection of his *Works*, he added this footnote:

I am sorry that I did not, in the execution of my self-created office as a reviewer, take an opportunity in this, or some other military work, to descant a little upon the miseries of war; and I think this has been unaccountably neglected in a work abounding in useful essays, and ever on the watch to propagate good and wise principles. It is not that human beings can live without occasional wars, but they may live with fewer wars, and take more just views of the evils which war inflicts upon mankind. If three men were to have their legs and arms broken, and were to remain all night exposed to the inclemency of weather, the whole country would be in a state of the most dreadful agitation. Look at the wholesale death of a field of battle, ten acres covered with dead, and half dead, and dying; and the shrieks and agonies of many thousand human beings. There is more of misery inflicted upon mankind by one year of war, than by all the civil peculations and oppressions of a century. Yet it is a state into which the mass of mankind rush with the greatest avidity, hailing official murderers, in scarlet, gold, and cocks' feathers, as the greatest and most glorious of human creatures. It is the business of every wise and good man to set himself against this passion for military glory, which really seems to be the most fruitful source of human misery.

What would be said of a party of gentlemen who were to sit very peaceably conversing for half an hour, and then were to fight for another half hour, then shake hands, and at the expiration of thirty minutes fight again? Yet such has been the state of the world between 1714 and 1815, a period in which there was in England as many years of war as peace. Societies have been instituted for the preservation of peace, and for lessening the popular love of war. They deserve every encouragement. The highest praise is due to Louis Philippe for his efforts to keep Europe in peace.

There had, however, been occasional anti-war and anti-colonial outbursts in the *Review* articles, one of them in an 1827 piece called 'Catholics':

It is not only the event of war we fear in the military struggle with Ireland; but the expense of war, and the expenses of the English government, are paving the way for future revolutions. The world never yet saw so extravagant a government as the Government of England. Not only is economy not practised – but it is despised; and the idea of it connected with disaffection, Jacobinism, and Joseph Hume. Every rock in the ocean where a cormorant can perch is occupied by our troops, has a governor, deputy-governor, storekeeper, and deputy-storekeeper – and will soon have an archdeacon and a bishop. Military colleges, with thirty-four professors, educating seventeen ensigns per annum, being half an ensign for each professor, with every species of nonsense, athletic, sartorial, and plumigerous. A just and necessary war costs this country about one hundred pounds a minute; whipcord fifteen thousand pounds; red tape seven thousand pounds; lace for drummers and fifers, nineteen thousand pounds; a pension to one man who has broken his head at the Pole; to another who has shattered his leg at the Equator; subsidies to Persia; secret service-money to Thibet; an annuity to Lady Henry Somebody and her seven daughters – the husband being shot at some place where we never ought to have had any soldiers at all; and the elder brother returning four members to Parliament. Such a scene of extravagance, corruption, and expense as must paralyse the industry, and mar the fortunes, of the most industrious, spirited people that ever existed.

There had also been his warning to the Americans (dated 1820, and quoted in chapter 3 of this book), never to go to war for reasons of supposed national pride or in the expectation of glory. The only truly predictable outcome of such folly, he argued, was higher taxes. This was something the British knew all too well, since it was wars against revolutionary France that had burdened them with the income tax in 1799 and every year since.

Sydney never wavered in his detestation of war. Today he would be seen as a fervent non-interventionist. A nation's prosperity, he believed, depended chiefly on its ability to mind its own business. There was no advantage to be won, and terrible dangers to be risked, in trying to rule the world, convert it, or police it. 'Pray vote against War if you possibly can,' he wrote to George Lamb in 1827, 'Nothing justifies War but a Box on the Ear – not a box on the ear by implication but a box on the ear physically corporally actually.'

He made the same point repeatedly, in many letters. Only a few years after Waterloo and the end of more than 20 years of war against revolutionary France, there was widespread clamour to despatch a British force to Spain to support the rebels there. Sydney wrote to Lady Grey:

> For God's sake, do not drag me into another war! I am worn down, and worn out, with crusading and defending Europe, and protecting mankind; I *must* think a little of myself. I am sorry for the Spaniards – I am sorry for the Greeks – I deplore the fate of the Jews; the people of the Sandwich Islands are groaning under the most detestable tyranny; Bagdad is oppressed; I do not like the present state of the Delta; Thibet is not comfortable. Am I to fight for all these people? The world is bursting with sin and sorrow. Am I to be champion of the Decalogue, and to be eternally raising fleets and armies to make all men good and happy? We have just done saving Europe, and I am afraid the consequence will be, that we shall cut each other's throats. No war, dear Lady Grey! – no eloquence; but apathy, selfishness, common sense, arithmetic! I beseech you, secure Lord Grey's swords and pistols, as the housekeeper did Don Quixote's armour. If there is another war, life will not be worth having.

'May the vengeance of Heaven' overtake all the Legitimates of Verona! but, in the present state of rent and taxes, they must be *left* to the vengeance of Heaven. I allow fighting in such a cause to be a luxury; but the business of a prudent, sensible man, is to guard against luxury.

There is no such thing as a 'just war,' or, at least, as a *wise* war.

In the same year, in another letter, he said this:

I am afraid we shall go to war: I am sorry for it. I see every day in the world a thousand acts of oppression which I should like to resent, but I cannot afford to play the Quixote. Why are the English to be the sole vindicators of the human race?   To Mrs Meynell, 18 Feb, 1823

Five years later he found something to praise in the policies of the Duke of Wellington:

I rather like his foreign politics, in opposition to the belligerent Quixotism of Canning. He has the strongest disposition to keep this country in profound peace, to let other nations scramble for freedom as they can, without making ourselves the liberty-mongers of all Europe; a very seductive trade, but too ruinous and expensive.

To J A Murray, 28 Nov, 1828

But in the last year of his life his fears remained: 'The English and French having saved a little money, will of course spend it in cutting each other's throats; and there have been such a number of warlike inventions since the last peace that the temptation to try them is irresistible.'

He was still worrying, though in a more light-hearted way, when he was nearly 70:

The smell of war is not over. I lament, and can conceive no greater misery. Among other evils, everybody must be ready for fighting; and I am not ready, but much the contrary. I am ten miles from the coast; a French steamer arrives in the night, and the first thing I hear in the morning is that the cushions of my pulpit are taken away, and my curate and churchwardens carried into captivity.

To Miss Mary Berry, Sept, 1840

Henry Phillpotts, Bishop of Exeter, 'so like Judas that I now firmly
believe in the apostolical succession'.

IX

Bishops

In an unrevised fragment found among Sydney's papers after his death, he describes a 'real bishop'.

> But I never remember in my time a real bishop – a grave, elderly man, full of Greek, with sound views of the middle voice and preterpluperfect tense, gentle and kind to his poor clergy, of powerful and commanding eloquence, in Parliament never to be put down when the great interests of mankind were concerned; leaning to the Government when it was right, leaning to the people when they were right; feeling that if the Spirit of God had called him to that high office, he was called for no mean purpose, but rather that seeing clearly, acting boldly, and intending purely, he might confer lasting benefit upon mankind.

Instead, with few exceptions, he saw the bishops as time-serving supporters of a reactionary Tory government. 'The liberality of Churchmen generally is like the quantity of matter in a cone – both get less and less as they move higher.' Bishop Philpotts of Exeter even caused Sydney to believe in the Apostolic Succession, 'there being no other way of accounting for the descent of the Bishop of Exeter from Judas Iscariot.'

Opportunity for elevation to the higher ranks of the clergy depended first on there being vacancies. Sydney wrote on 24 January 1831 to J A Murray,

> I think Lord Grey will give me some preferment if he stays in long enough – but the Upper Parsons live Vindictively – and evince their aversion to a Whigg Ministry by an improv'd health – the Bishop of Ely has the rancor to recover after three paralytic Strokes – and the Dean of Lichfield to be vigorous at 82 – and yet these are the men who are called Christians -

Preferment depended secondly on knowing the right people, especially the political party in power, and on being known as a loyal supporter of monarch and government. For most of Sydney's adult life the Tory party was in power. Preferring principle to promotion, he remained a country parson. Then in 1836 a brief interval of Whig government and the death of three bishops in six weeks provided the opportunity to elevate Sydney to the episcopate. It was not used. Lord Melbourne shirked the uproar that might ensue, but was later reported as saying that 'few things filled him with more regret than not putting Sydney on the Bench'. Two years before his death Sydney said to a visitor in his garden at Combe Florey,

They showed a want of moral courage in not making me a bishop, but I must own that it required a good deal. *They* know, *you* know, all who have lived and talked much with me must know, that I should have devoted myself heart and soul to my duties, and that the episcopal dignity would have sustained no loss in my keeping. But I have only myself to blame if I have been misunderstood.

In 1813 he had written to Francis Wrangham, 'Why are you an honest Man? you might have been Bishop of London – Will no time and no Example cure you? – Repent and do not go unmitrd to your Tomb -' Sydney gave no example, and went unmitred to *his* tomb.

Instead, he fought against the bishops, who were increasing their powers, even while they were hoping to make reforms in the Church.

A Letter to the Rt. Hon. Spencer Perceval, on a subject connected with his Bill, now under discussion in Parliament, for improving the situation of stipendiary curates.

Our first and greatest objection to such a measure, is the increase of power which it gives to the bench of Bishops, – an evil which may produce the most serious effects, by placing the whole body of the clergy under the absolute control of men who are themselves so much under the influence of the Crown. It is useless to talk of the power they anciently possessed. They have never possessed it since England has been what it now is. Since we have enjoyed practically a free constitution, the bishops have, in point of fact, possessed little or no power of oppression over their clergy.

It is in vain to talk of the good character of bishops. Bishops are men; not always the wisest of men; not always preferred for eminent virtues and talents, or for any good reason whatever known to the public. They are almost always devoid of striking and indecorous vices; but a man may be very shallow, very arrogant, and very vindictive, though a bishop; and pursue with unrelenting hatred a subordinate clergyman, whose principles he dislikes, and whose genius he fears. Bishops, besides, are subject to the infirmities of old age, like other men; and in the decay of strength and understanding, will be governed as other men are, by daughters and wives, and whoever ministers to their daily comforts. We have no doubt that such cases sometimes occur, and produce, wherever they do occur, a very capricious administration of ecclesiastical affairs. (I have seen in the course of my life, as the mind of the prelate decayed, wife bishops, daughter bishops, butler bishops, and even cook and housekeeper bishops.) *Edinburgh Review* 1810

Thoughts on the Residence of the Clergy
by John Sturges, LL.D.
Upon the propriety of investing the Bench of Bishops with
a power of enforcing residence we confess ourselves to
entertain very serious doubts. A bishop has frequently a very
temporary interest in his diocese: he has favours to ask; and
he must grant them. Leave of absence will be granted to
powerful intercession; and refused, upon stronger pleas, to
men without friends. Bishops are frequently men advanced
in years, or immersed in study. A single person who compels
many others to do their duty has much odium to bear and
much activity to exert. A bishop is subject to caprice, and en-
mity, and passion in common with other individuals; there is
some danger also that his power over the clergy may be converted to a political purpose. From innumerable causes,
which might be reasoned upon to great length, we are ap-
prehensive the object of the Legislature will be entirely frus-
trated in a few years, if it be committed to episcopal superintendence and care; though, upon the first view of the
subject, no other scheme can appear so natural and so wise.
Edinburgh Review 1803

Sydney's most impressive actions were fought in the *Edinburgh Review*
against the Bishop of Peterborough over the Church of England's traditional
acceptance of different theological viewpoints, and against the Bishop of
Lincoln, over concessions to Roman Catholics. This latter review (dealt with
in more detail in ch.12) begins:

It is a melancholy thing to see a man, clothed in soft raiment,
lodged in a public palace, endowed with a rich portion of
the product of other men's industry, using all the influence
of his splendid situation, however conscientiously, to
deepen the ignorance, and inflame the fury, of his fellow
creatures. These are the miserable results of that policy
which has been so frequently pursued for these fifty years
past, of placing men of mean, or middling abilities, in high
ecclesiastical stations. In ordinary times, it is of less importance who fills them; but when the bitter period arrives, in
which the people must give up some of their darling ab-
surdities; – when the senseless clamour, which has been
carefully handed down from father fool to son fool, can be
no longer indulged; – when it is of incalculable importance
to turn the people to a better way of thinking; the greatest
impediments to all amelioration are too often found among
those to whose councils, at such periods, the country ought
to look for wisdom and peace.
A bill for the former review was sent to Francis Jeffery, then Editor:

Francis Jeffrey Esq

Debtor to the Rev S Smith Clerk

To an attack upon a Bishop in No 74 – said Bishop being a Bigot & a Tyrant & for making said Bishop ridiculous & so improving him.

For this and two other reviews, he charged £129.5.6d

all executed in the best manner – good Language, witty & clear of Scotticisms, & very provoking according to order.

A PERSECUTING BISHOP.

1. *An Appeal to the Legislature and Public; or, the Legality of the Eighty-Seven Questions proposed by Dr Herbert Marsh, the Bishop of Peterborough, to Candidates for Holy Orders, and for Licenses, within that Diocese, considered.* Second Edition. London: Seely. 1821.

2. *A Speech, delivered in the House of Lords on Friday, June 7, 1822, by Herbert, Lord Bishop of Peterborough, on the Presentation of a Petition against his Examination Questions; with Explanatory Notes, a Supplement, and a Copy of the Questions.* London: Rivington. 1822. etc.

It is a great point in any question to clear away encumbrances, and to make a naked circle about the object in dispute, so that there may be a clear view of it on every side. In pursuance of this disencumbering process, we shall first acquit the Bishop of all wrong intentions. He has a very bad opinion of the practical effects of high Calvinistic doctrines upon the common people; and he thinks it his duty to exclude those clergymen who profess them from his diocese. There is no moral wrong in this. He has accordingly devised no fewer than *eighty-seven* interrogatories, by which he thinks he can detect the smallest taint of Calvinism that may lurk in the creed of the candidate; and in this also, whatever we may think of his reasoning, we suppose his purpose to be blameless. He believes, finally that he has legally the power so to interrogate and exclude; and in this perhaps he is not mistaken. His intentions then are good, and his conduct, perhaps, not amenable to the law. All this we admit in his favour: but against him we must maintain, that his conduct upon the points in dispute has been singularly injudicious, extremely harsh, and in its effects (though not in its intentions) very oppressive and vexatious to the clergy. . . .

The longer we live, the more we are convinced of the justice of the old saying, that an *ounce of mother wit is worth a pound of clergy*; that discretion, gentle manners, common sense, and good nature are, in men of high ecclesiastical station of far greater importance than the greatest skill in discriminating between sublapsarian and supralapsarian doctrines. Bishop Marsh should remember that all men wearing the mitre work by character, as well as doctrine; that a tender regard to men's rights and feelings, a desire to avoid sacred squabbles, a fondness for quiet, and an ardent wish to make everybody happy, would be of far more value to the Church of England than all his learning and vigilance of inquisition. The Irish Tithes will probably fall next session of Parliament; the common people are regularly receding from the Church of England – baptizing, burying, and con-firming for themselves. Under such circumstances, what would the worst enemy of the English Church require? – a bitter, bustling, theological Bishop, accused by his clergy of tyranny and oppression – the cause of daily petitions and daily debates in the House of Commons – the idoneous vehicle of abuse against the Establishment – a stalking-horse to bad men for the introduction of revolutionary opinions, mischievous ridicule, and irreligious feelings. Such will be the advantages which Bishop Marsh will secure for the English Establishment in the ensuing session. It is incon-ceivable how such a prelate shakes all the upper works of the Church, and ripens it for dissolution and decay. Six such Bishops, multiplied by eighty-seven, and working with five hundred and twenty-two questions, would fetch everything to the ground in less than six months. But what if it pleased Divine Providence to afflict every prelate with the spirit of putting eighty-seven queries, and the two Archbishops with the spirit of putting twice as many, and the Bishop of Sodor and Man with the spirit of putting only forty-three queries? – there would then be a grand total of two thousand three hundred and thirty-five interrogations flying about the Eng-lish Church; and sorely vexed would the land be with Question and Answer.

We will suppose this learned Prelate, without meanness or undue regard to his worldly interests, to feel that fair desire of rising in his profession, which any man, in any profession, may feel without disgrace. Does he forget that his character in the ministerial circles will soon become that of a violent impracticable man – whom it is impossible to place in the highest situations – who has been trusted with too much already, and must be trusted with no more? Ministers have something else to do with their time, and with the time of Parliament, than to waste them in debating squabbles between Bishops and their clergy. They naturally wish, and, on the whole, reasonably expect, that everything should go on silently and quietly in the Church. They have no objection to a learned Bishop; but they deprecate one atom more of learning than is compatible with moderation, good sense, and the soundest discretion. It must be the grossest ignorance of the world to suppose that the Cabinet has any pleasure in watching Calvinists.

The Bishop not only puts the questions, but he actually assigns the limits within which they are to be answered. Spaces are left in the paper of interrogations, to which limits the answer is to be confined; two inches to original sin, an inch and a half to justification, three quarters to predestination, and to free will only a quarter of an inch. But if his Lordship gives them an inch they will take an ell. His Lordship is himself a theological writer, and by no means remarkable for his conciseness. To deny space to his brother theologians, who are writing from the most difficult subjects, not from choice, but necessity; not for fame, but for bread; and to award rejection as the penalty of prolixity, does appear to us no slight deviation from Christian gentleness. . . .

We are not much acquainted with the practices of courts of justice; but, if we remember right, when a man is going to be hanged, the judge lets him make his defence in his own way, without complaining of its length. We should think a Christian Bishop might be equally indulgent to a man who is going to be ruined. The answers are required to be clear, concise, and correct – short, plain, and positive. In other words, a poor curate, extremely agitated at the idea of losing his livelihood, is required to write with brevity and perspicuity on the following subjects: – Redemption by Jesus Christ – Original Sin – Free Will – Justification – Justification in reference to its causes – Justification in reference to the time when it takes place – Everlasting Salvation – Predestination – Regeneration on the New Birth – Renovation, and the Holy Trinity. . . .

His Lordship boasts, that he has excluded only two curates. So the Emperor of Hayti boasted that he had only cut off two persons' heads for disagreeable behaviour at his table. In spite of the paucity of the visitors executed, the example operated as a considerable impediment to conversation; and the intensity of the punishment was found to be a full compensation for its rarity. How many persons have been deprived of curacies which they might have enjoyed, but for the tenour of these interrogatories? How many respectable clergymen have been deprived of the assistance of curates connected with them by blood, friendship, or doctrine, and compelled to choose persons for no other qualification than that they could pass through the eye of the Bishop's needle? Violent measures are not to be judged of merely by the number of times they have been resorted to, but by the terror, misery, and restraint which the severity is likely to have produced.

His lordship talks of the drudgery of wading through ten pages of answers to his eighty-seven questions. Who has occasioned this drudgery, but the person who means to be so much more active, useful, and important, than all other Bishops, by proposing questions which nobody has thought to be necessary but himself? But to be intolerably strict and harsh to a poor curate, who is trying to earn a morsel of hard bread, and then to complain of the drudgery of reading his answers, is much like knocking a man down with a bludgeon, and then abusing him for splashing you with his blood, and pestering you with his groans. It is quite monstrous, that a man who inflicts eighty-seven new questions in Theology upon his fellow-creatures should talk of the drudgery of reading their answers.

A Curate – there is something which excites compassion in the very name of a Curate!!! How any man of Purple, Palaces, and Preferment, can let himself loose against this poor working man of God, we are of a loss to conceive – a learned man in a hovel, with sermons and saucepans, lexicons and bacon, Hebrew books and ragged children – good and patient – a comforter and a preacher – the first and purest pauper of the hamlet, and yet showing, that, in the midst of his worldly misery, he has the heart of a gentleman, and the spirit of a Christian, and the kindness of a pastor; and this man, though he has exercised the duties of a clergyman for twenty years – though he has most ample testimonies of conduct from clergymen as respectable as any Bishop – though an Archbishop add his name to the list of witnesses, is not good enough for Bishop Marsh, but is pushed out in the street, with his wife and children, and his little furniture, to surrender his honour, his faith, his conscience, and his learning – or to starve!

An obvious objection to these innovations is that there can be no end to them. If eighty-three questions are assumed to be necessary by one Bishop, eight hundred may be considered as the minimum of interrogation by another. When once the ancient faith marks of the Church are lost sight of and despised, any misled theologian may launch out on the boundless sea of polemical vexation.

Sydney quotes several Anglican divines on the comprehensiveness of the English Church, ending with a passage from Thomas Fuller's *Church History*.

Children's clothes ought to be made of the biggest, because afterwards their bodies will grow up to their garments. Thus the Articles of this English Protestant Church, in the infancy thereof, they thought good to draw up in general terms, foreseeing that posterity would grow up to fill the same: I mean these holy men did prudently prediscover that differences in judgments would unavoidably happen in the Church, *and were loath to unchurch any and drive them off from an ecclesiastical communion for such petty differences, which made them pen the Articles in comprehensive words to take in all who, differing in the branches, meet in the root of the same religion.*

'Indeed most of them had formerly been sufferers themselves, and cannot be said, in compiling these Articles (an acceptable service, no doubt) to offer to God what cost them nothing, some having paid imprisonment, others exile, all losses in their estates, for this their experimental knowledge in religion, *which made them the more merciful and tender in stating those points*, seeing such who themselves have been most patient in bearing will be most pitiful in burdening the consciences of others.' – See Fuller's *Church History*, book ix., p. 72, folio ed.

But this generous and specific spirit gives no room for the display of zeal and theological learning. The gate of admission has been left too widely open. I may as well be without power at all, if I cannot force my opinions upon other people. What was purposely left indefinite, I must make finite and exclusive. Questions of contention and difference must be laid before the servants of the Church, and nothing like neutrality in theological metaphysics allowed to the ministers of the Gospel. *I come not to bring peace*, &c.

The Bishop, however, seems to be quite satisfied with himself, when he states that he has a *right to do* what he has done – just as if a man's character with his fellow creatures depended upon legal rights alone, and not upon a discreet exercise of those rights. A man may persevere in doing what he has a right to do, till the Chancellor shuts him up in Bedlam, or till the mob pelt him as he passes. It must be presumed that all men whom the law has invested with rights, Nature has invested with common sense to use those rights. For these reasons, children have no rights till they have gained some common sense, and old men have no rights after they lose their common sense. All men are at all times accountable to their fellow creatures for the discreet exercise of every right they possess.

Prelates are fond of talking of *my* see, *my* clergy, *my* diocese, as if these things belonged to them as their pigs and dogs belong to them. They forget that the clergy, the diocese, and the Bishops themselves, all exist, only for the public good; that the public are a third and principal party in the whole concern. It is not simply the tormenting Bishop *versus* the tormented Curate, but the public against the system of tormenting; as tending to bring scandal upon religion and religious men. By the late alteration in the laws, the labourers in the vineyard are given up to the power of the inspectors of the vineyard. If he have the meanness and malice to do so, an inspector may worry and plague to death any labourer against whom he may have conceived an antipathy. As often as such cases are detected, we believe they will meet, in either House of Parliament, with the severest reprehension. The noblemen and gentlemen of England will never allow their parish clergy to be treated with cruelty, injustice, and caprice, by men who were parish clergymen themselves yesterday, and who were trusted with power for very different purposes.

The Bishop of Peterborough complains of the insolence of the answers made to him. This is certainly not true of Mr Grimshawe, Mr Neville, or of the author of the Appeal. They have answered his Lordship with great force, great manliness, but with perfect respect. Does the Bishop expect that humble men, as learned as himself, are to be driven from their houses and homes by his new theology, and then to send him letters of thanks for the kicks and cuffs he has bestowed upon them? Men of very small incomes, be it known to his Lordship, have very often very acute feelings; and a Curate trod on feels a pang as great as when a Bishop is refuted.

This pencil drawing, on a page at the beginning of the Book of Common Prayer, was presumably made by John Marshall during a service in St Paul's 28 April 1839. Marshall, at that time a young man of 21, was at University College studying anatomy and surgery, and later became a distinguished surgeon.

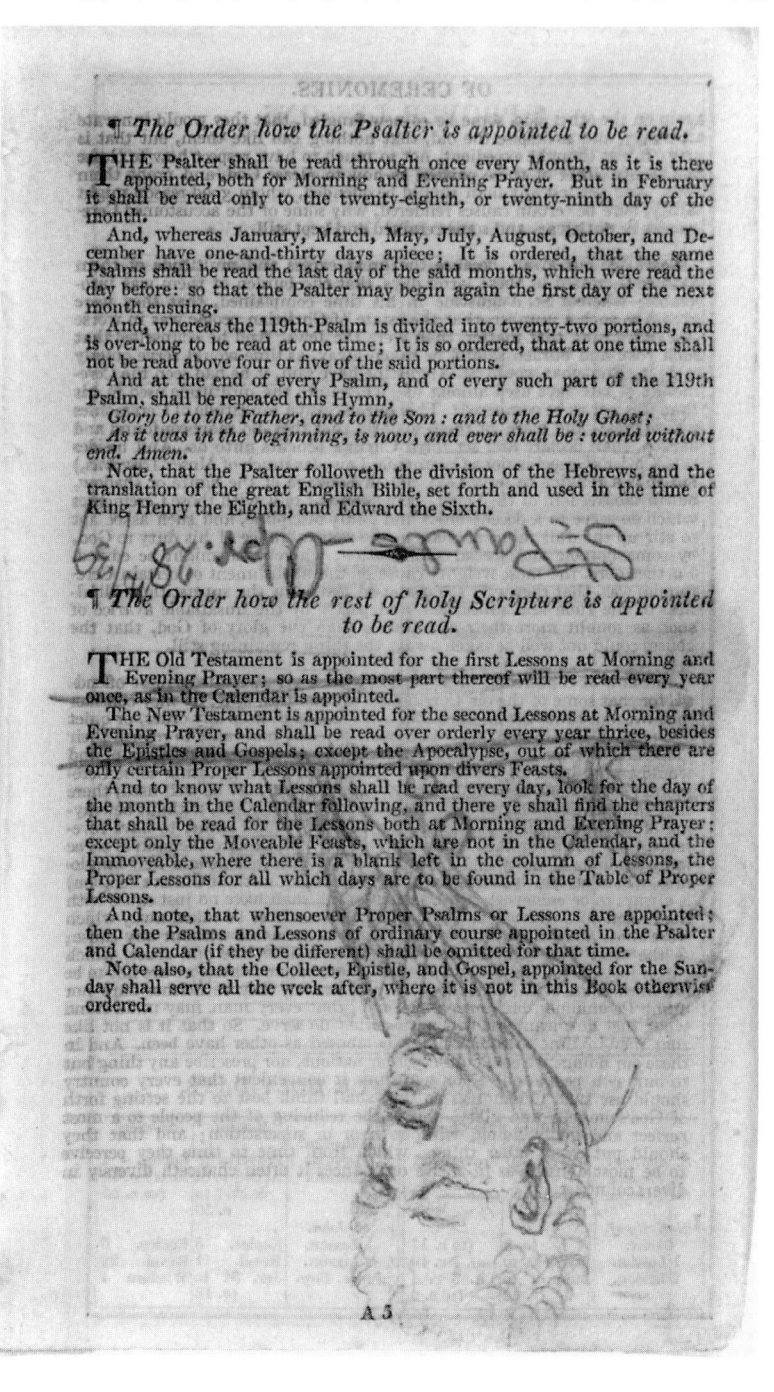

¶ The Order how the Psalter is appointed to be read.

THE Psalter shall be read through once every Month, as it is there appointed, both for Morning and Evening Prayer. But in February it shall be read only to the twenty-eighth, or twenty-ninth day of the month.

And, whereas January, March, May, July, August, October, and December have one-and-thirty days apiece; It is ordered, that the same Psalms shall be read the last day of the said months, which were read the day before: so that the Psalter may begin again the first day of the next month ensuing.

And, whereas the 119th Psalm is divided into twenty-two portions, and is over-long to be read at one time; It is so ordered, that at one time shall not be read above four or five of the said portions.

And at the end of every Psalm, and of every such part of the 119th Psalm, shall be repeated this Hymn,

Glory be to the Father, and to the Son : and to the Holy Ghost;
As it was in the beginning, is now, and ever shall be : world without end. Amen.

Note, that the Psalter followeth the division of the Hebrews, and the translation of the great English Bible, set forth and used in the time of King Henry the Eighth, and Edward the Sixth.

¶ The Order how the rest of holy Scripture is appointed to be read.

THE Old Testament is appointed for the first Lessons at Morning and Evening Prayer; so as the most part thereof will be read every year once, as in the Calendar is appointed.

The New Testament is appointed for the second Lessons at Morning and Evening Prayer, and shall be read over orderly every year thrice, besides the Epistles and Gospels; except the Apocalypse, out of which there are only certain Proper Lessons appointed upon divers Feasts.

And to know what Lessons shall be read every day, look for the day of the month in the Calendar following, and there ye shall find the chapters that shall be read for the Lessons both at Morning and Evening Prayer: except only the Moveable Feasts, which are not in the Calendar, and the Immoveable, where there is a blank left in the column of Lessons, the Proper Lessons for all which days are to be found in the Table of Proper Lessons.

And, note, that whensoever Proper Psalms or Lessons are appointed; then the Psalms and Lessons of ordinary course appointed in the Psalter and Calendar (if they be different) shall be omitted for that time.

Note also, that the Collect, Epistle, and Gospel, appointed for the Sunday shall serve all the week after, where it is not in this Book otherwise ordered.

A 5

X

Preachers and their Sermons

Sydney reviewed several published sermons in the *Edinburgh Review*. Of the Anniversary Sermon of the Royal Humane Society by W Langford D.D. in 1802 he writes:

An accident, which happened to the gentleman engaged in reviewing this sermon, proves, in the most striking manner, the importance of this charity for restoring to life persons in whom the vital power is suspended. He was discovered, with Dr Langford's discourse lying open before him, in a state of the most profound sleep; from which he could not, by any means, be awakened for a great length of time. By attending, however, to the rules prescribed by the Humane Society, flinging in the smoke of tobacco, applying hot flannels, and carefully removing the discourse itself to a great distance, the critic was restored to his disconsolate brothers.

The only account he could give of himself was, that he remembers reading on, regularly, till he came to the following pathetic description of a drowned tradesman; beyond which, he recollects nothing:-

'But to the individual himself, as a man, let us add the interruption to all the temporal business in which his interest was engaged. To him indeed, now apparently lost, the world is as nothing; but it seldom happens, that man can live for himself alone: society parcels out its concerns in various connections; and from one head issue waters which run down in many channels. – The spring being suddenly cut off, what confusion must follow in the streams which have flowed from its source? It may be, that all the expectations reasonably raised of approaching prosperity, to those who have embarked in the same occupation, may at once disappear; and the important interchange of commercial faith be broken off, before it could be brought to any advantageous conclusion.'

This extract will suffice for the style of the sermon. The charity itself is above all praise.

And of the Spital Sermon preached at Christ Church upon Easter Tuesday 1800 by Samuel Parr LL.D., to which are added notes:

Whoever has had the good fortune to see Dr Parr's wig, must have observed, that while it trespasses a little on the orthodox magnitude of perukes in the anterior parts, it scorns even Episcopal limits behind, and swells out into a boundless convexity of frizz, the μεγα θαυμα of barbers, and the terror of the literary world. After the manner of his wig, the Doctor has constructed his sermon, giving us a discourse of no common length, and subjoining an immeasurable mass of notes, which appear to concern every learned thing, every learned man, and almost every unlearned man since the beginning of the world.

With such comments one might wonder at the number of sermons which issued from the press. In his review of 'A Thanks giving for Plenty, and a Warning against Avarice', a sermon by the Revd Robert Nares published in 1802, Sydney begins with an explanation.

For the swarm of ephemeral sermons which issue from the press, we are principally indebted to the vanity of popular preachers, who are puffed up by female praises into a belief, that what may be delivered, with great propriety, in a chapel full of visitors and friends, is fit for the deliberate attention of the public, who cannot be influenced by the decency of a clergyman's private life, flattered by the sedulous politeness of his manners, or misled by the fallacious circumstances of voice and action. A clergyman cannot be always considered as reprehensible for preaching an indifferent sermon; because, to the active piety, and correct life, which the profession requires, many an excellent man may not unite talents of that species of composition: but every man who prints, imagines he gives to the world something which they had not before, either in matter or style; that he has brought forth new truths, or adorned old ones; and when, in lieu of novelty and ornament, we can discover nothing but trite imbecility, the law must take its course, and the delinquent suffer that mortification from which vanity can rarely be expected to escape, when it chooses dulness for the minister of its gratifications.

The learned author, after observing that a large army praying would be a much finer spectacle than a large army fighting, and after entertaining us with the old anecdote of Xerxes, and the flood of tears, proceeds to express his sentiments on the late scarcity, and the present abundance: then, stating the manner in which the Jews were governed by the immediate interference of God, and informing us, that other people expect not, nor are taught to look for, miraculous interference, to punish or reward them, he proceeds to talk of the visitation of Providence, for the purposes of trial, warning, and correction, as if it were a truth of which he had never doubted.

Still, however, he contends, though the Deity does interfere, it would be presumptuous and impious to pronounce
the purposes for which he interferes; and then adds, that it
has pleased God, within these few years, to give us a most
awful lesson of the vanity of agriculture and importation
without piety, and that he has proved this to the conviction
of every thinking mind.

'Though he interpose not (says Mr Nares) by positive
miracle, he influences by means unknown to all but himself,
and directs the winds, the rain, and glorious beams of heaven
to execute his judgment, or fulfil his merciful designs.' –
Now, either the wind, the rain, and the beams, are here represented to act, as they do in the ordinary course of nature,
or they are not. If they are, how can their operations be considered as a judgment on sins: and if they are not, what are
their extraordinary operations, but positive miracles? So that
the Archdeacon, after denying that anybody knows *when,
how,* and *why* the Creator works a miracle, proceeds to
specify the *time, instrument,* and *object* of a miraculous
scarcity; and then, assuring us that the elements were
employed to execute the judgments of Providence, denies
that this is any proof of a positive miracle.

Having given us this specimen of his talents for theological metaphysics, Mr Nares commences his attack upon
the farmers.

In his review of *Discourses on Various Subjects* by Thomas Rennel, D.D.,
Master of the Temple in the same year, Sydney begins by writing of sermons
in general, before commenting on the fourteen that comprised the *Discourses.*

The great object of modern sermons is to hazard nothing;
their characteristic is, decent debility; which alike guards
their authors from ludicrous errors, and precludes them from
striking beauties. Every man of sense, in taking up an English
sermon, expects to find it a tedious essay, full of commonplace morality: and if the fulfilment of such expectations
be meritorious, the clergy have certainly the merit of not
disappointing their readers. Yet it is curious to consider,
how a body of men so well educated, and so magnificently
endowed as the English clergy, should distinguish themselves so little in a species of composition to which it is
their peculiar duty, as well as their ordinary habit, to attend.
To solve this difficulty, it should be remembered, that the
eloquence of the Bar and of the Senate force themselves into
notice, power, and wealth – that the penalty which an individual client pays for choosing a bad advocate, is the loss of
his cause – that a prime minister must infallibly suffer in

the estimation of the public, who neglects to conciliate eloquent men, and trusts the defence of his measures to those
who have not adequate talents for that purpose, whereas,
the only evil which accrues from the promotion of a clergyman to the pulpit, which he has no ability to fill as he ought,
is the fatigue of the audience, and the discredit of that species of public instruction; an evil so general, that no individual patron would dream of sacrificing to it his particular
interest. The clergy are generally appointed to their situations by those who have no interest that they should please
the audience before whom they speak; while the very reverse
is the case in the eloquence of the Bar, and of Parliament.
We by no means would be understood to say, that the clergy
should owe their promotion principally to their eloquence,
or that eloquence ever could, consistently with the constitution of the English Church, be made a common cause of
preferment. In pointing out the total want of connection
between the privilege of preaching, and the power of preaching well, we are giving no opinion as to whether it might, or
might not, be remedied; but merely stating a fact. . . .

Dr Rennel is apt to put on the appearance of a holy bully,
an evangelical swaggerer, as if he could carry his point
against infidelity by big words and strong abuse, and kick
and cuff men into Christians. It is a very easy thing to talk
about the shallow impostures, and the silly ignorant soph-
isms of Voltaire, Rousseau, Condorcet, D'Alembert, and
Volney, and to say that Hume is not worth answering. This
affectation of contempt will not do. While these pernicious
writers have power to allure from the Church great numbers
of proselytes, it is better to study them diligently, and to
reply to them satisfactorily, than to veil insolence, want of
power, or want of industry, by a pretended contempt; which
may leave infidels and wavering Christians to suppose such
writers are abused, because they are feared; and not answered, because they are unanswerable. While every body
was abusing and despising Mr Godwin, and while Mr
Godwin was, among a certain description of understandings,
increasing every day in popularity, Mr Malthus took the
trouble of refuting him: and we hear no more of Mr Godwin.
We recommend this example to the consideration of Dr
Rennel, who seems to think it more useful, and more pleasant, to rail than to fight.

After the world had returned to its sober senses upon
the merits of the ancient philosophy, it is amusing enough
to see a few *bad heads* bawling for the restoration of ex-

ploded errors and past infatuation. We have some dozen of plethoric phrases about Aristotle, who is, in the estimation of the Doctor, *et rex et sutor bonus*, and every thing else; and to the neglect of whose works he seems to attribute every moral and physical evil under which the world has groaned for the last century. Dr Rennel's admiration of the ancients is so great, that he considers the works of Homer to be the region and depository of natural law, and natural religion. Now, if, by natural religion, is meant the will of God collected from his works, and the necessity man is under of obeying it; it is rather extraordinary that Homer should be so good a natural theologian, when the divinities he has painted are certainly a more drunken, quarrelsome, adulterous, intriguing, lascivious set of beings, than are to be met with in the most profligate court in Europe. There is, every now and then, some plain coarse morality in Homer; but the most bloody revenge, and the most savage cruelty in warfare, the ravishing of women, and the sale of men, &c., &c., &c., are circumstances which the old bard seems to relate as the ordinary events of his times, without ever dreaming that there could be much harm in them; and if it be urged that Homer took his ideas of right and wrong from a barbarous age, that is just saying, in other words, that Homer had very imperfect ideas of natural law.

Having exhausted all his powers of eulogium upon the times that are gone, Dr Rennel indemnifies himself by the very novel practice of declaiming against the present age. It is an *evil age* – an *adulterous age* – an *ignorant age* – an *apostate age* – and a *foppish age*. Of the propriety of the last epithet, our readers may perhaps be more convinced, by calling to mind a class of fops not usually designated by that epithet – men clothed in profound black, with large canes, and strange amorphous hats – of big speech, and imperative presence – talkers about Plato – great affecters of senility – despisers of women and all the graces of life – fierce foes to common sense – abusive of the living, and approving no one who has not been dead for at least a century. Such fops, as vain, and as shallow as their fraternity in Bond Street, differ from these only as Gorgonius differed from Rufillus.

In the ninth Discourse (p.226), we read of St Paul, that he had 'an heroic zeal, directed, rather than bounded, by the nicest discretion – a conscious and commanding dignity, softened by the meekest and most profound humility.' This is intended for a fine piece of writing; but it is without meaning: for, if words have any limits, it is a *contradiction in terms* to say of the *same* person, at the *same* time, that he is nicely discreet, and heroically zealous; or that he is profoundly humble, and imperatively dignified: and if Dr Rennel means that St Paul displayed these qualities at different times, then could not any one of them direct or soften the other. . . .

Of Dr Rennel's talents as a reasoner, we certainly have formed no very high opinion. Unless dogmatical assertion, and the practice (but too common among theological writers) of taking the thing to be proved, for part of the proof, can be considered as evidence of a logical understanding, the specimens of argument Dr Rennel has afforded us are very insignificant.

After reading these reviews, we can understand Sydney writing 'Preaching has become a bye-word for long and dull conversation of any kind; and whoever wishes to imply, in any piece of writing, the absence of everything agreable and inviting, calls it a sermon.' The chief reason for this, he says, is the bad choice of subjects for the pulpit. In 1824 Sydney acted as Chaplain to the High Sheriff at the York Assizes and preached two Assize Sermons. For the first he chose as his text Acts chapter 23 verse 3: 'Sittest thou here to judge me after the Law, and commandest thou me to be smitten, contrary to the Law,' and before the two presiding judges pleaded powerfully for the proper administration of justice by disinterested men, who temper justice with mercy and acknowledge their accountability to God. He reveals en passant what he thinks preaching should be about:

And let no man say, 'Why teach such things? Do you think they must not have occurred to those to whom they are a concern? I answer to this, that no man preaches novelties and discoveries; the object of preaching is, constantly to remind mankind of what mankind are constantly forgetting; not to supply the defects of human intelligence, but to fortify the feebleness of human resolutions, to recall mankind from the by-paths where they turn, into that broad path of salvation which all know, but few tread. These plain lessons the humblest ministers of the gospel may teach, if they are honest, and the most powerful Christians will ponder, if they are wise.

In a letter to his friend Archdeacon Wrangham, he writes,

My dear Sr. -
Don't use hard Words – and say odd things in the pulpit – as you ask me for my Critique it is this – and I say it because no man respects more your attainments, and liberal Sentiments than I do – but in Words – you have peregrinity and Sesquipediality and it is very odd to say that Cain and Abel

sold things to each other and to talk about *Ardent Spirits*. –
I give you great credit for honesty. and preservation of your
principles – which I believe you will maintain to the last –
and this in men who are *marketable* is a great merit – I have
been in Town these 3 Weeks – and remain some time -

sincerely Yrs
Sydney Smith

However, as well as the matter of sermons there is also the way they are
preached:

> To this cause of the unpopularity of sermons may be added
> the extremely ungraceful manner in which they are deliver-
> ed. The English, generally remarkable for doing very good
> things in a very bad manner, seem to have reserved the mat-
> urity and plenitude of their awkwardness for the pulpit. A
> clergyman clings to his velvet cushion with either hand,
> keeps his eye riveted upon his book, speaks of the ecstasies
> of joy and fear with a voice and a face which indicate neither,
> and pinions his body and soul into the same attitude of limb
> and thought, for fear of being called theatrical and affected.
> The most intrepid veteran of us all dares no more than wipe
> his face with his cambric sudarium; if, by mischance, his
> hand slip from its orthodox grip of the velvet, he draws it
> back as from liquid brimstone, or the caustic iron of the
> law, and atones for this indecorum by fresh inflexibility and
> more rigorous sameness. Is it wonder, then, that every semi-
> delirious sectary who pours forth his animated nonsense
> with the genuine look and voice of passion should gesticul-
> ate away the congregation of the most profound and learned
> divine of the Established Church, and in two Sundays preach
> him bare to the very sexton? Why are we natural everywhere
> but in the pulpit? No man expresses warm and animated
> feelings anywhere else, with his mouth alone, but with his
> whole body; he articulates with every limb, and talks from
> head to foot with a thousand voices. Why this holoplexia
> on sacred occasions alone? Why call in the aid of paralysis
> to piety? Is it a rule of oratory to balance the style against
> the subject, and to handle the most sublime truths in the
> dullest language and the driest manner? Is sin to be taken
> from men, as Eve was from Adam, by casting them into a
> deep slumber? Or from what possible perversion of common
> sense are we all to look like field-preachers in Zembla, holy
> lumps of ice, numbed in quiescence, and stagnation, and
> mumbling?

It is theatrical to use action, and it is Methodistical to
use action.

> But we have cherished contempt for sectaries, and per-
> severed in dignified tameness so long, that while we are
> freezing common sense for large salaries in stately churches,
> amidst whole acres and furlongs of empty pews, the crowd
> are feasting on ungrammatical fervour and illiterate anim-
> ation in the crumbling hovels of Methodists. If influence
> over the imagination can produce these powerful effects; if
> this be the chain by which the people are dragged captive at
> the wheel of enthusiasm, why are we, who are rocked in
> the cradle of ancient genius, who hold in one hand the book
> of the wisdom of God, and in the other grasp that eloquence
> which ruled the Pagan world, why are we never to rouse, to
> appeal, to inflame, to break through every barrier, up to the
> very haunts and chambers of the soul. . . . There is, I grant,
> something discouraging at present to a man of sense in the
> sarcastical phrase of popular preacher; but I am not entirely
> without hope that the time may come when energy in the
> pulpit will be no longer considered as a mark of superficial
> understanding; when animation and affectation will be
> separated; when churches will cease (as Swift says) to be
> public dormitories; and sleep be no longer looked upon as
> the most convenient vehicle of good sense.

Sydney's own preaching was the very opposite of 'clinging to his velvet
cushion'.

> When I began to thump the cushion of my pulpit, on first
> coming to Foston, as is my wont when I preach, the accum-
> ulated dust of a hundred and fifty years made such a cloud,
> that for some minutes I lost sight of my congregation.

or, as he put it in rhyme to Lady Woodhouselee:

> Tis mine, with all my consecrated dress on
> To read the evening and the morning lesson;
> With band bi-forkèd, and with visage calm
> To join the bawling, quav'ring Clerk in Psalm.
> With brawny fist the velvet lump to beat,
> And rouse the faithful, snoring at my feet!

Little did the lady wearing a crimson velvet gown know the danger she was
in!

> Conversing in the evening, with a small circle, round Miss
> Berry's tea-table (who, though far advanced towards the four-
> score years and ten which she afterwards attained, was still
> remarkable for her vigour of mind and beauty of person),
> my father observed the entrance of a no less remarkable
> person, both for talents and years, dressed in a beautiful
> crimson velvet gown. He started up to meet his fine old
> friend, exclaiming, 'Exactly the colour of my preaching cush-

ion!' and leading her forward to the light, he pretended to
be lost in admiration, saying, 'I really can hardly keep my
hands off you; I shall be preaching on you, I fear,' etc., and
played with the subject to the infinite amusement of his old
friend and the little circle assembled round her.

He was a 'bould' preacher, as Saba, his daughter, tells in her *Memoir*.

'You must preach, Mr Smith,' said Mrs W. (it was Saturday). 'We must go and try the pulpit, then,' said he, 'to see if
it suits me.' So to the church we walked; and how he amused
us by his droll way of trying the pulpit, as he called it; – his
criticisms on the little old-fashioned sounding-board, which
seemed ready to fall on his head, and which, he said, would
infallibly extinguish him! 'I can't bear,' said he, 'to be im-
prisoned in the true orthodox way in my pulpit, with my
head just peeping above the desk. I like to look down upon
my congregation, – to fire into them. The common people
say I am a *bould preacher*, for I like to have my arms free,
and to thump the pulpit. A singular *contretemps* happened
to me once, when, to effect this, I had ordered the clerk to
pile up some hassocks for me to stand on. My text was, 'We
are perplexed, but not in despair; persecuted, but not forsaken; cast down, but not destroyed.' I had scarcely uttered
these words, and was preparing to illustrate them, when I
did so practically, and in a way I had not all all anticipated.
My fabric of hassocks suddenly gave way: down I fell, and
with difficulty prevented myself from being precipitated
into the arms of my congregation; who, I must say, behaved
very well, and recovered their gravity sooner than I could
have expected.

Even in his early days in the sacred ministry, when he sought pulpits in London,
the same metaphor was there of 'firing', 'discharging':

Two or three random sermons I have discharged, and though
I perceived that the greater part of the congregation thought
me mad. The clerk was as pale as death in helping me off
with my gown, for fear I should bite him.

Few of Sydney's sermons were published: one or two from special
occasions, a slender volume from his Edinburgh days, and a slightly larger
one from his years at St Paul's and Combe Florey. They are eloquently expressed, moving in their sincerity, and wise in their counsels. Two short
samples from a sermon at St Paul's must suffice.

LUKE, XVIII. 10.

'I thank thee, Lord, that I am not as other men are, and even
as this publican!' Upon this I ground my first rule. Avoid
comparisons, which are such a fertile source of spiritual
pride. If you live a Christian life, and others do not, it is

impossible you should not notice the difference, but beware that you do not make the perception of that difference a source of inward pride. The evil of such a conduct, and the folly of such a conduct, is, that you perform Christian actions from motives which are not Christian. You are charitable, why? and you are devout, why? Not because God has ordained it, not because it conforms with the mandate of our blessed Saviour; but because you wish to be better than that publican! You are, in reality, though unconsciously, substituting for the true principles of religion mere worldly vanity; and losing Christian rewards, though you perform Christian actions: act as you are acting; it is not the action wants changing, but the mind. Purify your motives, elevate your views, forget the publican; do what Christ bids you, because Christ *has* bidden you; think of your own soul, do not pollute yourself with wretched worldly vanities, and degrading considerations whether you have passed this man, or that man, in the path of righteousness; look not to the small distance between you and actual sin, but to the immeasurable distance between you and infinite purity.

And then open the Gospel, read a page of it, and see what little you have done. You have given a little, you have resisted temptation a little; is this enough? Is that a foundation for spiritual pride? Are you pure in heart? Are you fit to see God? Are you yet of that number whose souls no torment shall touch? Come rather with a deep blush of holiness at the smallness of the offering you have placed upon the altar; do not look upon that altar and say I have brought more than my brother! Let your life be what it may, – if you come to boast to God and not to pray to God, – if you come to despise your fellow suppliant, and not to humble yourself, – you know the words of the text, 'The wretched publican goes down to his house justified rather than you.'

Avoid not only to make comparisons in your own favour, but, if you are good and religious, do not judge other men too severely, nor watch them too scrupulously. It is not suitable that religion should wear a rigid aspect, that men less perfect than yourself, should suspect that you are looking out for their imperfections, that what is bad in them will be accurately noticed, and what is innocent possibly be mistaken. Connect rather your own exemption from faults, with habitual indulgence to, the faults of others: your own character is fixed. You are known to be serious and attentive to your Christian duties; you can afford to be indulgent to others, you do not want the assistance of comparison. . . .

Who can help being struck with a real Christian coming out to show himself in the haunts of the world? Humble, of tried sanctity, arrogating nothing, not affecting humility, but really wishing to place you in general estimation above himself, – interpreting all you say kindly, not watching for the evil of your nature, but delighted by the good, – indulgent to all other infirmities than his own, radiating with kindness, seeking by every word to promote general satisfaction, and to communicate innocent pleasure, throwing the mantle of the world over a pure heart, and walking gaily among men the secret servant of God. These are the effects which I have seen, and which you have seen, when truly religious men will condescend to add a little worldly wisdom to their high principles, and to be as wise as the serpent, as well as innocent as the dove. The effect which is produced by such a wise and amiable Christian, avoiding all spirit of party, all moroseness, singularity of manner, and living graciously among the promiscuous characters which the world produces, is of the greatest possible importance to religion. Why is that man always so cheerful and contented? why is he received with such real pleasure by his fellow-creatures? why is he always so kind and indulgent? why is he so much respected? How is it possible that young persons, that bad persons, that unhappy persons, should not ask these questions, and asking the question, how long will it be before the solution is gained? – that he is a religious man, not a Pharisee,. not one who thanks God that he is not as other men are, but an humble, unassuming, zealous Christian, who knows that it is his duty to make the ways of religion as lovely in the eyes of his fellow-creatures as they are grateful to his Redeemer and his Judge.

Of his preaching in St Paul's in November he writes, 'My sentences are frozen as they come out of my mouth and are thawed in the course of the sermon, making strange and unexpected assertions in various parts of the church.'

IN PRISON AND YE CAME UNTO ME

Elizabeth Fry in Newgate Prison, which Sydney visited with her. 'She is
very unpopular with the clergy. . . . We long to burn her alive.'

XI

Dissenters and Missionaries

The Church must be distinguished from religion itself; we might be Christians without any Established Church at all, as some countries of the world are at this day. A church establishment is only an instrument for teaching religion, but an instrument of admirable contrivance and of vast utility. The Church of England is the wisest and most enlightened sect of Christians; I think so, or I would not belong to it another hour. But is it possible for me to believe that every Christian out of the pale of that Church will be consigned after this life to the never-ending wrath of God? If I were to preach such doctrines, who would hear me? Can I paint God as the protector of one Christian creed, dead to all prayers, blind to all woes but ours? – God, whom the Indian Christian, whom the Armenian Christian, whom the Greek Christian, whom the Catholic, whom the Protestant, adore in a varied manner, in another climate, with a fresh priest and a changed creed. Are you and I to live again, and are these Christians as well as us not to live again? Foolish, arrogant man has said this, but God has never said this. He calls for the just in Christ. He tells us that through that name He will reward every good man, and accept every just action; that if you take up the cross of Christ he will reward you for every kind deed, repay you sevenfold for every example of charity, carefully note and everlastingly recompense the justice, the honour, the integrity, the benevolence of your present life. And yet, though God is the God of all Christians, each says to the other, He is not your God, but my God; not the God of the just in Christ, but the God of Calvin, the God of Luther, or the God of the Papal Crown.

The true Christian, amid all the diversities of opinion, searches for the holy in desire, for the good in council, for the just in works; and he loves the good, under whatever temple, at whatever altar he may find them.

If I have *read well my Gospel*, it is in such wise we should imitate the patient forbearance of our common Father, who pities the frailties we do not pity, who forgives the error we do not forgive, who maketh His sun to rise on the evil and on the good, and sendeth rain on the just and the unjust.

Lady Holland, *Memoir*

In 1828 Sydney, by then a Canon of Bristol Cathedral, preached before the Mayor and Corporation in the Cathedral on 5 November, when the Church of England used 'A Form of Prayer with Thanksgiving for the happy Deliverance of the King and the Three Estates of the Realm from the traitorous and bloody intended Massacre by Gunpowder'. It was an annual occasion for anti-Roman Catholic sentiment to have its fling, but Sydney chose for his text two verses from St Paul's Epistle to the Colossians:

'Put on, as the elect of God, kindness, humbleness of mind, meekness, long-suffering; forbearing one another and forgiving one another.'

A great deal of mischief is done by not attending to the limits of interference with each other's religious opinions, – by not leaving to the power and wisdom of God, that which belongs to God alone. Our holy religion consists of some doctrines which influence practice, and of others which are purely speculative. If religious errors be of the former description, they may, perhaps, be fair objects of human interference; but if the opinion be merely theological and speculative, there the right of human interference seems to end, because the necessity for such interference does not exist. Any error of this nature is between the Creator and the creature, – between the Redeemer and the redeemed. If such opinions are not the best opinions which can be found, God Almighty will punish the error, if mere error seemeth to the Almighty a fit object of punishment. Why may not a man wait if God waits?

He concluded:

The arguments, then, which I have adduced in support of the great principles of religious charity are, that violence upon such subjects is rarely or ever found to be useful; but generally to produce effects opposite to those which are intended. I have observed that religious sects are not to be judged from the representations of their enemies; but that they are to be heard for themselves, in the pleadings of their best writers, not in the representations of those whose intemperate zeal is a misfortune to the sect to which they belong. If you will study the principles of your religious opponents, you will often find your contempt and hatred lessened in proportion as you are better acquainted with what you despise. Many religious opinions, which are purely speculative, are without the limits of human interference. In the numerous sects of Christianity, interpreting our religion in very opposite manners, all cannot be right. Imitate the forbearance and long-suffering of God, who throws the mantle of his mercy over all, and who will probably save, on the

last day, the piously right, and the piously wrong, seeking
Jesus in humbleness of mind. Do not drive religious sects to
the disgrace (or to what they foolishly think the disgrace) of
formally disavowing tenets they once professed, but concede something to human weakness; and, when the tenet is
virtually given up, treat it as if it were actually given up;
and always consider it to be very possible that you yourself
may have made mistakes, and fallen into erroneous opinions,
as well as any other sect to which you are opposed. If you
put on these dispositions, and this tenor of mind, you cannot
be guilty of any religious fault, take what part you will in
the religious disputes which appear to be coming on in the
world. If you choose to perpetuate the restrictions upon your
fellow-creatures, no one has a right to call you bigoted; if
you choose to do them away, no one has any right to call
you lax and indifferent; you have done your utmost to do
right, and whether you err, or do not err, in your mode of
interpreting the Christian religion, you show at least that
you have caught its heavenly spirit, – that you have put on,
as the elect of God, kindness, humbleness of mind, meekness, long-suffering, forbearing one another, and forgiving
one another.

I have thus endeavoured to lay before you the uses and
abuses of this day; and, having stated the great mercy of
God's interference, and the blessings this Country has
secured to itself in resisting the errors, and follies, and superstitions of the Catholic church, I have endeavoured that this
just sense of our own superiority should not militate against
the sacred principles of Christian charity. That charity,
which I ask for others, I ask for also for myself. I am sure I
am preaching before those who will think (whether they
agree with me or not) that I have spoken conscientiously,
and from good motives, and from honest feelings, on a very
difficult subject, – not sought for by me, but devolving upon
me in the course of duty; – in which I should have been
heartily ashamed of myself, (as you would have been
ashamed of me,) if I had thought only how to flatter and
please, or thought of any thing but what I hope I always do
think of in the pulpit, – that I am placed here by God to tell
truth, and to do good.

I shall conclude my sermon, (pushed I am afraid already
to an unreasonable length,) by reciting to you a very short
and beautiful Apologue, taken from the Rabbinical writers.
It is, I believe, quoted by Bishop Taylor in his 'Holy Living
and Dying.' I have not now access to that book, but I quote it

to you from memory; and should be made truly happy if you would quote it to others from memory also.

'As Abraham was sitting in the door of his tent, there came unto him a wayfaring man; and Abraham gave him water for his feet, and set bread before him. And Abraham said unto him, 'let us now worship the Lord our God, before we eat of this bread.' And the wayfaring man said unto Abraham, 'I will not worship the Lord thy God, for thy God is not my God; but I will worship my God, even the God of my fathers.' But Abraham was exceeding wroth; and he rose up to put the wayfaring man forth from the door of his tent. And the Voice of the Lord was heard in the tent, – 'Abraham, Abraham, have I borne with this man for three score and ten years, and canst not thou bear with him for one hour?' '

Lady Holland writes:

I have heard that this sermon occasioned an immense sensation at the time, 'and the cathedral, from that period, whenever he was to preach (though previously almost deserted), was filled to suffocation. A crowd collected round the doors long before they were opened, and the heads of the standers in the aisle were so thick-set you could not have thrust in another; and I saw the men holding up their hats above their heads, that they might not be crushed by the pressure.'

The only Dissenters Sydney really admired were the Quakers. When an infectious disease spread rapidly in Thornton village (neighbouring Foston and part of his cure), he was much struck by the heroic conduct of the Quakers, who, amid general panic, constantly attended the sick, as he did. 'Are you aware of the danger?' he asked. 'Oh, we have no fears; we are in the hands of God, thou knowest,' came the reply.

He once visited Newgate Prison with the Quaker, Elizabeth Fry, and wrote afterwards

There is a spectacle which this town now exhibits, that I will venture to call the most solemn, the most Christian, the most affecting which any human being ever witnessed. To see that holy woman in the midst of the wretched prisoners; to see them all calling earnestly upon God, soothed by her voice, animated by her look, clinging to the hem of her garment; and worshiping her as the only being who has ever loved them, or taught them, or noticed them, or spoken to them of God! This is the sight which breaks down the pageant of the world; which tells us that the short hour of life is passing away, and that we must prepare by some good deeds to meet God; that it is time to give, to pray, to comfort; to go, like this blessed woman, and do the work of our heavenly Saviour, Jesus, among the guilty, among the broken-hearted and the sick, and to labour in the deepest and darkest wretchedness of life.

He added, 'She is very unpopular with the clergy; examples of living, active virtue disturb our repose, and give birth to distressing comparisons: we long to burn her alive.' Sydney also much admired their treatment of the insane (see chapter 6).

But he also teased them for their solemnity.

'A Quaker baby?'

'A Quaker baby?' he said. 'Impossible. There is no such thing; there never was; they are always born broad-brimmed and in full quake.'

He wrote in their style to Martha Davis, who kept a cheese shop in Taunton, near his parish of Combe Florey:

Dear Martha, -

Strange times! but what is life, but the valley of the shadow of death? Lord Melbourne's speech at Melbourne is excellent, & I recommend it to thee & the Friends. Oh Martha! what are talents without prudence & discretion? Look at friend Brougham; – Nature has taken more pains with him than the best Dairyman with the best cheese in the shop; & what is he now? Martha, I hope the fall of Brougham will be a warning to Peter (her shop boy), & that he will not wax proud as he becomes wiser in cheese and butter but keep his heart down as he rises before men. Martha – I am better in health, as I hope thou art: thy health is ruined by going from shop to cheese loft without a bonnet; & in this I see no signs of worldly wisdom.

Martha, mind & save me three beautiful cheeses. – I depend on thee & will write when & where they are to be sent; but they must be of the first quality. Martha, Sir Robert Peel is not arrived, but nevertheless put by the cheeses, & so farewell.

SYDNEY SMITH.

29th Novr, 1834.

Sydney's fight for Roman Catholics deserves a chapter to itself, but one other Church, at the opposite extreme, whose cause he supported was the Unitarian. Their name implies their inability to accept the doctrine of the Trinity, and yet, to marry, they had to make promises and receive blessings in the name of the Father, Son and Holy Ghost. Sydney writes to Francis Jeffrey, editor of the *Edinburgh Review*:

April, 1820

My dear Jeffrey,

For the number next but one, I have engaged to write an article on Ireland, which shall contain all the information I can collect, detailed as well as I know how to detail it.

The Unitarians think the doctrine of the Trinity to be a profanation of the Scriptures; you compel them to marry in your churches, or rather, I should say, we compel them to marry in our churches; and when the male and female Dissenter are kneeling before the altar, much is said to them by the priest, of this, to them, abhorred doctrine. They are about to petition Parliament that their marriages may be put upon the same footing as those of Catholics and Quakers. The principles of religious liberty which I have learnt (perhaps under you) make me their friend in this question; and if you approve, I will write an article upon it. Upon the receipt of your letter in the affirmative, I will write to the dissenting king, William Smith, for information. Pray have the goodness to answer by return of post, or as soon after as you can, if it is but a word; as despatch in these matters, and in my inaccessible situation, is important.

Sydney Smith

Unitarians, too, he teased. Dr Blake, a staunch Unitarian at Taunton, complained to him,

'O, Mr Smith, I am far from well. I have got a cold aguish feeling all over me, and though I sit by a good fire, I cannot keep myself warm.'

'I can cure you, Doctor. Cover yourself with the Thirty Nine Articles and you will soon have a delicious glow all over you.'

But he let the last laugh be against himself. As he lay ill during August 1844 he lamented, 'I feel so weak both in body and mind that I verily believe, if the knife were put into my hands, I should not have strength or energy enough to slide it into a Dissenter.'

Methodism

Sydney's most vitriolic language was deployed against Methodists. In reviewing *Causes of the Increase of Methodism and Dissension* by Robert Acklem Ingram in 1808, he provides many extracts from Evangelical and Methodistical magazines of the previous year,

Works which are said to be circulated to the amount of 18,000 or 20,000 each, every month; and which contain the sentiments of Arminian and Calvinistic methodists, and of the *evangelical* clergymen of the Church of England. We shall use the general term of Methodism, to designate these three classes of fanatics, not troubling ourselves to point out the finer shades and nicer discriminations of lunacy, but treating them all as in one general conspiracy against common sense, and rational orthodox Christianity.

It is not wantonly, or with the most distant intention of

trifling upon serious subjects, that we call the attention of the public to these sorts of publications. Their circulation is so enormous, and so increasing, – they contain the opinions, and display the habits of so many human beings, – that they cannot but be objects of curiosity and importance. The common and the middling classes of people are the purchasers; and the subject is religion, – though not that religion certainly which is established by law, and encouraged by national provision. This may lead to unpleasant consequences, or it may not; but it carries with it a sort of aspect, which ought to insure to it serious attention and reflection.

It is impossible to arrive at any knowledge of a religious sect, by merely detailing the settled articles of their belief: it may be the fashion of such a sect to insist upon some articles very slightly; to bring forward others prominently; and to consider some portion of their formal creed as obsolete. As the knowledge of the jurisprudence of any country can never be obtained by the perusal of volumes which contain some statues that are daily enforced, and others that have been silently antiquated: in the same manner, the practice, the preaching, and the writing of sects, are comments absolutely necessary to render the perusal of their creed of any degree of utility.

It is the practice, we believe, with the orthodox, both in the Scotch and the English Churches, to insist very rarely, and very discreetly, upon the particular instances of the interference of Divine Providence. They do not contend that the world is governed only by general laws, – that a Superintending Mind never interferes for particular purposes; but such purposes are represented to be of a nature very awful and sublime, – when a guilty people are to be destroyed, – when an oppressed nation is to be lifted up, and some remarkable change introduced into the order and arrangement of the world. With this kind of theology we can have no quarrel; we bow to its truth; we are satisfied with the moderation which it exhibits; and we have no doubt of the salutary effect which it produces upon the human heart. Let us now come to those special cases of the interference of Providence, as they are exhibited in the publications before us. One extract must suffice:

> 'A clergyman, not far distant from the spot on which these lines were written, was spending an evening –
> not in his closet, wrestling with his Divine Master for the communication of that grace which is so peculiarly

necessary for the faithful discharge of the ministerial function, – not in his study, searching the sacred oracles of divine truth for materials wherewith to prepare for his public exercises and feed the flock under his care, – not in pastoral visits to that flock, to inquire into the state of their souls, and endeavour, by his pious and affectionate conversation, to conciliate their esteem, and promote their edification, – but at the *card table.*' – After stating that, when it was his turn to deal, he dropt down dead, 'It is worthy of remark (says the writer) that within a very few years this was the third character in the neighbourhood which had been summoned from the card table to the bar of God.'

Evangelical Magazine p.262.

Upon the spirit evinced by these extracts, we shall make a few comments.

1. It is obvious, that this description of Christians entertain very erroneous and dangerous notions of the present judgments of God. A belief, that Providence interferes in all the little actions of our lives, refers all merit and demerit to bad and good fortune; and causes the successful man to be always considered as a good man, and the unhappy man as the object of divine vengeance. It furnishes ignorant and designing men with a power which is sure to be abused: – the cry of, a *judgment*, a *judgment*, it is always easy to make, but not easy to resist. It encourages the grossest superstitions; for if the Deity rewards and punishes on every slight occasion, it is quite impossible, but that such a helpless being as man will set himself and work to discover the will of Heaven in the appearances of outward nature, and to apply all the phenomena of thunder, lightning, wind, and every striking appearance to the regulation of his conduct; as the poor Methodist, when he rode into Piccadilly in a thunder storm, and imagined that all the uproar of the elements was a mere hint to him not to preach at Mr Romaine's chapel. Hence a great deal of error, and a great deal of secret misery. This doctrine of a theocracy must necessarily place an excessive power in the hands of the clergy; it applies so instantly and so tremendously to men's hopes and fears, that it must make the priest omnipotent over the people, as it always has done where it has been established. It has a great tendency to check human exertions, and to prevent the employment of those secondary means of effecting an object which Providence has placed in our power. The doctrine of the immediate and perpetual interference of Divine Prov-

idence, is not true. If two men travel the same road, the one to rob, the other to relieve a fellow-creature who is starving; will any but the most fanatic contend, that they do not both run the same chance of falling over a stone, and breaking their legs? and is it not matter of fact, that the robber often returns, safe, and the just man sustains the injury? Have not the soundest divines of both Churches always urged this unequal distribution of good and evil, in the present state, as one of the strongest natural arguments for a future state of retribution? Have not they contended, and well and admirably contended, that the supposition of such a state is absolutely necessary to our notion of the justice of God, – absolutely necessary to restore order to that moral confusion which we all observe and deplore in the present world? The man who places religion upon a false basis is the greatest enemy to religion. If victory is always to the just and good, – how is the fortune of impious conquerors to be accounted for? Why do they erect dynasties, and found families which last for centuries? The reflecting mind whom you have inst-ructed in this manner, and for present effect only, naturally comes upon you hereafter with difficulties of this sort; he finds he has been deceived; and you will soon discover that, in breeding up a fanatic, you have unwittingly laid the foun-dation of an atheist. The honest and the orthodox method is to prepare young people for the world, as it actually exists; to tell them that they will often find vice perfectly successful, virtue exposed to a long train of afflictions; that they must bear this patiently, and look to another world for its rectifi-cation.

2. The second doctrine which it is necessary to notice among the Methodists, is the doctrine of inward impulse and emotions, which, it is quite plain, must lead, if univers-ally insisted upon, and preached among the common people, to every species of folly and enormity. When a human being believes that his internal feelings are the monitions of God, and that these monitions must govern his conduct; and when a great stress is purposely laid upon these inward feelings in all the discourses from the pulpit; it is of course imposs-ible to say to what a pitch of extravagance mankind may not be carried, under the influence of such dangerous doctrines.

3. The Methodists hate pleasure and amusements; no theatre, no cards, no dancing, no punchinello, no dancing dogs, no blind fiddlers; – all these amusements of the rich and of the poor must disappear, wherever these gloomy people get a footing. It is not the abuse of pleasure which

they attack, but the interspersion of pleasure, however much it is guarded by good sense and moderation; – it is not only wicked to hear the licentious plays of Congreve, but wicked to hear Henry the Fifth, or the School for Scandal; – it is not only dissipated to run about to all the parties in London and Edinburgh, – but dancing is not *fit for a being who is preparing himself for Eternity. Ennui*, wretchedness, melancholy, groans and sighs, are the offerings which these unhappy men make to a Deity, who has covered the earth with gay colours, and scented it with rich perfumes; and shown us, by the plan and order of his works, that he has given to man something better than a bare existence, and scattered over his creation a thousand superfluous joys, which are totally unnecessary to the mere support of life.

4. The Methodists lay very little stress upon practical righteousness. They do not say to their people, Do not be deceitful; do not be idle; get rid of your bad passions; or at least (if they do say these things) they say them very seldom. Not that they preach faith without works; for if they told the people, that they might rob and murder with impunity, the civil magistrate must be compelled to interfere with such doctrine: – but they say a great deal about faith, and very little about works. What are commonly called the mysterious parts of our religion, are brought into the fore-ground, much more than the doctrines which lead to practice; – and this among the lowest of the community.

5. The Methodists are always desirous of making men more religious than it is possible, from the constitution of human nature, to make them. If they could succeed as much as they wish to succeed, there would be at once an end of delving and spinning, and of every exertion of human industry. Men must eat, and drink, and work; and if you wish to fix upon them high and elevated notions, as the *ordinary* furniture of their minds, you do these two things; – you drive men of warm temperaments mad, – and you introduce, in the rest of the world, a low and shocking familiarity with words and images, which every real friend to religion would wish to keep sacred. *The friends of the dear Redeemer who are in the habit of visiting the Isle of Thanet* – (as in the extract we have quoted) – Is it possible that this mixture of the most awful, with the most familiar images, so common among Methodists now, and with the enthusiasts in the time of Cromwell, must not, in the end, divest religion of all the deep and solemn impressions which it is calculated to produce? In a man of common imagination (as we have before

observed), the terror, and the feeling which it first excited, must necessarily be soon separated: but, where the fervour of impression is long preserved, piety ends in Bedlam. Accordingly, there is not a madhouse in England, where a considerable part of the patients have not been driven to insanity by the extravagance of these people. We cannot enter such places without seeing a number of honest artisans, covered with blankets, and calling themselves angels and apostles, who, if they had remained contented with the instruction of men of learning and education, would still have been sound masters of their own trade, sober Christians, and useful members of society.

Missionaries

In the same year Sydney reviewed several books on Christianity in India. Two years earlier two battalions of sepoys had rebelled at Vellore and massacred some British soldiers. The government of Madras found the cause of the uprising in the spread of a rumour that the British government wished to convert them by forcible means to Christianity. Sydney studied the transactions of the Baptist Missionary Society and found the missionaries in India to be of similar ilk to the Methodists at home.

We see from the massacre at Vellore what a powerful engine attachment to religion may be rendered in Hindostan. The rumours might all have been false; but that event shows they were tremendously powerful when excited. The object, therefore, is not only not to do any thing violent and unjust upon subjects of religion, but not to give any strong colour to jealous and disaffected natives for misrepresenting your intentions.

All these observations have tenfold force, when applied to an empire which rests so entirely upon opinion. If physical force could be called in to stop the progress of error, we could afford to be misrepresented for a season; but 30,000 white men living in the midst of 70 millions of sable subjects, must be always in the right, or at least never represented as grossly in the wrong. Attention to the prejudices of the subject is wise in all governments, but quite indispensable in a government constituted as our empire in India is constituted; where an uninterrupted series of dexterous conduct is not only necessary to our prosperity, but to our existence.

The duty of conversion is less plain, and less imperious, when conversion exposes the convert to great present misery. An African, or an Otaheite proselyte, might not perhaps be less honoured by his countrymen if he became a Christian;

a Hindoo is instantly subjected to the most perfect degradation. A change of faith might increase the immediate happiness of any other individual; it annihilates for ever all the *human* comforts which a Hindoo enjoys. The eternal happiness which you proffer him, is therefore less attractive to him than to any other heathen, from the life of misery by which he purchases it.

Conversion is no duty at all, if it merely destroys the old religion, without really and effectually teaching the new one. Brother Ringletaube may write home that he makes a Christian, when, in reality, he ought only to state that he has destroyed a Hindoo. Foolish and imperfect as the religion of a *Hindoo* is, it is at least some restraint upon the intemperance of human passions. It is better a Brahman should be respected, than that nobody should be respected. A Hindoo had better believe that a deity, with an hundred legs and arms, will reward and punish him hereafter, than that he is not to be punished at all. Now, when you have destroyed the faith of a Hindoo, are you quite sure that you will graft upon his mind fresh principles of action, and make him any thing more than a nominal Christian?

For ourselves, if there were a fair prospect of carrying the gospel into regions where it was before unknown, – if such a project did not expose the best possessions of the country to extreme danger, and if it was in the hands of men who were discreet as well as devout, we should consider it to be a scheme of true piety, benevolence, and wisdom: but the baseness and malignity of fanaticism shall never prevent us from attacking its arrogance, its ignorance, and its activity. For what vice can be more tremendous than that which, while it wears the outward appearance of religion, destroys the happiness of man, and dishonours the name of God?

One paragraph in particular was to be singled out by a Mr Styles:

The Hindoos have some very savage customs, which it would be desirable to abolish. Some swing on hooks, some run *kimes* through their hands, and widows burn themselves to death: but these follies (even the last) are quite voluntary on the part of the sufferers. We dislike all misery, voluntary or involuntary; but the difference between the torments which a man chooses, and those which he endures from the choice of others, is very great.

Sydney's philippics against Methodism and the Indian Missions brought a reply, which he reviewed in 1809.

Strictures on two Critiques in the Edinburgh Review, on the
Subject of Methodism and Missions; with Remarks on the
Influence of Reviews, in general, on Morals and Happiness.
By John Styles. 8vo. London: 1809.

To our attack upon the melancholy tendency of Methodism, Mr Styles replies, 'that a man must have studied in the *schools of Hume, Voltaire, and Kotzebue,* who can plead in behalf of the theatre; that, at fashionable ball-rooms and assemblies, seduction is drawn out to a system; that dancing excites the fever of the passions, and raises a delirium too often fatal to innocence and peace; and that, for the poor, instead of the common rough amusements to which they are now addicted, there remain the simple beauties of nature, the gay colours and scented perfumes of the earth.' These are the blessings which the common people have to expect from their Methodistical instructors. They are pilfered of all their money – shut out from all their dances and country wakes – and are then sent penniless into the fields, to gaze on the clouds, and smell to dandelions!

While Mr Styles is severe upon the indolence of the Church, he should recollect that his Methodists are the ex-party; that it is not in human nature, that any persons who quietly possess power, can be as active as those who are pursuing it. The fair way to state the merit of the two parties is, to estimate what the exertions of the lachrymal and suspirious clergy would be, if they stepped into the endow-ments of their competitors. The moment they ceased to be paid by the groan – the instant that Easter offerings no longer depended upon jumping and convulsions – Mr Styles may assure himself, that the character of his darling preachers would be totally changed; their bodies would become quiet, and their minds reasonable.

It is not true, as this bad writer is perpetually saying, that the world hates piety. That modest and unobtrusive piety, which fills the heart with all human charities, and makes a man gentle to others, and severe to himself, is an object of universal love and veneration. But mankind hate the lust of power, when it is veiled under the garb of piety; – they hate canting and hypocrisy; – they hate advertisers, – and quacks in piety; – they do not choose to be insulted; – they love to tear folly and impudence from that altar, which should only be a sanctuary for the wretched and the good.

Having concluded his defence of Methodism, this fanatic-al writer opens upon us his Missionary battery, firing away with the most incessant fury, and calling names, all the time, as loud as lungs accustomed to the eloquence of the tub usually vociferate. In speaking of the cruelties which their religion entails upon the Hindoos, Mr Styles is peculiarly severe upon us for not being more shocked at their piercing their limbs with *kimes*. This is rather an unfair mode of alarming his readers with the idea of some unknown instrument. He represents himself as having paid considerable attention to the manners and customs of the Hindoos; and, therefore, the peculiar stress he lays upon this instrument is naturally calculated to produce, in the minds of the humane, a great degree of mysterious terror. A drawing of the *kime* was imperiously called for; and the want of it is a subtle evasion, for which Mr Styles is fairly accountable. As he has been silent on this subject, it is for us to explain the plan and nature of this terrible and unknown piece of mechanism. A *kime*, then, is neither more nor less than a false print in the Edinburgh Review of a *knife*; and from this blunder of the printer has Mr Styles manufactured this Dædalean instrument of torture, called a *kime*! We were at first nearly persuaded by his arguments against *kimes*; we grew frightened; – we stated to ourselves the horror of not sending missionaries to a nation which used *kimes*; – we were struck with the nice and accurate information of the Tabernacle upon this important subject: – but we looked in the errata, and found Mr Styles to be always Mr Styles – always cut off from every hope of mercy, and remaining for ever himself.

Mr Styles is right in saying we have abolished many practices of the Hindoos since, the establishment of our empire; but then we have always consulted the Brahmins, whether or not such practices were conformable with their religion; and it is upon the authority of their condemnation that we have proceeded to abolition.

To the whole of Mr Styles's observations upon the introduction of Christianity into India, we have one short answer: – it is not Christianity which is introduced there, but the debased mummery and nonsense of Methodists, which has little more to do with the Christian religion than it has to do with the religion of China.

What is the use, too, of telling us what these men endure? Suffering is not a merit, but only useful suffering. Prove to us that they are fit men, doing a fit thing, and we are ready to praise the missionaries; but it gives us no pleasure to hear that a man has walked a thousand miles with peas in his shoes, unless we know why and wherefore, and to what good purpose he has done it. . . .

In answer to all the low malignity of this author, we have only to reply,. that we are, as we always have been, sincere friends to the conversion of the Hindoos. We admit the Hindoo religion to be full of follies, and full of enormities; – we think conversion a great duty; and should think it, if it could be effected, a great blessing; but our opinion of the missionaries and of their employer is such, that we most firmly believe, in less than twenty years, for the conversion of a few degraded wretches, who would be neither Methodists nor Hindoos, they would infallibly produce the massacre of every European in India; the loss of our settlements; and, consequently, of the chance of that slow, solid, and temperate introduction of Christianity, which the superiority of the European character may ultimately effect in the Eastern world. The Board of Control (all Atheists, and disciples of Voltaire, of course) are so entirely of our way of thinking, that the most peremptory orders have been issued to send all the missionaries home upon the slightest appearance of disturbance. Those who have sons and brothers in India may now sleep in peace. Upon the transmission of this order, Mr Styles is said to have destroyed himself with a *kime.*

Despite his strength of feeling about Methodists, Sydney still maintained the right of dissenters to preach their gospel in the ways they thought best. When Viscount Sidmouth sought to bring in a bill which would subject dissenting ministers to examination, and to limit their movement, Sydney defended their rights.

Hints on Toleration, in Five Essays, &c., suggested for the Consideration of Lord Viscount Sidmouth, and the Dissenters. By Philagatharches. London: 1810.

If a prudent man see a child playing with a porcelain cup of great value, he takes the vessel out of his hand, pats him on the head, tells him his mamma will be sorry if it is broken, and gently cheats him into the use of some less precious substitute. Why will Lord Sidmouth meddle with the Toleration Act, when there are so many other subjects in which his abilities might be so eminently useful – when inclosure bills are drawn up with such scandalous negligence – turnpike roads so shamefully neglected – and public conveyances illegitimately loaded in the face of day, and in defiance of the wisest legislative provisions? We confess our trepidation at seeing the Toleration Act in the hands of Lord Sidmouth; and should be very glad if it were fairly back in the statute-book, and the sedulity of this well-meaning nobleman diverted into another channel.

The alarm and suspicion of the Dissenters upon these

measures are wise and rational. They are right to consider the Toleration Act as their palladium; and they may be certain that, in this country, there is always a strong party ready, not only to prevent the further extension of tolerant principles, but to abridge (if they dared) their present operation within the narrowest limits. Whoever makes this attempt will be sure to make it under professions of the most earnest regard for mildness and toleration, and with the strongest declarations of respect for King William, the Revolution, and the principles which seated the House of Brunswick on the throne of these realms; – and then will follow the clauses for whipping Dissenters, imprisoning preachers, and subjecting them to rigid qualifications, &c. &c. &c. The infringement on the militia acts is a mere pretence. The real object is, to diminish the number of Dissenters from the Church of England, by abridging the liberties and privileges they now possess. This is the project which we shall examine; for we sincerely believe it to be the project in agitation. The mode in which it is proposed to attack the Dissenters, is, first, by exacting greater qualifications in their teachers; next, by preventing the inter-change or itinerancy of preachers, and fixing them to one spot.

It can never, we presume, be intended to subject dissenting ministers to any kind of *theological* examination. A teacher examined in doctrinal opinions, by another teacher who differs from him, is so very absurd a project, that we entirely acquit Lord Sidmouth of any intention of this sort. We rather presume his Lordship to mean, that a man who professes to teach his fellow-creatures should at least have made some progress in human learning; – that he should not be wholly without education; – that he should be able at least to read and write. If the test is of this very ordinary nature, it can scarcely exclude many teachers of religion; and it was hardly worth while, for the very insignificant diminution of numbers which this must occasion to the dissenting clergy, to have raised all the alarm which this attack upon the Toleration Act has occasioned.

A dissenting minister, of vulgar aspect and homely appearance, declares that he entered into that holy office because he felt a call; and a clergyman of the Establishment smiles at him for the declaration. But it should be remembered, that no minister of the Establishment is admitted into orders, before he has been expressly interrogated by the bishop, whether he feels himself called to that sacred office. The doctrine of calling, or inward feeling, is quite orthodox in the English Church; – and in arguing this subject in Parliament, it will hardly be contended, that the Episcopalian only is the judge when that call is genuine, and when it is only imaginary.

The attempt at making the dissenting clergy stationary, and persecuting their circulation, appears to us quite as unjust and inexpedient as the other measure of qualifications. It appears a gross inconsistency to say – 'I admit that what you are doing is legal, – but you must not do it thoroughly and effectually. I allow you to propagate your heresy, – but I object to all means of propagating it which appear to be useful and effective.' If there are any other grounds upon which the circulation of the dissenting clergy is objected to, let these grounds be stated and examined; but to object to their circulation, merely because it is the best method of effecting the object which you allow them to effect, does appear to be rather unnatural and inconsistent.

Nothing dies so hard and rallies so often as intolerance. The fires are put out, and no living nostril has scented the nidor of a human creature roasted for faith; – then, after this, the prison-doors were got open, and the chains knocked off; – and now Lord Sidmouth only begs that men who disagree with him in religious opinions may be deprived of all civil offices, and not be allowed to hear the preachers they like best. Chains and whips he would not hear of; but these mild gratifications of his bill every orthodox mind is surely entitled to. The hardship would indeed be great, if a churchman were deprived of the amusement of putting a dissenting parson in prison. We are convinced Lord Sidmouth is a very amiable and well-intentioned man: his error is not the error of his heart, but of his time, *above which few men ever rise.* It is the error of some four of five hundred thousand English gentlemen, of decent education and worthy characters, who conscientiously believe that they are punishing, and continuing incapacities, for the good of the State; while they are, in fact (though without knowing it), only gratifying that insolence, hatred, and revenge, which all human beings are unfortunately so ready to feel against those who will not conform to their own sentiments.

But Dissenters also show intolerance, and Sydney concludes his essay with comments upon Philagatharches (whom he describes as 'a stern, subacid Dissenter') and his like.

Philagatharches is an instance (not uncommon, we are sorry to say, even among the most rational of the Protestant Dissenters) of a love of toleration combined with a love of persecution. He is a dissenter, and earnestly demands religious liberty for that body of men; but as for the Catholics, he would not only continue their present disabilities, but load them with every new one that could be conceived. He expressly says that an Atheist or a Deist may be allowed to propagate their doctrines, but not a Catholic; and then proceeds with all the customary trash against that sect which nine schoolboys out of ten now know how to refute. So it is with Philagatharches; – so it is with weak men in every sect. It has ever been our object, and (in spite of misrepresentation and abuse) ever *shall* be our object, to put down this spirit – to protect the true interests, and to diffuse the true spirit, of toleration. To a well-supported national Establishment, effectually discharging its duties, we are very sincere friends. If any man, after he has paid his contribution to this great security for the existence of religion in any shape, choose to adopt a religion of his own, that man should be permitted to do so without let, molestation, or disqualification for any of the offices of life. We apologise to men of sense for sentiments so trite; and patiently endure the anger which they will excite among those with whom they will pass for original.

XII

Ireland and Roman Catholic Emancipation

Sydney devoted more time and energy to working for the emancipation of Roman Catholics than to any other cause. An 'unrevised fragment' on the Irish Roman Catholic Church (which he planned to make into a pamphlet) was found among his papers after his death. 'If it serve no other purpose,' says the Editor of his collected works, 'it will at least prove that his *last*, as well as his earliest efforts, were exerted for the promotion of religious freedom.' – and, inextricably woven with this, for the good of the people of Ireland.

His earliest expression of sympathy for the Irish is found in an *Edinburgh Review* of 1803, the first full year of publication. He reviewed an *Essay on Irish Bulls* by R.L. Edgeworth and Maria Edgeworth. He begins, 'We hardly know what to say about this rambling, scrambling book; but that we are quite sure the author, when he began any sentence in it, had not the smallest suspicion of what it was about to contain.' But he ends, 'Whatever the deficiencies of the book, they are, in our estimation, amply atoned for by its merits, but none more than that lively feeling of compassion which pervades it for the distresses of the wild, kind hearted, blundering poor of Ireland.'

Twenty six years were to elapse before the Roman Catholic Emancipation Act was passed in April 1829. Sydney heard the news at the bedside of his dying son, Douglas. Later he wrote:

> I do not retract one syllable (or one iota) of what I have said or written upon the Catholic question. What was wanted for Ireland was emancipation, time and justice, abolition of present wrongs; time for forgetting past wrongs, and that continued and even justice which would make oblivion wise. It is now only difficult to tranquillise Ireland, before emancipation it was impossible. As to the danger from Catholic doctrines, I must leave such apprehensions to the respectable anility of these realms. I will not meddle with it.

CATHOLICS

*History of the Penal Laws against the Irish Catholics,
from the Treaty of Limerick to the Union.*

By Henry Parnell, Esq., M.P.

> The various publications which have issued from the press in favour of religious liberty, have now nearly silenced the arguments of their opponents; and, teaching sense to some, and inspiring others with shame, have left those only on

the field who can neither learn nor blush.

But, though *the argument* is given up, and the justice of the Catholic cause admitted, it seems to be generally conceived, that their case, at present, is utterly hopeless; and that, to advocate it any longer, will only irritate the oppressed, without producing any change of opinion in those by whose influence and authority that oppression is continued. To this opinion, unfortunately too prevalent, we have many reasons for not subscribing.

We are by no means convinced, that the decorous silence recommended upon the Catholic question would be rewarded by those future concessions, of which many persons appear to be so certain. We have a strange incredulity where persecution is to be abolished, and any class of men restored to their indisputable rights. When we see it done, we will believe it. Till it is done, we shall always consider it to be highly improbable – much too improbable – to justify the smallest relaxation in the Catholics themselves, or in those who are well-wishers to their cause. When the fanciful period at present assigned for the emancipation arrives, new scruples may arise – fresh forbearance be called for – and the operations of common sense be deferred for another generation. Toleration never had a present tense, nor taxation a future one. The answer which Paul received from Felix, he owed to the subject on which he spoke. When justice and righteousness were his theme, Felix told him to go away, and he would hear him some other time. All men who have spoken to courts upon such disagreeable topics, have received the same answer. Felix, however, trembled when he gave it; but his fear was ill directed. He trembled at the subject – he ought to have trembled at the delay.

Edinburgh Review, 1808

Sydney rehearses the oppressive and savage laws against the Irish Roman Catholics which continued in operation from William III's reign until almost the end of the eighteenth century. There remained the Corporation and Test Acts from the reign of Charles II, whereby office holders in government in England and Ireland had to take not only the oath of supremacy, but also the sacrament in the Church of England and to declare against the doctrine of transsubstantiation. Toleration Acts had provided exemptions for Protestant Dissenters, and from 1727 annual bills to indemnify Dissenters who had 'forgotten' to take the sacrament were passed, but these did not apply to Roman Catholics.

Rewards are given by the same act for the discovery of Popish clergy; – £50 for discovering a Popish bishop; £20 for a common Popish clergyman; £10 for a Popish usher! Two justices of the peace can compel any Papist above 18 years of age to disclose every particular which has come to his knowledge respecting Popish priests, celebration of mass, or Papist schools. – Imprisonment for a year if he refuses to answer. – Nobody can hold property in trust for a Catholic. – Juries, in all trials growing out of these statues, to be Protestants. – No Papist to take more than two apprentices, except in the linen trade. – All the Catholic clergy to give in their names and places of abode at the quarter-sessions, and to keep no curates. – Catholics not to serve on grand juries.

Such is the rapid outline of a code of laws which reflects indelible disgrace upon the English character, and explains but too clearly the cause of that hatred in which the English name has been so long held in Ireland. It would require centuries to efface such an impression: and yet, when we find it fresh, and operating at the end of a few years, we explain the fact by every cause which can degrade the Irish, and by none which can remind us of our own scandalous policy. With the folly and the horror of such a code before our eyes, – with the conviction, of recent and domestic history, that mankind are not to be lashed and chained out of their faith, – we are striving to teaze and worry them into a better theology. Heavy oppression is removed; light insults and provocations are retained; the scourge does not fall upon their shoulders, but it sounds in their ears. And this is the conduct we are pursuing, when it is still a great doubt whether this country alone may not be opposed to the united efforts of the whole of Europe. It is really difficult to ascertain which is the most utterly destitute of common sense, – the capricious and arbitrary stop we have made in our concessions to the Catholics, or the precise period we have chosen for this grand effort of obstinate folly.

Contemporary with this review came the *Peter Plymley letters*, ten in all. Abraham Hayward, in his review of Lady Holland's *Memoirs* writes,

In the summer of 1807, he and the family were the temporary occupants of a cottage at Sunning, near Reading. 'I believe it was about this period,' she states, 'that a letter from Peter Plymley to his brother Abraham on the subject of the Irish Catholics appeared suddenly in the London world. Its effect, I have been told, was like a spark on a heap of gunpowder. It was quickly followed by another and another; each increasing the eagerness and curiosity of the public. Every effort was made on the part of the existing Government to find out the author in vain: the secret was well kept.

Their success can be understood when we read Lord Murray's tribute: 'After

Pascal's Letters, it is the most instructive piece of wisdom in the form of irony ever written, and had the most important and lasting effect.'

From Letter I

I found in your letter the usual remarks about fire, fagot, and bloody Mary. Are you aware, my dear Priest, that there were as many persons put to death for religious opinions under the mild Elizabeth as under the bloody Mary? The reign of the former was, to be sure, ten times as long; but I only mention the fact, merely to show you that something depends upon the age in which men live, as well as on their religious opinions. Three hundred years ago, men burnt and hanged each other for these opinions. Time has softened Catholic as well as Protestant: they both required it; though each perceives only his own improvement, and is blind to that of the other. We are all the creatures of circumstances. I know not a kinder and better man than yourself; but you (if you had lived in those times) would certainly have roasted your Catholic: and I promise you, if the first exciter of this religious mob had been as powerful then as he is now, you would soon have been elevated to the mitre. I do not go the length of saying that the world has suffered as much from Protestant as from Catholic persecution; far from it: but you should remember the Catholics had all the power, when the idea first started up in the world that there could be two modes of faith; and that it was much more natural they should attempt to crush this diversity of opinion by great and cruel efforts, than that the Protestants should rage against those who differed from them, when the very basis of their system was complete freedom in all spiritual matters.

From Letter II

Dear Abraham,

The Catholic not respect an oath! why not? What upon earth has kept him out of Parliament, or excluded him from all the offices whence he is excluded, but his respect for oaths? There is no law which prohibits a Catholic to sit in Parliament. There could be no such law; because it is impossible to find out what passes in the interior of any man's mind. Suppose it were in contemplation to exclude all men from certain offices who contended for the legality of taking tithes: the only mode of discovering that fervid love of decimation which I know you to possess would be to tender you an oath against that damnable doctrine, that it is lawful for a spiritual man to take, abstract, appropriate, sunduct, or lead away the tenth calf, sheep, lamb, ox, pigeon, duck. &c. &c. &c., and every other animal that ever existed, which of course the lawyers would take care to enumerate. Now this oath I am sure you would rather die than take; and so the Catholic is excluded from Parliament because he will not swear that he disbelieves the leading doctrines of his religion! The Catholic asks you to abolish some oaths which oppress him; your answer is, that he does not respect oaths. They why subject him to the test of oaths? The oaths keep him out of Parliament; why, then, he respects them. Turn which way you will, either your laws are nugatory, or the Catholic is bound by religious obligations as you are: but no eel in the well-sanded fist of a cook-maid, upon the eve of being skinned, ever twisted and writhed as an orthodox parson does when he is compelled by the gripe of reason to admit any thing in favour of a Dissenter.

A distinction, I perceive, is taken, by one of the most feeble noblemen in Great Britain, between persecution and the deprivation of political power; whereas there is no more distinction between these two things than there is between him who makes the distinction and a booby. If I strip off the relic-covered jacket of a Catholic, and give him twenty stripes. . . . I persecute: if I say, Every body in the town where you live shall be a candidate for lucrative and honourable offices, but you, who are a Catholic. . . . I do not persecute! – What barbarous nonsense is this! as if degradation was not as great an evil as bodily pain, or as severe poverty: as if I could not be as great a tyrant by saying, You shall not enjoy – as by saying, You shall suffer. The English, I believe, are as truly religious as any nation in Europe; I know no greater blessing: but it carries with it this evil in its train, that any villain who will bawl out. '*The Church is in danger!*' may get a place, and a good pension; and that any administration who will do the same thing may bring a set of men into power who, at a moment of stationary and passive piety, would be hooted by the very boys in the streets. But it is not all religion; it is, in great part, the narrow and exclusive spirit which delights to keep the common blessings of sun, and air, and freedom from other human beings. 'Your religion has always been degraded; you are in the dust, and I will take care you never rise again. I should enjoy less the possession of an earthly good, by every additional person to whom it was extended.' You may not be aware of it yourself, most reverend Abraham, but you deny their freedom to the Catholics upon the same principle that Sarah your wife

refuses to give the receipt for a ham or a gooseberry dump-
ling: she values her receipts, not because they secure to her
a certain flavour, but because they remind her that her neighbours want it: – a feeling laughable in a priestess, shameful
in a priest; venial when it withholds the blessings of a ham,
tyrannical and execrable when it narrows the boon of religious freedom.

The Napoleonic Wars were the background to the Letters; and the invasion
of Ireland was good French military strategy, for here were an oppressed
people, ripe for rebellion. Sydney's fears were, not realised, and he called
Great Britain an 'anemocracy' – ruled by the winds, which prevented the
French from landing.

From Letter III

You ask me, if I think it possible for this country to survive
the recent misfortunes of Europe? – I answer you, without
the slightest degree of hesitation: that if Bonaparte lives,
and a great deal is not immediately done for the conciliation
of the Catholics, it does seem, to me absolutely impossible
but that we must perish; and take this with you, that we
shall perish without exciting the slightest feeling of present
or future compassion, but fall amidst the hootings and
revilings of Europe, as a nation of blockheads, Methodists,
and old women. If there were any great scenery, any heroic
feelings, any blaze of ancient virtue, any exalted death, any
termination of England that would be ever remembered, ever
honoured in that western world, where liberty is now retiring, conquest would be more tolerable, and ruin more sweet;
but it is double miserable to become slaves abroad, because
we would be tyrants at home; to persecute, when we are
contending against persecution; and to perish, because we
have raised up worse enemies within, from our own bigotry,
than we are exposed to without, from the unprincipled
ambition, of France. It is, indeed, a most silly and affecting
spectacle to rage at such a moment against our own kindred
and our own blood; to tell them they cannot be honourable
in war, because they are conscientious in religion; to stipul-
ate (at the very moment when we should buy their hearts
and swords at any price) that they must hold up the right
hand in prayer, and not the left; and adore one common
God, by turning to the east rather than to the west.

What is it the Catholics ask of you? Do not exclude us
from the honours and emoluments of the state, because we
worship God in one way, and you worship him in another.

From Letter IV

Our conduct to Ireland, during the whole of this war, has been that of a man who subscribes to hospitals, weeps at charity sermons, carries out broth and blankets to beggars, and then comes home and beats his wife and children. We had compassion for the victims of all other oppression and injustice, except our own. If Switzerland was threatened, away went a Treasury Clerk with a hundred thousand pounds for Switzerland; large bags of money were kept constantly under sailing orders; upon the slightest demonstration towards Naples, down went Sir William Hamilton upon his knees, and begged for the love of St Januarius they would help us off with a little money; all the arts of Machiavel were resorted to, to persuade Europe to borrow; troops were sent off in all directions to save the Catholic and Protestant world; the Pope himself was guarded by a regiment of English dragoons; if the Grand Lama had been at hand, he would have had another; every Catholic Clergyman who had the good fortune to be neither English nor Irish, was immediately provided with lodging, soap, crucifix, missal, chapel-beads, relics, and holy water; if Turks had landed, Turks would have received an order from the Treasury for coffee, opium, korans, and seraglios. In the midst of all this fury of saving and defending, this crusade, for conscience and Christianity, there was a universal agreement among all descriptions of people to continue every species of internal persecution; to deny at home every just right that had been denied before; to pummel poor Dr Abraham Rees and his Dissenters; and to treat the unhappy Catholics of Ireland as if their tongues were mute, their heels cloven, their nature brutal, and designedly subjected by Providence to their Orange masters.

From Letter IV (cont.)

[King George III was utterly opposed to Roman Catholic Emancipation, believing that his assent would be a violation of his Coronation Oath.]

How is a minister of this country to act when the conscientious scruples of his Sovereign prevent the execution, of a measure deemed by him absolutely necessary to the safety of the country? His conduct is quite clear – he should resign. But what is his successor to do? – Resign. But is the King to be left without ministers, and is he in this manner to be compelled to act against his own conscience? Before I answer this, pray tell me in my turn, what better defence is there against the machinations of a wicked, or the errors of a weak, Monarch, than the impossibility of finding a minister who will lend himself to vice and folly? Every English Monarch, in such a predicament, would sacrifice his opinions and views to such a clear expression of the public will; and it is one method in which the Constitution aims at bringing about such a sacrifice. You may say, if you please, the ruler of a state is forced to give up his object, when the natural love of place and power will tempt no one to assist him in its attainment; this may be force; but it is force without injury, and therefore without blame. I am not to be beat out of these obvious reasonings, and ancient constitutional provisions, by the term conscience. There is no fantasy, however wild, that a man may not persuade himself that he cherishes from motives of conscience; eternal war against impious France, or rebellious America, or Catholic Spain, may in times to come be scruples of conscience. One English Monarch may, from scruples of conscience, wish to abolish every trait of religious persecution; another Monarch may deem it his absolute and indispensable duty to make a slight provision for Dissenters out of the revenues of the Church of England. So that you see, Brother Abraham, there are cases where it would be the duty of the best and most loyal subjects to oppose the conscientious scruples of their Sovereign, still taking care that their actions were constitutional, and their modes respectful.

Do not imagine by these observations that I am not loyal: without joining in the common cant of the best of kings, I respect the King most sincerely as a good man. His religion is better than the religion of Mr Perceval, his old morality very superior to the old morality of Mr Canning, and I am quite certain he has a safer understanding than both of them put together. Loyalty, within the bounds of reason and moderation, is one of the great instruments of English happiness; but the love of the King may easily become more strong than the love of the kingdom, and we may lose sight of the public welfare in our exaggerated admiration of him who is appointed to reign only for its promotion and support. I detest Jacobinism; and if I am doomed to be a slave at all, I would rather be the slave of a king than a cobbler. God save the King, you say, warms your heart like the sound of a trumpet. I cannot make use of so violent a metaphor; but I am delighted to hear it, when it is the cry of genuine affection; I am delighted to hear it when they hail not only the individual man, but the outward and living sign of all English blessings. These are noble feelings, and the heart of every good man must go with them; but God save the King, in these times, too often means God save my pension and my place, God give my sisters an allowance out of the privy purse, make me clerk of the irons, let me survey the meltings, let me live upon the fruits of other men's industry, and fatten upon the plunder of the public.

From Letter V

The effects of penal laws, in matters of religion, are never confined to those limits in which the legislature intended they should be placed: it is not only that I am excluded from certain offices and dignities because I am a Catholic, but the exclusion carries with it a certain stigma, which degrades me in the eyes of the monopolising sect, and the very name of my religion becomes odious. These effects are so very striking in England, that I solemnly believe blue and red baboons to be more popular here than Catholics and Presbyterians; they are more understood, and there is a greater disposition to do something for them. When a country squire hears of an ape, his first feeling is to give it nuts and apples; when he hears of a Dissenter, his immediate impulse is to commit it to the county jail to shave its head, to alter its customary food, and to have it privately whipped. This is no caricature, but an accurate picture of national feelings, as they degrade and endanger us at this very moment. The Irish Catholic gentleman would bear his legal disabilities with greater temper, if these were all he had to bear – if they did not enable every Protestant cheesemonger and tide-waiter to treat him with contempt. He is branded on the forehead with a red-hot iron, and treated like a 'spiritual felon, because, in the highest of all considerations, he is led by the noblest of all guides, his own disinterested conscience.

Why are nonsense and cruelty a bit the better because they are enacted? If Providence, which gives wine and oil, had blessed us with that tolerant spirit which makes the countenance more pleasant and the heart more glad than these can do; if our Statute Book had never been defiled with such infamous laws, the sepulchral Spencer Perceval would have been hauled through the dirtiest horse-pond in Hampstead, had he ventured to propose them. But now persecution is good, because it exists; every law which originated in ignorance and malice, and gratifies the passions from whence it sprang, we call the wisdom of our ancestors: when such laws are repealed, they will be cruelty and madness; till they are repealed, they are policy and caution.

In Letters V and X Sydney contrasts the position of Protestant Dissenters with that of Roman Catholics.

I cannot imagine why the friends to the Church Establishment should entertain such a horror of seeing the doors of Parliament flung open to the Catholics, and view so passively the enjoyment of that right by the Presbyterians and by every other species of Dissenter. In their tenets, in their Church government, in the nature of their endowments, the Dissenters are infinitely more distant from the Church of England than the Catholics are; yet the Dissenters have never been excluded from Parliament. There are 45 members in one House, and 16 in the other, who always are Dissenters. There is no law which would prevent every member of the Lords and Commons from being Dissenters. The Catholics could not bring into Parliament half the number of the Scotch members; and yet one exclusion is of such immense importance, because it has taken place; and the other no human being thinks of, because no one is accustomed to it. I have often thought, if the *wisdom of our ancestors* had excluded all persons with red hair from the House of Commons, of the throes and convulsions it would occasion to restore them to their natural rights. What mobs and riots would it produce! To what infinite abuse and obloquy would the capillary patriot be exposed; what wormwood would distil from Mr Perceval, what froth would drop from Mr Canning; how (I will not say *my*, but *our* Lord Hawkesbury, for he belongs to us all) – how our Lord Hawkesbury would work away about the hair of King William and Lord Somers, and the authors of the great and glorious Revolution; how Lord Eldon would appeal to the Deity and his own virtues, and to the hair of his children: some would say that red-haired men were superstitious; some would prove they were atheists; they would be petitioned against as the friends of slavery, and the advocates for revolt; in short, such a corrupter of the heart and understanding is the spirit of persecution, that these unfortunate people (conspired against by their fellow-subjects of every complexion), if they did not emigrate to countries where hair of another colour was persecuted, would be driven to the falsehood of perukes, or the hypocrisy of the Tricosian Fluid.

It is not by any means necessary, as you contend, to repeal the Test Act if you give relief to the Catholic: what the Catholics ask for is to be put on a footing with the Protestant Dissenters, which would be done by repealing that part of the law which compels them to take the oath of supremacy and to make the declaration against transubstantiation: they would then come into parliament as all other Dissenters are allowed to do, and the penal laws to which they were exposed for taking office would be suspended every year, as they have been for this half century past towards Protestant Dissenters. Perhaps, after all, this is the best method, – to continue the persecuting law, and to suspend it every year, – a method which, while it effectually destroys the persecution itself, leaves to the great mass of mankind the exquisite gratification of supposing that they are enjoying some advantage from which a particular class of their fellow creatures are excluded. We manage the Corporation and Test Acts at present much in the same manner as if we were to persuade parish boys who had been in the habit of beating an ass to spare the animal, and beat the skin of an ass stuffed with straw; this would preserve the semblance of tormenting without the reality, and keep boy and beast in good humour.

From Letter IX

[Concerning a poverty-stricken priesthood and people, – people who had to pay their tithes to the incumbents of the Church of Ireland, as well as support their own priests.]

I admit that nothing can be more reasonable than to expect that a Catholic priest should starve to death, genteelly and pleasantly, for the good of the Protestant religion; but is it equally reasonable to expect that he should do so for the Protestant pews, and Protestant brick and mortar? On an Irish Sabbath, the bell of a neat parish church often summons to church only the parson and an occasionally conforming clerk; while, two hundred yards off, a thousand Catholics are huddled together in a miserable hovel, and pelted by all the storms of heaven. Can any thing be more distressing than to see a venerable man pouring forth sublime truths in tattered breeches, and depending for his food upon the little offal he gets from his parishioners? I venerate a human being who starves for his principles, let them be what they may; but starving for any thing is not at all to the taste of the honourable flagellants: strict principles, and good pay, is the motto of Mr Perceval: the one he keeps in great measure for the faults of his enemies, the other for himself.

I cannot describe the horror and disgust which I felt at hearing Mr Perceval call upon the then ministry for measures of vigour in Ireland. If I lived at Hampstead upon stewed meats and claret; if I walked to church every Sunday before eleven young gentlemen of my own begetting, with their faces washed, and their hair pleasingly combed: if the Almighty had blessed me with every earthly comfort, – how awfully would I pause before I sent forth the flame and the sword over the cabins of the poor, brave, generous, open-hearted peasants of Ireland! How easy it is to shed human blood – how easy it is to persuade ourselves that it is our duty to do so – and that the decision has cost us a severe struggle – how much in all ages have wounds and shrieks and tears been the cheap and vulgar resources of the rulers of mankind – how difficult and how noble it is to govern in kindness and to found an empire upon the everlasting basis of justice and affection! – But what do men call vigour? To let loose hussars and to bring up artillery, to govern with lighted matches, and to cut, and push, and prime – I call this, not vigour, but the *sloth of cruelty and ignorance*. The vigour I love consists in finding out wherein subjects are aggrieved, in relieving them, in studying the temper and genius of a people, in consulting their prejudices, in select-ing proper persons to lead, and manage them, in the laborious, watchful, and difficult task of increasing public happiness by allaying each particular discontent. In this way Hoche pacified La Vendée – and in this way only will Ireland ever be subdued. But this, in the eyes of Mr Perceval, is imbecility and meanness: houses are not broken open – women are not insulted – the people seem all to be happy; they are not rode over by horses, and cut by whips. Do you call this vigour? – Is this government?

At this time the bishops and the inferior clergy, almost to a man, were strongly opposed to any relaxation of the laws which disadvantaged Roman Catholics. In his own archdeaconry in Yorkshire Sydney had attended two meetings of the local clergy held for the purpose of petitioning Parliament against the emancipation of Roman Catholics, and his counterpetitions were signed in the first instance by two other clergymen and in the second by himself alone!

The Bishop of Lincoln, whose clergy had requested his charge to them to be published, maintained that Roman Catholicism *was* already tolerated in England.

A Charge delivered to the Clergy of the Diocese of Lincoln, at the Triennial *Visitation of that Diocese in May, June, and July,* 1812. By George Tomline, D.D., F.R.S., Lord Bishop of Lincoln. London: Cadell and Co. 4to.

We must begin with denying the main position upon which the Bishop of Lincoln has built his reasoning. – *The Catholic religion is not tolerated in England.* No man can be fairly said to be permitted to enjoy his own worship who is punished for exercising that worship. His Lordship seems to have no other idea of punishment than lodging a man in the *Poultry Compter*, or flogging him at the cart's tail, or fining him a sum of money; – just as if incapacitating a man from enjoying the dignities and emoluments to which men of similar condition and other faith may fairly aspire, was not frequently the most severe and galling of all punishments. This limited idea of the nature of punishment is the more extraordinary, as *incapacitation* is actually one of the most common punishments in some branches of our law. The sentence of a court-martial frequently purports, that a man is rendered for ever *incapable* of serving his Majesty, &c. &c.; and a person not in holy orders, who performs the functions of a clergyman, is rendered for ever *incapable* of holding any preferment in the Church. There are indeed many species of offence for which no punishment more apposite and judicious could be devised. It would be rather extraordinary, however, if the court, in passing such a sentence, were to assure the culprit, 'that such incapacitation was not by them considered as a punishment; that it was only exercising a right inherent in all governments, of determining who should be eligible for office and who ineligible.' His Lordship thinks the toleration complete, because he sees a permission in the statutes for the exercise of the Roman Catholic worship. He sees the permission – but he does not choose to see the consequences to which they are exposed who avail themselves of this permission. It is the liberality of a father who says to a son, 'Do as you please, my dear boy; follow your own inclination. Judge for yourself, you are free as air. But remember, if you marry that lady, I will cut you off with a shilling.' We have scarcely ever read a more solemn and frivolous statement, than the Bishop of Lincoln's antithetical distinction between persecution and the denial of political power.

'It is a principle of our constitution, that the King should have advisers in the discharge of every part of his royal functions – and is it to be imagined, that Papists would advise measures in support of the cause of Protestantism? A similar observation may be applied to the two Houses of Parliament: would Popish peers or Popish members of the House of Commons, enact laws for the security of the Protestant government? Would they not rather repeal the whole Protestant code, and make Popery again the established religion of the country?' – (p.14.)

And these are the apprehensions which the clergy of the diocese have prayed my Lord to make public.

Kind providence never sends an evil without a remedy: – and arithmetic is the natural cure for the passion of fear. If a coward can be made to count his enemies, his terrors may be reasoned with, and he may think of ways and means of counteraction. Now, might it not have been expedient that the Reverend Prelate, before he had alarmed his Country Clergy with the idea of so large a measure as the repeal of Protestantism, should have counted up the probable number of Catholics who would be seated in both Houses of Parliament? Does he believe that there would be ten Catholic Peers, and thirty Catholic Commoners? But, admit double that number (and more, Dr Duigenan himself would not ask) – will the Bishop of Lincoln seriously assert, that he thinks the whole Protestant code in danger of repeal from such an admixture of Catholic legislators as this? Does he forget, amid the innumerable answers which may be made to such sort of apprehensions, what a picture he is drawing of the weakness and versatility of Protestant principles? – that a handful of Catholics, in the bosom of a Protestant legislature, are to overpower the ancient jealousies, the fixed opinions, the inveterate habits of twelve millions of people? – that the King is to apostatize, the Clergy to be silent, and the parliament to be taken by surprise? – that the nation are to go to bed over night, and to see the Pope walking arm in arm with Lord Castlereagh the next morning? – One would really suppose, from the Bishop's fears, that the civil defences of mankind were, like their military bulwarks, transferred by superior skill and courage, in a few hours, from the vanquished to the victor – that the destruction of a church was like the blowing up of a mine – deans, prebendaries, church-wardens, and overseers, all up in the air in an instant. The Bishop has not stated the true and great security for any course of human actions. It is not the word of the law, nor the spirit of the Government, but the general way of thinking among the people, especially when that way of thinking is ancient, exercised upon high interests, and connected with striking passages in history. The Protestant Church does not rest upon the little narrow foundations where the Bishop of Lincoln supposes it to be placed; if it did, it would not be worth saving. It rests upon the general opinion entertained by a free and reflecting people, that the doctrines of the Church are true, her pretensions moderate, and her exhortations useful.

Another species of false reasoning, which pervades the Bishop of Lincoln's Charge, is this: He states what the interests of men are, and then takes it for granted that they will eagerly and actively pursue them; laying totally out of the question the probability or improbability of their effecting their object, and the influence which this balance of chances must produce upon their actions. For instance, it is the interest of the Catholics that our Church should be subservient to theirs. Therefore, says his Lordship, the Catholics will enter into a conspiracy against the English Church. But, is it not also the decided interest of his Lordship's butler that he should be Bishop, and the Bishop, his butler? That the crozier and the corkscrew should change hands, – and the washer of the bottles which they had emptied become the diocesan of learned divines? What has prevented this change, so beneficial to the upper domestic, but the extreme improbability of success, if the attempt were made; an improbability so great, that we will venture to say, the very notion of it has scarcely once entered into the understanding of the good man. Why then is the Reverend Prelate, who lives on so safely and contentedly with *John*, so dreadfully alarmed at the Catholics? And why does he so completely forget, in their instance alone, that men do not merely strive to obtain a thing because it is good, but always mingle with the excellence of the object a consideration of the chance of gaining it. *Edinburgh Review* 1813

IRELAND
1. *Whitelaw's History of the City of Dublin.*
4to. Cadell and Davies.
2. *Observations on the State of Ireland, principally directed to its Agriculture and Rural Population: in a Series of Letters written on a Tour through that Country. In 2 vols. By J. C. Curwen, Esq., M.P. London: 1818*
3. *Gambel's Views of Society in Ireland.*

So great, and so long has been the misgovernment of that country, that we verily believe the empire would be much stronger, if every thing was open sea between England and the Atlantic, and if *skates and cod-fish* swam over the fair land of Ulster. Such jobbing, such profligacy – so much direct tyranny and oppression – such an abuse of God's gifts – such a profanation of God's name for the purposes of bigotry and party spirit, cannot be exceeded in the history of civilised Europe, and will long remain a monument of infamy and shame to England. But it will be more useful to suppress the indignation which the very name of Ireland inspires, and to consider impartially those causes which have marred this fair portion of the creation, and kept it wild and savage in the midst of improving Europe.

Such, then, is Ireland at this period, – a land more barbarous than the rest of Europe, because it has been worse treated and more cruelly oppressed. Many of the incapacities and privations to which the Catholics were exposed, have been removed by law; but, in such instances, they are still incapacitated and deprived by custom. Many cruel and oppressive laws are still enforced against them. A ninth part of the population engrosses all the honours of the country; the other nine pay a tenth of the product of the earth for the support of a religion in which they do not believe. There is little capital in the country. The great and rich men are called by business, or allured by pleasure, into England; their estates are given up to factors, and the utmost farthing of rent extorted from the poor, who, if they give up the land, cannot get employment in manufactures, or regular employment in husbandry. The common people use a sort of food so very cheap, that they can rear families, who cannot procure employment, and who have little more of the comforts of life than food. The Irish are light-minded – want of employment has made them idle – they are irritable and brave – have a keen remembrance of the past wrongs they have suffered, and the present wrongs they are suffering, from England. The consequence of all this is, eternal riot and insurrection, a whole army of soldiers in time of profound peace, and general rebellion whenever England is busy with other enemies, or off her guard! And thus it will be while the same causes continue to operate, for ages to come, – and worse and worse as the rapidly increasing population of the Catholics becomes more and more numerous.

The remedies are, time and justice; and that justice consists in repealing all laws which make any distinction between the two religions; in placing over the government of Ireland, not the stupid, amiable, and insignificant noblemen who have too often been sent there, but men who feel deeply the wrongs of Ireland, and who have an ardent wish to heal them; who will take care that Catholics, when eligible, shall be elected; who will share the patronage of Ireland proportionally among the two parties, and give to just and liberal laws the same vigour of execution which has hitherto been reserved only for decrees of tyranny, and the enactments of oppression. The injustice and hardship of supporting two Churches must be put out of sight, if it cannot or ought not to be cured. The political economist, the moralist, and the satirist, must combine to teach moderation and superintendence to the great Irish proprietors. Public talk and clamour may do something for the poor Irish, as it did for the slaves in the West Indies. Ireland will become more quiet under such treatment, and then more rich, more comfortable, and more civilised; and the horrid spectacle of folly and tyranny, which it at present exhibits, may in time be removed from the eyes of Europe.   *Edinburgh Review* 1820

1. *A Plain Statement of the Political Claims of the Roman Catholics* by Lord Nugent
2. *A letter to Viscount Milton M.P.*
3. *Charge* by the Archbishop of Cashel

Of all human nonsense, it is surely the greatest to talk of respect to the late king – respect to the memory of the Duke of York – by not voting for the Catholic question. Bad, enough to burn widows when the husband dies – bad enough to burn horses, dogs, butlers, footmen, and coachmen, on the funeral pile of a Scythian warrior – but to offer up the happiness of seven millions of people to the memory of the dead, is certainly the most insane sepulchral oblation of which history makes mention. The best compliment to these deceased princes, is to remember their real good qualities, and to forget (as soon as we can forget it) that these good qualities were tarnished by limited and mistaken views of religious liberty.

A distinction is set up between civil rights and political power, and applied against the Catholics: the real difference between these two words is, that civil comes from a Latin word, and political from a Greek one; but if there be any difference in their meaning, the Catholics do not ask for political power, but for *eligibility* to political power. The Catholics have never prayed or dreamt of praying, that so many of the Judges and King's Counsel should necessarily be Catholics; but that no law should exist which prevented them from becoming so if a Protestant King chose to make them so.

Formerly a poor man might be removed from a parish if there was the slightest danger of his becoming chargeable; a hole in his coat or breeches excited suspicion. The churchwardens said, 'He *has* cost us nothing, but *may* cost us something; and we must not live even in the apprehension of evil.' All this is changed; and the law now says, 'Wait till you are hurt; time enough to meet the evil when it comes;

you have no right to do a certain evil to others, to prevent an uncertain evil to yourselves.' The Catholics, however, are told that what they *do* ask is objected to, from the fear of what they *may* ask; that they must do without that which is *reasonable*, for fear they should ask what is *unreasonable*. 'I would give you a penny (says the miser to the beggar) if I was quite sure you would not ask me for half a crown.'

The real evil they dread is the destruction of the Church of Ireland, and through that, of the Church of England. To which we reply, that such danger must proceed from the regular proceedings of Parliament, or be effected by insurrection and rebellion. The Catholics, restored to civil functions, would, we believe, be more likely to cling to the Church than to Dissenters. If not, both Catholics and Dissenters must be utterly powerless against the overwhelming English interest and feelings in the House. Men are less inclined to run into rebellion, in proportion as they have less to complain of; and, of all other dangers, the greatest to the Irish and English Church establishments, and to the Protestant faith throughout Europe, is *to leave Ireland in its present state of discontent.*

If the intention is to wait to the last, before concession is made, till the French or Americans have landed, and the Holy standard has been unfurled, we ought to be sure of the terms which can be obtained at such a crisis. This game was played in America. Commissioners were sent in one year to offer and to press what would have been most thankfully received the year before; but they were always too late. The rapid concessions of England were outstripped by the more rapid exactions of the colonies; and the commissioners returned with the melancholy history, that they had humbled themselves before the rebels in vain. If you ever mean to concede at all, do it when every concession will be received as a favour. To wait till you are forced to treat, is as mean in principle as it is dangerous in effect.

Edinburgh Review 1827

In 1837 Sydney preached a Sermon on the Duties of the Queen in St Paul's Cathedral:

I hope the Queen will love the National Church, and protect it; but it must be impressed upon her mind, that every sect of Christians have as perfect right to the free exercise of their worship as the Church itself – that there must be no invasion of the privileges of other sects, and no contemptuous disrespect of their feelings – that the altar is the very ark and citadel of freedom.

Some persons represent old age as miserable, because it brings with it the pains and infirmities of the body; but what gratification to the mind may not old age bring with it in this country of wise and rational improvement? I have lived to see the immense improvements of the Church of England – all its powers of persecution destroyed – its monopoly of civil offices expunged from the book of the law, and all its unjust and exclusive immunities levelled to the ground. The Church of England is now a rational object of love and admiration – it is perfectly compatible with civil freedom – it is an institution for worshipping God, and not a cover for gratifying secular insolence, and ministering to secular ambition. It will be the duty of those to whom the sacred trust of instructing our youthful Queen is instrusted, to lead her attention to these great improvements in our religious establishments; and to show to her how possible, and how wise it is, to render the solid advantages of a national Church compatible with the civil rights of those who cannot assent to its doctrines.

Then again, our youthful Ruler must be very slow to believe all the exaggerated and violent abuse which religious sects indulge in against each other. She will find, for instance, that the Catholics, the great object of our horror and aversion, have (mistaken as they are) a great deal more to say in defence of their tenets than those imagine who indulge more in the luxury of invective than in the labour of inquiry – she will find in that sect, men as enlightened, talents as splendid, and probity as firm, as in our own Church: and she will soon learn to appreciate, at its just value, that exaggerated hatred of sects which paints the Catholic faith (the religion of two thirds of Europe) as utterly incompatible with the safety, peace, and order of the world.

On 31 January, 1844 Sydney wrote to Mrs Grote

'If I take this dose of calomel, shall I be well immediately?' 'Certainly not,' replies the physician. 'You have been in bed these six weeks; how can you expect such a sudden cure? But I can tell you you will never be well without it, and that it will tend materially to the establishment of your health.' So, the pay to the Catholic Clergy. They will not be immediately satisfied by the measure but, they will never be satisfied without it, and it will have a considerable tendency to produce that effect. It will not supersede other medicines, but it is an indispensable preliminary to them.

This was the substance of the fragment on the Irish Roman Catholic Church, found among his papers after his death.

The revenue of the Irish Roman Catholic Church is made up of half-pence, potatoes, rags, bones, and fragments of old clothes; and those, Irish old clothes. They worship often in hovels, or in the open air, from the *want* of any place of worship. Their religion is the religion of three fourths of the population! Not far off, in a well-windowed and well-roofed house, is a well-paid Protestant clergyman, preaching to stools and hassocks, and crying in the wilderness; near him the clerk, near him the sexton, near him the sexton's wife – furious against the errors of Popery, and willing to lay down their lives for the great truths established at the Diet of Augsburg.

There is a story in the Leinster family which passes under the name of 'She is not well.'

A Protestant clergyman, whose church was in the neighbourhood, was a guest at the house of that upright and excellent man the Duke of Leinster. He had been staying there three or four days; and on Saturday night, as they were all retiring to their rooms, the Duke said, 'We shall meet tomorrow at breakfast.' – 'Not so' (said our Milesian Protestant); 'your hour, my lord, is a little too late for me; I am very particular in the discharge of my duty, and your breakfast will interfere with my Church.' The Duke was pleased with the very proper excuses of his guest, and they separated for the night; – his Grace perhaps deeming his palace more safe from all the evils of life for containing in its bosom such an exemplary son of the Church. The first person, however, whom the Duke saw in the morning upon entering the breakfast-room was our punctual Protestant, deep in rolls and butter, his finger in an egg, and a large slice of the best Tipperary ham secured on his plate. 'Delighted to see you, my dear Vicar,' said the Duke, 'but I must say as much surprised as delighted.' – 'Oh, don't you know what has happened?' said the sacred breakfaster. '*She is not well.*' – 'Who is not well?' said the Duke: 'you are not married – you have no sister living – I'm quite uneasy; tell me who is not well.' – 'Why the fact is, my lord Duke, that my congregation consists of the clerk, the sexton, and the sexton's wife. Now the sexton's wife is in very delicate health: when she cannot attend, we cannot muster the number mentioned in the rubric; and we have, therefore, no service on that day. The good woman had a cold and sore throat this morning, and, as I breakfasted but slightly, I thought I might as well hurry back to the regular family dejeuner.' I don't know that the gentleman behaved improperly; but such a church is hardly worth an insurrection and civil war every ten years.

Daniel O'Connell strove for the repeal of the 1800 Act of Union which made Ireland and England one kingdom. Sydney disagreed with him.

What is the object of all government? The object of all government is roast mutton, potatoes, claret, a stout constable, an honest justice, a clear highway, a free chapel. What trash to be bawling in the streets about the Green Isle, the Isle of the Ocean; the bold anthem of *Erin go bragh*! A far better anthem would be Erin go bread and cheese, Erin go cabins that will keep out the rain, Erin go pantaloons without holes in them! What folly to be making eternal declamations about governing yourselves! If laws are good and well administered, is it worth while to rush into war and rebellion in order that no better laws may be made in another place? Are you an Eton boy, who has just come out, full of Plutarch's Lives, and considering in every case how Epaminondas or Philopoemen would have acted, or are you our own dear Daniel, drilled in all the business and bustle of life? I am with you heart and soul in my detestation of all injustice done to Ireland. Your priests shall be fed and paid, the liberties of your Church be scrupulously guarded, and in civil affairs the most even justice be preserved between Catholic and Protestant. Thus far I am a thorough rebel as well as yourself; but when you come to the perilous nonsense of *Repeal*, in common with every honest man who has five grains of common sense, I take my leave.

It turns out that there is no law to prevent entering into diplomatic engagements with the Pope. The sooner we become acquainted with a gentleman who has so much to say to eight million of our subjects the better! Can any thing be so childish and absurd as a horror of communicating with the Pope, and all the hobgoblins we have imagined of premunires and outlawries for this contraband trade in piety? Our ancestors (strange to say wiser than ourselves) have left us to do as we please, and the sooner Government do, what they *can* do legally, the better. A thousand opportunities of doing good in Irish affairs have been lost, from our having no avowed and dignified agent at the Court of Rome. If it depended upon me, I would send the Duke of Devonshire there to-morrow, with nine chaplains and several tons of Protestant theology. I have no love of popery, but the Pope is at all events better than the idol of Juggernaut, whose chaplains I believe we pay, and whose chariot I dare say is made in Long Acre. We pay £10,000 a year to our ambassador at Constantinople, and are startled with the idea of communicating diplomatically with Rome, deeming the

Sultan a better Christian than the Pope!

I maintain that it is shocking and wicked to leave the religious guides of six millions of people in such a state of destitution! – to bestow no more thought upon them than upon the clergy of the Sandwich Islands! If I were a member of the Cabinet, and met my colleagues once a week to eat birds and beasts, and to talk over the state of the world, I should begin upon Ireland before the soup was finished, go on through fish, turkey, and saddle of mutton, and never end till the last thimbleful of claret had passed down the throat of the incredulous Haddington: but there they sit, week after week; there they come, week after week; the Piccadilly Mars, the Scotch Neptune, Themis Lyndhurst, the Tamworth Baronet, dear Goody, and dearer Gladdy, and think no more of paying the Catholic clergy, than a man of real fashion does of paying his tailor! And there is no excuse for this in fanaticism. There is only one man in the Cabinet who objects from reasons purely fanatical, because the Pope is the Scarlet Lady, or the Seventh Vial, or the Little Horn. All the rest are entirely of opinion that it *ought* to be done – that it is the one thing needful; but they are afraid of bishops, and county meetings, newspapers, and pamphlets, and reviews; all fair enough objects of apprehension, but they must be met, and encountered, and put down. It is impossible that the subject can be much longer avoided, and that every year is to produce a deadly struggle with the people, and a long trial in time of peace with O' somebody, the patriot for the time being, or the general, perhaps, in time of a foreign war.

We consider the Irish clergy as factious, and as encouraging the bad anti-British spirit of the people. How can it be otherwise? They live by the people; they have nothing to live upon but the voluntary oblations of the people; and they must fall into the same spirit as the people, or they would be starved to death. No marriage; no mortuary masses; no unctions to the priest who preached against O'Connell!

Give the clergy a maintenance separate from the will of the people, and you will then enable them to oppose the folly and madness of the people. The objection to the State provision does not really come from the clergy, but from the agitators and repealers: these men see the immense advantage of carrying the clergy with them in their agitation, and of giving the sanction of religion to political hatred; they know that the clergy, moving in the same direction with the people, have an immense influence over them; and they are very wisely afraid, not only of losing this co-operating power, but of seeing it, by a State provision, arrayed against them. I am fully convinced that a State payment to the Catholic clergy, by leaving to that laborious and useful body of men the exercise of their free judgment, would be the severest blow that Irish agitation could receive.

For advancing these opinions, I have no doubt I shall be assailed by Sacerdos, Vindex, Latimer, Vates, Clericus, Aruspex, and be called atheist, deist, democrat, smuggler, poacher, highwayman, Unitarian, and Edinburgh reviewer! Still, *I am in the right*, – and what I say, requires excuse for being trite and obvious, not for being mischievous and para-doxical. I write for three reasons: first, because I really wish to do good; secondly, because if I don't write, I know nobody else will; and thirdly, because it is the nature of the animal to write, and I cannot help it. Still, in looking back I see no reason to repent. What I have said *ought* to be done, generally *has* been done, but always twenty or thirty years too late; done, not of course because I have said it, but because it was no longer *possible* to avoid doing it. Human beings cling to their delicious tyrannies, and to their exquisite nonsense, like a drunkard to his bottle, and go on till death stares them in the face. The monstrous state of the Catholic church in Ireland will probably remain till some monstrous ruin threat-ens the very existence of the Empire, and Lambeth and Fulham are cursed by the affrighted people.

Fragment

I have always compared the Protestant Church in Ireland (and I believe my friend Thomas Moore stole the simile from me) to the institution of butchers' shops in all the villages of our Indian empire. 'We *will* have a butcher's shop in every village, and you, Hindoos, shall pay for it. We know that many of you do not eat meat at all, and that the sight of beef-steaks is particularly offensive to you; but still, a stray European may pass through your village, and want a steak or a chop: the shop *shall* be established; and you shall pay for it.' This is English legislation for Ireland!! There is no abuse like it in all Europe, in all Asia, in all the discovered parts of Africa, and in all we have heard of Timbuctoo! It is an error that requires 20,000 armed men for its protection in time of peace; which costs more than a million a year; and which, in the first French war, in spite of the puffing and panting of fighting steamers, will and *must* break out into desperate rebellion.

The less a clergyman exacts of his people, – the more his

payments are kept out of sight, the less will be the friction with which he exercises the functions of his office. A poor Catholic may respect a priest the more who marries, baptizes, and anoints; but he respects him because he associates with his name and character the performance of sacred duties, not because he exacts heavy fees for doing so. Double fees would be a very doubtful cure for scepticism; and though we have often seen the tenth of the earth's produce carted away for the benefit of the clergyman, we do not remember any very lively marks of satisfaction and delight which it produced in the countenance of the decimated person. I am thoroughly convinced that State payments to the Catholic clergy would remove a thousand causes of hatred between the priest and his flock, and would be as favourable to the increase of his useful authority, as it would be fatal to his factious influence over the people.

In his biography *The Smith of Smiths*, Hesketh Pearson passes this verdict:

If Sydney's advice had been taken, and the Catholic clergy had been paid, another century's hatred and bloodshed would have been avoided, and Ireland would never have become a republic.

XIII

Health and Happiness

Sydney believed that men were meant to be happy. So many seemed set on preventing their own attainment of happiness or that of others by false religion and morality (see his comments on the Society for the Suppression of Vice, Chapter 6), or, – and on this he dwells from his own experience – by over indulgence in food and drink, shared largely in his day by those who could afford such. In his letters, and the conversations and notes included in his daughter's *Memoir*, we find his understanding of the nature of happiness, and, since he was convinced of the close connection between health and happiness, a deal of medical matters.

A LITTLE MORAL ADVICE:
A Fragment on the Cultivation and Improvement
of the Animal Spirits.

It is surprising to see for what foolish causes men hang themselves. The most silly repulse, the most trifling ruffle of temper, or derangement of stomach, anything seems to justify an appeal to the razor or the cord. I have a contempt for persons who destroy themselves. Live on, and look evil in the face; walk up to it, and often you will not find it at all; for it will recede as you advance. Any fool may be a suicide. When you are in a melancholy fit, first suspect the body, appeal to rhubarb and calomel, and send for the apothecary; a little bit of gristle sticking in the wrong place, an untimely consumption of custard, excessive gooseberries, often cover the mind with clouds and bring on the most distressing views of human life.

I start up at two o'clock in the morning, after my first sleep, in an agony of terror, and feel all the weight of life upon my soul. It is impossible that I can bring up such a family of children, my sons and daughters will be beggars; I shall live to see those whom I love exposed to the scorn and contumely of the world! – But stop, thou child of sorrow, and humble imitator of Job, and tell me on what you dined. Was not there soup and salmon, and then a plate of beef, and then duck, blanc-mange, cream cheese, diluted with beer, claret, champagne, hock, tea, coffee, and noyeau? And after all this, you talk of the *mind* and the evils of life! These kind of cases do not need meditation, but magnesia. Take short views of life. What am I to do in these times with such a family of children? So I argued, and lived dejected and with little hope; but the difficulty vanished as life went on. An uncle died, and left me some money; an aunt died, and left me more; my daughter married well; I had two or three appointments, and before life was half over became a prosperous man. And so will you. Every one has uncles and aunts who are mortal; friends start up out of the earth; time brings a thousand chances in your favour; legacies fall from the clouds. Nothing so absurd as to sit down and wring your hands because all the good which may happen to you in twenty years has not taken place at this precise moment.

The greatest happiness which can happen to any one is to cultivate a love of reading. Study is often dull because it is improperly managed. I make no apology for speaking of myself, for as I write anonymously nobody knows who I am, and if I did not, very few would be the wiser – but every man speaks more firmly when he speaks from his own experience. I read four books at a time; some classical book perhaps on Monday, Wednesday, and Friday mornings. The 'History of France,' we will say, on the evenings of the same days. On Tuesday, Thursday, and Saturday, Mosheim or Lardner, and in the evening of those days, Reynolds' Lectures, or Burns' Travels. Then I have always a standing book of poetry, and a novel to read when I am in the humour to read nothing else. Then I translate some French into English one day, and re-translate it the next; so that I have seven or eight pursuits going on at the same time, and this produces the cheerfulness of diversity, and avoids that gloom which proceeds from hanging a long while over a single book. I do not recommend this as a receipt for becoming a learned man, but for becoming a cheerful one.

Nothing contributes more certainly to the animal spirits than benevolence. Servants and common people are always about you; make moderate attempts to please everybody, and the effort will insensibly lead you to a more happy state of mind. Pleasure is very reflective, and if you give it you will feel it. The pleasure you give by kindness of manner returns to you, and often with compound interest. The receipt for cheerfulness is not to have one motive only in the day for living, but a number of little motives; a man who from the time he rises till bedtime conducts himself like a gentleman, who throws some little condescension into his manner to superiors, and who is always contriving to soften the distance between himself and the poor and ignorant, is always improving his animal spirits, and adding to his happiness.

I recommend lights as a great improver of animal spirits. How is it possible to be happy with two mould candles ill-snuffed? You may be virtuous, and wise, and good, but two candles will not do for animal spirits. Every night the room in which I sit is lighted up like a town after a great naval victory, and in this cereous galaxy and with a blazing fire, it is scarcely possible to be low-spirited, a thousand pleasing images spring up in the mind, and I can see the little blue demons scampering off like parish boys pursued by the beadle.

MANAGEMENT OF THE BODY:
Digestion the Secret of Life

The longer I live, the more I am convinced that the apothecary is of more importance than Seneca; and that half the unhappiness in the world proceeds from little stoppages, from a duct choked up, from food pressing in the wrong place, from a vext duodenum, or an agitated pylorus.

The deception, as practised upon human creatures, is curious and entertaining. My friend sups late; he eats some strong soup, then a lobster, then some tart, and he dilutes these esculent varieties with wine. The next day I call upon him. He is going to sell his house in London, and to retire into the country. He is alarmed for his eldest daughter's health. His expenses are hourly increasing, and nothing but a timely retreat can save him from ruin. All this is the lobster: and when over-excited nature has had time to manage this testaceous encumbrance, the daughter recovers, the finances are in good order, and every rural idea effectually excluded from the mind.

In the same manner old friendships are destroyed by toasted cheese, and hard salted meat has led to suicide. Unpleasant feelings of the body produce correspondent sensations in the mind, and a great scene of wretchedness is sketched out by a morsel of indigestible and misguided food. Of such infinite consequence to happiness is it to study the body!

I have nothing new to say upon the management which the body requires. The common rules are the best: – exercise without fatigue; generous living without excess; early rising, and moderation in sleeping. These are the apothegms of old women; but if they are not attended to, happiness becomes so extremely difficult that very few persons can attain to it. In this point of view, the care of the body becomes a subject of elevation and importance. A walk in the fields, an hour's less sleep, may remove all those bodily vexations and disquietudes which are such formidable enemies to virtue;

and may enable the mind to pursue its own resolves without that constant train of temptations to resist, and obstacles to overcome, which it always experiences from the bad organisation of its companion. Johnson says, every man is a rascal when he is sick; meaning, I suppose, that he had no benevolent dispositions at that period towards his fellow-creatures, but that his notions assume a character of greater affinity to his bodily feelings, and that, *feeling* pain, he becomes malevolent; and if this be true of great diseases, it is true in a less degree of the smaller ailments of the body.

Get up in a morning, walk before breakfast, pass four or five hours of the day in some active employment; then eat and drink over-night, lie in bed till one or two o'clock, saunter away the rest of the day in doing nothing! – can any two human beings be more perfectly dissimilar than the same individual under these two different systems of corporeal management? and is it not of as great importance towards happiness to pay a minute attention to the body, as it is to study the wisdom of Chrysippus and Crantor?

Lady Holland, *Memoir*

I am convinced digestion is the great secret of life; and that character, talents, virtues and qualities are powerfully affected by beef, mutton, piecrust, and rich soups. I have often thought I could feed or starve men into many virtues and vices, and affect them more powerfully with my instruments of cookery than Timotheus could do formerly with his lyre.

Letter to Arthur Kinglake, 30 September, 1837

You are, I hear, attending more to diet than heretofore. If you wish for anything like happiness in the fifth act of life, eat and drink about one-half what you *could* eat and drink. Did I ever tell you my calculation about eating and drinking? Having ascertained the weight of what I could live upon, so as to preserve health and strength, and what I did live upon, I found that, between ten and seventy years of age, I had eaten and drunk forty four-horse waggon-loads of meat and drink more than would have preserved me in life and health! The value of this mass of nourishment I considered to be worth seven thousand pounds sterling. It occurred to me that I must, by my voracity, have starved to death fully a hundred persons. This is a frightful calculation, but irresistibly true; and I think, dear Murray, your waggons would require an additional horse each!

Letter to J. A. Murray, 29 September, 1843

The weather also has its effect!

Very high and very low temperatures extinguish all human

sympathy and relations. It is impossible to feel any affection beyond 78 and below 20 Farenheit; human nature is too solid or too liquid beyond these limits. Man only lives to shiver or to perspire. God send that the glass may fall, and restore me to my regard for you which in the temperate zone is invariable.　　　　To Lady Georgiana Morpeth Melancholy commonly flies to the future for its aliment, and must be encountered in this sort of artifice by diminishing the range of our views. I have a large family coming on, my income is diminishing, and I shall fall into pecuniary difficulties. Well! but you are not now in pecuniary difficulties. Your eldest child is only seven years old; it must be two or three years before your family make any additional demands on your purse. Wait till the time comes. Much may happen in the interval to better your situation; and if nothing does happen, at least enjoy two or three years of ease and uninterruption which are before you. You are uneasy about your eldest son in india; but it is now June, and at the earliest the fleet will not come in till September; it may bring accounts of his prosperity, but at all events there are eight or nine weeks before you can hear news. Why are they to be spent as if you had heard the worst? The habit of taking very short views of human life may be acquired by degrees, and a great sum of happiness is gained by it. It becomes as customary at last to view things on the good side of the question as it was before to despond and to extract misery from every passing event.　　　　Lady Holland, *Memoir*

Reading and being occupied

He was accustomed to declare that he was at a loss to understand how any reflecting man could trust himself in the solitude of the country without clinging to the love of knowledge as his sheet anchor. He held that, though the best books were apt to become a little languid and soporific at times, there was at least this advantage over conversation, that a man and his book generally kept the peace with tolerable success, and that if they did quarrel, the man could at all events shut his book and toss it into a corner of the room – an action not always quite so safe or easy to do in the case of a living folio.

Stuart Reid, *The Life and Times of Sydney Smith* 1896

To his first pupil, Michael Hicks Beach, he wrote c.1800

I hope you sometimes take a book in hand; and as I have often told you – to enjoy the pleasures of doing nothing, we must do something. Idle people know nothing of the pleasures of idleness; it is a very difficult accomplishment to acquire in perfection.

OF OCCUPATION.

A good stout bodily machine being provided, we must be actively occupied, or there can be little happiness.

If a good useful occupation be *not* provided, it is so ungenial to the human mind to do nothing, that men occupy themselves *perilously*, as with gaming; or *frivolously*, as with walking up and down a street at a watering-place, and looking at the passers-by; or *malevolently*, as by teazing their wives and children. It is impossible to support, for any length of time, a state of perfect *ennui*; and if you were to shut a man up for any length of time within four walls, without occupation, he would go mad. If idleness do not produce vice or malevolence, it commonly produces melancholy.

A stockbroker or a farmer have no leisure for imaginary wretchedness; their minds are usually hurried away by the necessity of noticing external objects, and they are guaranteed from that curse of idleness, the eternal disposition to think of themselves.

If we have no necessary occupation, it becomes extremely difficult to make to ourselves occupations as entirely absorbing as those which necessity imposes.

The profession which a man makes for himself is seldom more than a half profession, and often leaves the mind in a state of vacancy and inoccupation. We must lash ourselves up however, as well as we can, to a notion of its great importance; and as the dispensing power is in our own hands, we must be very jealous of remission and of idleness.

It may seem absurd that a gentleman who does not live by the profits of farming should rise at six o'clock in the morning to look after his farm; or, if botany be his object, that he should voyage to Iceland in pursuit of it. He is the happier however for his eagerness; his mind is more fully employed, and he is much more effectually guaranteed from all the miseries of *ennui*.

When a very clever man, or a very great man, takes to cultivating turnips and retiring, it is generally an imposture. The moment men cease to talk of their turnips, they are wretched and full of self-reproach. Let every man be *occupied*, and occupied in the highest employment of which his nature is capable, and die with the consciousness that *he has done his best*!   Lady Holland, *Memoir*

Benevolence

Sydney practised what he preached and was loved by his children and servants, by the poor in his parish as well as his well to do friends. His daughter, Saba, provides instances in her Memoir of his kindness to his parishioners; his letters provide ample evidence of the pleasure he gave to his friends.

'After luncheon may I have the honour of driving you round my wood?' (addressing one of the ladies). 'David, bring me my hat.' And with his crutch-stick in his hand, he sallied forth into his parish. My father writes, 'I lay a particular stress upon visiting the poor in person. He who only knows the miseries of mankind at second-hand and by description has but a faint idea of what is really suffered in the world.' He practised diligently what he preached, and always seemed to carry comfort and pleasure into every cottage he entered, for he brought what the poor value so highly, and so seldom obtain – *sympathy*. He appeared, and was, interested in their concerns. When he sat down in a cottage, nothing escaped his eye: Solomon's Temple in rockwork, – the Prodigal Son on the wall, – the old woman in the inglenook, – the dirty, rosy infant on the floor, all came in for a share of his notice.

'Why, John, I took you for a general officer at least, in that new red waistcoat; but, John, I think there is a touch of pride in those brass buttons, don't you?' 'Na, your honour, there beant,' said John, highly gratified, and grinning from ear to ear. 'Well, and how do you do?' to the old woman. 'Oh! the stuff your honour sent did me a world of good.' 'Ah, I thought it would reach the right *spot*, Dame; well, then, you must send the bottle for some more.'

'At this time,' writes Mrs Marcet, 'he was in the habit of spending half an hour every morning with a young workman who was in the last stage of consumption; 'part of that time,' he said, 'was spent in preparing him for another world, and part in endeavouring to render his last days in this as cheerful and as happy as he could.' He used to stop and talk to the children of the village as he passed along the road. He always kept a box of sugar-plums in his pocket for these occasions, and often some rosy-faced urchin was made happy by sharing its contents, or obtaining a penny to buy a tart. 'Let it be large and full of juice, Johnny,' he would say, 'so that it may run down both corners of the mouth.' Stopping another: 'What do you call me? who am I?' 'Why, we calls you the Parson Doctor.' 'Oh, you little rogue!' pinching his cheek smilingly, and holding up his fist at him, 'I will send you a dose when I go home.'

Sydney's daughter, Saba, provides an example of his tact:

> After our settlement at Foston, an old lady, the widow of an artist, a woman of some fortune, large dimensions, considerable talents, and much oddity, came to establish herself in a small cottage at no great distance, and was so delighted with her neighbour, that she kindly offered to drop in (as she said) frequently to tea. My father, though the most sociable of human beings, felt rather alarmed at this threatened invasion of his privacy; yet, unwilling to hurt the old lady, he at last bethought himself of writing to her a most comical letter, full of all sorts of imaginary facts, accepting her offer, only begging to have full notice of her approach: 'for,' said he, 'at home I sit in an old coat, which may have a hole in it; now I like to appear before you in my best. When alone we have the black kettle, we should have the urn for you; Bunch would have on her clean apron and her hair brushed, etc. etc.' This answered very well for both parties.

A comfortable house

> From thence to Lambton. And here I ask, what use of wealth so luxurious and delightful as to light your house with gas? What folly, to have a diamond necklace or a Correggio, and not to light your house with gas! The splendour and glory of Lambton Hall make all other houses mean. How pitiful to submit to a farthing-candle existence, when science puts such intense gratification within your reach! Dear lady, spend all your fortune in a gas-apparatus. Better to eat dry bread by the splendour of gas than to dine on wild beef with wax candles. Letter to Lady Mary Bennet

> My dear Murray,
> Jeffrey has written to me to say he means to dedicate his Essays to me. This I think a very great honour, and it pleases me very much. I am sure he ought to resign. He has very feeble health; a mild climate would suit the state of his throat. Mrs Jeffrey thinks he could not employ himself. Wives know a great deal about husbands; but, if she is right, I should be surprised. I have thought he had a canine appetite for books, though this sometimes declines in the decline of life. I am beautifying my house in Green-street; a comfortable house is a great source of happiness. It ranks immediately after health and a good conscience.
> Cheerfulness and good spirits depend in a great degree upon bodily causes, but much may be done for the promotion of this turn of mind. Persons subject to low spirits should

make the rooms in which they live as cheerful as possible; taking care that the paper with which the wall is covered should be of a brilliant, lively colour, hanging up pictures or prints, and covering the chimney-piece with beautiful china. A bay-window looking upon pleasant objects, and, above all, a large fire whenever the weather will permit, are favourable to good spirits, and the tables near should be strewed with books and pamphlets. To this must be added as much eating and drinking as is consistent with health; and some manual employment for men, – as gardening, a carpenter's shop, the turning-lathe, &c. Women have always manual employment enough, and it is a great source of cheerfulness. Fresh air, exercise, occupation, society and travelling are powerful remedies.

Friendship the greatest source of happiness

Life is to be fortified by many friendships. To love, and to be loved, is the greatest happiness of existence. If I lived under the burning sun of the equator, it would be a pleasure to me to think that there were many human beings on the other side of the world who regarded and respected me; I could and would not live if I were alone upon the earth, and cut off from the remembrance of my fellow-creatures. It is not that a man has occasion often to fall back upon the kindness of his friends; perhaps he may never experience the necessity of doing so; but we are governed by our imaginations, and they stand there as a solid and impregnable bulwark against all the evils of life.

Friendships should be formed with persons of all ages and conditions, and with both sexes. I have a friend who is a bookseller, to whom I have been very civil, and who would do anything to serve me; and I have two or three small friendships among persons in much humbler walks of life, who, I verily believe, would do me a considerable kindness according to their means. It is a great happiness to form a sincere friendship with a woman; but a friendship among persons of different sexes rarely or ever takes place in this country. The austerity of our manners hardly admits of such a connection; – compatible with the most perfect innocence, and a source of the highest possible delight to those who are fortunate enough to form it.   Lady Holland, *Memoir*

Sydney's women friends meant much to him. One such was Mrs Austin who made the first collection of his letters, published conjointly with Lady Holland's *Memoir*. In 1836 he wrote to her, 'If I am remov'd by an indigestion, retain some good natur'd recollections of an ecclesiastic who knows your value, – likes your society, and who would have been very much in love with you – if common sense – and all laws human and divine had not guarded him from an accident so formidable.'

Sydney made some of his best friends in Edinburgh and kept them the rest of his life, and indeed hoped still to enjoy them in the next. Leaving Edinburgh for London, he wrote, 'My good fortune will be very great if I should ever again fall into the society of so liberal, correct, and instructed men, and live with them on such terms of friendship as I have done.'

Sydney's friends were inevitably a source of laughter, but he was never unkind and none took offence. In her Autobiography Harriet Martineau writes,

I do not believe that any body ever took amiss his quizzical descriptions of his friends. I am sure I never did: and when I now recal his fun of that sort, it seems to me too innocent to raise an uneasy feeling. There were none, I believe, whom he did not quizz; but I never heard of any hurt feelings. He did not like precipitate speech; and among the fastest talkers in England were certain of his friends and acquaintance; – Mr Hallam, Mr Empson, Dr Whewell, Mr Macaulay and myself. None of us escaped his wit. His account of Mr Empson's method of out-pouring stands, without the name, in Lady Holland's Life of her father. His praise of Macaulay is well known: – 'Macaulay is improved! Macaulay improves! I have observed in him of late, – flashes of silence!' His account of Whewell is something more than wit: – 'Science is his forte: omniscience is his foible.' As for his friend Hallam, he knew he might make free with his characteristics, of oppugnancy and haste among others, without offence, In telling us what a blunder he himself made in going late to a dinner-party, and describing how far the dinner had proceeded, and how every body was engaged, he said, 'And there was Hallam, with his mouth full of cabbage and contradiction!' Nothing could be droller than his description of all his friends in influenza, in the winter of 1832-3; and of these, Hallam was the drollest of all that I remember. 'And poor Hallam was tossing and tumbling in his bed when the watchman came by and called 'Twelve o'clock and a starlight night.' Here was an opportunity for controversy when it seemed most out of the question! Up jumped Hallam, with 'I question that, – I question that! Starlight! I see a star, I admit; but I doubt whether that constituted starlight.' Hours more of tossing and tumbling; and then comes the watchman again: 'Past two o'clock, and a cloudy morning.' 'I question that, – I question that,' says Hallam. And he rushes to the window, and throws up the sash, – influenza notwithstanding. 'Watchman! do you mean to call this a cloudy morning? I see a star. And I question its being past two o'clock: I question it, – I question it!" And so on.

In his old age Sydney wrote to Lady Holland,

It is a bore, I admit, to be past seventy, for you are left for execution, and are daily expecting the death-warrant; but, as you say, it is not anything very capital we quit. We are, at the close of life, only hurried away from stomach-aches, pains in the joints, from sleepless nights and unamusing days, from weakness, ugliness, and nervous tremors; but we shall all meet again in another planet, cured of all our defects. Rogers will be less irritable; Macaulay more silent; Hallam will assent; Jeffrey will speak slower; Bobus will be just as he is; I shall be more respectful to the upper clergy; but I shall have as lively a sense as I now have of all your kindness and affection for me.

One of Sydney's dear friends was Georgiana, Viscountess Morpeth, who suffered from depression. In his letter to her on cures for depression he reiterates a number of his recipes for Health and Happiness.

Foston, Feb. 16th, 1820

Dear Lady Georgiana,

Nobody has suffered more from low spirits than I have done – so I feel for you.

1st. Live as well (and drink as much wine) as you dare.

2nd. Go into the shower-bath with a small quantity of water at a temperature low enough to give you a slight sensation of cold, 75° or 80°.

3rd. Amusing books.

4th. Short views of human life – not further than dinner or tea.

5th. Be as busy as you can.

6th. See as much as you can of those friends who respect and like you.

7th. And of those acquaintances who amuse you.

8th. Make no secret of low spirits to your friends, but talk of them freely – they are always worse for dignified concealment.

9th. Attend to the effects tea and coffee produce upon you.

10th. Compare your lot with that of other people.

11th. Don't expect too much from human life – a sorry business at the best.

12th. Avoid poetry, dramatic representations (except comedy), music, serious novels, melancholy sentimental people, and everything likely to excite feeling or emotion not ending in active benevolence.

13th. *Do good*, and endeavour to please everybody of every degree.
14th. Be as much as you can in the open air without fatigue.
15th. Make the room where you commonly sit, gay and pleasant.
16th. Struggle by little and little against idleness.
17. Don't be too severe upon yourself, or underrate yourself, but do yourself justice.
18th. Keep good blazing fires.
19th. Be firm and constant in the exercise of rational religion.
20th. Believe me, dear Lady Georgiana.

Dining and Dosing

Sydney enjoyed dining out, and was constantly being invited to do so, especially when in London. He delighted, not only in company, but in food, and was himself no mean chef, – his verse recipe for salad became very popular. 'Of the tribe of Falstaff', his girth increased with age. Gout afflicted him and he sought to relieve it. Several letters express his gratitude for gifts of food.

Foston, Sept. 1817

Dear Davenport,
You have no idea what a number of handsome things were said of you when your six partridges were consumed today. Wit, literature, and polished manners were ascribed to you – some good quality for each bird. You never met with a more favourable jury. I conclude the *éloge* with my best thanks for your kind and flattering attention. We all, however, objected to your equipage; longevity is incompatible with driving two horses at length. Man is frequently cut off even in buggies; an inch to the right or the left may send you to the Davenports of ages past, and put half Cheshire in mourning.

Ever most truly yours
Sydney Smith

A Postscript to Mrs Baring about the gift of a bottle of wine
Many thanks. It shall have a week of forbearance, and shall then descend into that ancient and venerable depository for wine – the stomach of the priest.

His 'Recipe for a Salade'
To make this condiment your poet begs
The pounded yellow of two hard-boiled eggs;
Two boiled potatoes, passed through kitchen sieve,
Smoothness and softness to the salad give.
Let onion atoms lurk within the bowl,

And, half-suspected, animate the whole.
Of mordant mustard add a single spoon,
Distrust the condiment that bites so soon;
But deem it not, thou man of herbs, a fault
To add a double quantity of salt;
Four times the spoon with oil of Lucca crown,
And twice with vinegar procured from town;
And lastly o'er the flavoured compound toss
A magic soupçon of anchovy sauce.
Oh, green and glorious! Oh, herbaceous treat!
'Twould tempt the dying anchorite to eat;
Back to the world he'd turn his fleeting soul,
And plunge his fingers in the salad-bowl!
Serenely full, the epicure would say,
'Fate cannot harm me, I have dined today'.

The consequence of dining out

In 1840 Sydney wrote from London to Richard York that 'I dine out eight or nine times every week. If people will talk across the table it is agreeable but I hate whispering to the lady next to me – when I have asked her whether she has lately been to the opera, I am knocked up entirely and don't know what else to say – and I know she hates me for being a large fat parson and for not [being] slim and elegant. One of the greatest evils of old age is the advance of the stomach over the rest of the body. It looks like the accumulation of thousands of dinners and luncheons. It looks like a pregnant woman in a cloth waistcoat and as if I were near my time and might reasonably look for twins.'

The primary punishment was gout. He writes to Lady Carlisle in 1840

I am pretty well, except gout, asthma, and pains in all the bones, and all the flesh, of my body. What a very singular disease gout is! It seems as if the stomach fell down into the feet. The smallest deviation from right diet is immediately punished by limping and lameness, and the innocent ankle and blameless instep are tortured for the vices of the nobler organs. The stomach having found this easy way of getting rid of inconveniences, becomes cruelly despotic, and punishes for the least offences. A plum, a glass of champagne, excess in joy, excess in grief, – any crime, however small, is sufficient for redness, swelling spasms, and large shoes.

Dieting continued to be necessary, and in 1844 he writes again:

My dear Lady Carlisle,

From your ancient goodness to me, I am sure you will be glad to receive a bulletin from myself, informing you that I am making a good progress; in fact, I am in a regular train of promotion from gruel, vermicelli, and sago, I was promoted to panada, from thence to minced meat, and (such is the effect of good conduct) I was elevated to a mutton-chop. My breathlessness and giddiness are gone – chased away by the gout. If you hear of sixteen or eighteen pounds of human flesh, they belong to me. I look as if a curate had been taken out of me. I am delighted to hear such improved accounts of my fellow-sufferer at Castle Howard. Lady Holland is severe in her medical questions; but I detail the most horrible symptoms, at which she takes flight.

and to Harriet Martineau

My dear Miss Martineau, – What an admirable provision of Providence is the gout! What prevents human beings from making the body a larder or a cellar, but the gout? When I feel a pang, I say, 'I know what this is for. I know what you mean. I understand the hint!' and so I endeavour to extract a little wisdom from pain.   Sydney Smith

'You must take a walk on an empty stomach,' Rogers declares was the advice of Sydney Smith's medical man to him on one occasion. The patient quietly looked up with a glance of inquiry, and naïvely uttered but one word – 'Whose?'

Abstaining from 'fermented liquors' helped.

Many thanks my dear Lady Holland for your kind anxiety respecting my health. I not only was never better, but never half so well: indeed I find that I have been very ill all my life without knowing it. Let me state some of the goods arising from abstaining from all fermented liquors. 1st sweet sleep; having never known what sleep was I sleep like a baby or a ploughboy. If I wake, no needless terror, no black views of life, but pleasing hope and pleasing recollection: Holland House, past and to come. If I dream, it is not of lyons and tygers, but of Love* – and Tithes. 2ndly I can take longer walks and make greater exertions without fatigue. My understanding is improved, and I comprehend Political Economy. I see better without wine and spectacles than when I use both. Only one evil ensues from it: I am in such extravagant spirits that I must loose blood, or look out for some one who will bore and depress me. Pray leave off wine – the stomach quite at rest; no heartburn, no pain, nor distension.

I am better in health avoiding all fermented Liquors, and drinking nothing but London Water with a million of insects in every drop; he who drinks a tumbler of London Water has literally in his stomach more animated beings than there are men, Women and Children on the face of the Globe.

Doses of colchicum also kept the gout in check, though somewhat uncertainly. On observing some of the autumn crocus in flower he stopped: 'There!' he said, 'who would guess the virtue of that little plant? But I find the power of colchicum so great, that if I feel a little gout coming on, I go into the garden, and hold out my toe to that plant, and it gets well directly. I never do more without orders from head-quarters. Oh! when I have the gout, I feels as if I was walking on my eyeballs.'

In 1842 he wrote to Lady Morgan,

I had last week an attack of gout, which is receding from me (as the bailiff from the house of an half-pay captain) dissatisfied, and terrified by the powers of colchicum.

More Medical Matters

In 1835 Sydney writes from Combe Florey to his son-in-law, Dr (later Sir Henry) Holland.

I am suffering from my old complaint, the Hay-fever (as it is calld). My fear is of perishing by deliquescence. – I melt away in Nasal and Lachrymal profluvia. My remedies are warm Pediluvium, Cathartics, topical application of a watery solution of Opium to eyes ears, and the interior of the nostrils. The membrane is so irritable, that light, dust, contradiction, an absurd remark, the sight of a dissenter, – anything, sets me a sneezing and if I begin sneezing at 12, I don't leave off till two o'clock – and am heard distinctly in Taunton when the wind sets that way at a distance of 6 miles. Turn your mind to this little curse. If Consumption is too powerful for Physicians at least they should not suffer themselves to be outwitted by such little upstart disorders as the Hay-fever.

I am very glad you married my daughter, for I am sure you are both very happy, and I assure you I am proud of my son-in-law.

I have ordered a Brass Knocker against you come and we have a case of Chronic Bronchitis next door – some advanced cases of Dyspepsia not far off – and a considerable promise of acute Rheumatism at no great distance – a neighbouring Squire has water forming on the chest so that I hope <things> will be comfortable and your visit not unpleasant.

I did not think that Copplestone with all his nonsense could have gone down to Tar-water. I have as much belief in it as I have in Holy water. – it is the water has done the business, not the tar. They could not induce the sensual prelate [the Dean of St Paul's] to drink water but by mixing it up with nonsense and disguising the simplicity of the receipt. You must have a pitch battle with him about his tar-water, and teach him what he has never learnt – the rudiments of common sense. Kindest love to dear Saba. Ever your affectionate father

Sydney Smith

Of illness among the aristocracy
Knowing (as you do my dear Lady Grey) Lady Holland so well, and having known her so long, you will I am sure be sorry to hear the misfortune which has befallen her. You know how long she has been alarmed by diseases of the heart; terrified to an agony by some recent death from that cause, she was determined that Brodie should examine the chest thoroughly with a stethoscope. He spent a long time there, bestowed the greatest attention upon the case, and ended with saying that in the course of his practice he had never witnessed a more decided case of healthy circulation, and that she had not a single complaint belonging to her. I have seen her since, and never saw anyone so crestfallen and desponding. She did all she could to get me to help her to some fresh complaint, but I was stubborn.

I saw the other day John Lord Ponsonby who looks old I think but well, he seems in very good Spirits and determined to amuse himself for the rest of his Life, a resolution which I have long since adopted, and which I recommend to you. Quinine is not a greater Specific for ague than Lady Morley is for Lord Grey. She is a very charming remedy and is enough to make any disease popular for which she is prescribed.

Illness must be peculiarly disagreeable to the Duchess of Sutherland, as I take it all Duchesses descend when they die, and there are some peculiar circumstances in the life of that Lady that will certainly not occasion any exemption in her favor. The defunct Duke must by this time be well informed of her infidelities and their first meeting in Tartarus will not therefore be of the most agreeable description.

And among the poor of his parish
Sydney had attended medical lectures in Oxford and during his stay in Edinburgh, and in his parish of Foston he put them to good use, as also his theories about diet.

I know all drugs, all simples and all pills;

I cure diseases, and I send no bills.
The poor old women now no lameness know;
Rheumatics leave their hand, the gout their toe.
Fell atrophy has fled from Foston's vale,
And health, and peace, and joy and love prevail.

Sydney was also much concerned for the general welfare of the poor in his parish. While at Edinburgh, with many opportunities of comparing the common diet of the poor in England and Scotland, he had thought carefully about providing cheap, nourishing food and had written that 'I am in hopes to carry these ideas into execution at some future time, and become master cook, as well as master parson, of my village'. He was convinced by his Scottish experience that the best means of helping them to better their condition was by educating them in the best use of available resources rather than by charitable doles of food.

One of the practical ways in which he helped his parishioners was by dividing several acres of his glebe into sixteenths, and letting them out cheaply – a very early example of a beneficial scheme which later became widespread. His daughter wrote of these plots for the poor (to which Sydney later added 'Dutch gardens for spade cultivation') that 'It becomes quite a pretty sight afterwards to see these small gardens (which were just enough to supply a cottager with potatoes, and sometimes to enable him to keep a pig) filled at dawn with women and children cultivating them before they went to their day's labour.' Late in the century, they were still gratefully remembered as 'Sydney's orchards'. (see Alan Bell *Sydney Smith* 1980)

When a visitor arrived to see his servant, Annie Kay, he delighted in describing his remedies to her:

'Bring me my medicine-book, Annie Kay. Kay is my apothecary's boy, and makes up my medicines.' Kay appears with the book. 'I am a great doctor; would you like to hear some of my medicines?' 'Oh yes, Mr Sydney.' 'There is the Gentlejog, a pleasure to take it, – the Bull-dog, for more serious cases, – Peter's puke, – Heart's delight, the comfort of all the old women in the village, – Rub-a-dub, a capital embrocation, – Dead-stop, settles the matter at once, – Up-with-it then needs no explanation; and so on. Now, Annie Kay, give Mrs Spratt a bottle of Rub-a-dub; and to Mr Coles a dose of Dead-stop and twenty drops of laudanum.'

'This is the house to be ill in' (turning to us); 'indeed everybody who comes is expected to take a little something; I consider it a delicate compliment when my guests have a slight illness here. We have contrivances for everything.

As the 'Parson Doctor' Sydney addressed the minds of his flock also.

I endeavour in vain to give my parishioners more cheerful ideas of religion; to teach them that God is not a jealous, childish, merciless tyrant; that he is best served by a regular tenour of good actions, – not by bad singing, ill-composed prayers, and eternal apprehensions. But the luxury of false religion is, to be unhappy!

Some Rules of Life

Sydney's daughter, Saba, includes in her Memoir of her Father some 'slight, unfinished fragments' from his diary.

MAXIMS AND RULES OF LIFE

Remember that every person, however low, has *rights* and *feelings*. In all contentions, let peace be rather your object, than triumph: value triumph only as the means of peace.

Remember that your children, your wife, and your servants, have rights and feelings; treat them as you would treat persons who could turn again. Apply these doctrines to the administration of justice as a magistrate. Rank poisons make good medicines; error and misfortune may be turned into wisdom and improvement.

Do not attempt to frighten children and inferiors by passion; it does more harm to your own character than it does good to them; the same thing is better done by firmness and persuasion.

If you desire the common people to treat you as a gentleman, you must conduct yourself as a gentleman should do to them.

When you meet with neglect, let it rouse you to exertion, instead of mortifying your pride. Set about lessening those defects which expose you to neglect, and improve those excellences which command attention and respect.

Against general fears, remember how very precarious life is, take what care you will; how short it is, last as long as it ever does.

Rise early in the morning, not only to avoid self-reproach, but to make the most of the little life that remains; not only to save the hours lost in sleep, but to avoid that languor which is spread over mind and body for the whole of that day in which you have lain late in bed.

Passion gets less and less powerful after every defeat. Husband energy for the real demand which the dangers of life make upon it.

Not only is religion calm and tranquil, but it has an extensive atmosphere round it, whose calmness and tranquility must be preserved, if you would avoid misrepresentation.

Find fault, when you must find fault, in private, if possible; and some time after the offence, rather than at the time. The blamed are less inclined to resist, when they are blamed without witnesses; both parties are calmer, and the accused party is struck with the forbearance of the accuser, who has seen the fault, and watched for a private and proper time for mentioning it.

Don't be too severe upon yourself and your own failings; keep on, don't faint, be energetic to the last.

Portrait of Sydney Smith by Briggs, 1840

XIV

Epilogue

The Annual Register for 1845 provided this obituary for Sydney:

When his 'quips and cranks' are lost and forgotten, it will be remembered that he supported the Roman Catholic claims, and that they were conceded; that he strenuously assailed the Game Laws, and that they underwent great modification; that he compelled a large portion of the public to acknowledge the mischief of our penal settlements; that he became the advocate of the wretched chimney sweepers, and their miseries were alleviated; that he contended against many of the unjust measures of the Church Reform Bill, and they were amended; that, whereas before his time, a man accused at the bar of a criminal court might be hanged before he had been half heard, now every prisoner has the benefit of a defence by counsel. It will further be freely acknowledged that no public writer was more successful than he in denouncing a political humbug, or demolishing a literary pretender; that he was on the whole an upright and benevolent man; and, as the world goes, a disinterested politician; that he had opportunities of improving his fortune, which he rejected; and, that, having lived with unostentatious respectability, he died without accumulating wealth.

A. Chevrillon in his book *Sydney Smith et la Renaissance des Idées libérales en Angleterre au XIX siècle* (Paris 1894) emphasises Sydney's wider influence in addition to these particular achievements. He quotes Lord Cockburn's *Memorial of his own time*: 'The change in an individual passing from youth to adulthood is not greater than the change which occurred in England from 1815 to 1830.' He continues,

By an inner labour, the English soul was transformed, a wind of pity began to blow, the heart of the nation expanded. By his writings in the midst of a régime of terror, at the moment when the crowd condemned as a revolutionary every man who raised his voice on behalf of the wretched, by his articles Sydney Smith inaugurated the great humanitarian movement of nineteenth-century England. . . . Like Sydney Smith at Foston and Combe Florey the English middle classes took a serious view of their duty towards the less fortunate. In fact in the nineteenth century, and in the nineteenth century alone, there appeared this noble type of gentleman. The

Whig idea as Sydney Smith conceived it was put into practice without being too much distorted, and this period is one of the fine movements of England when gentlemen govern for the sake of the common people.[1]

With this expansion of the English heart came, he writes, a corresponding freeing of their understanding from all abhorrence of reform, in which was always seen danger to 'Church and King'. So deeply rooted were these prejudices that J.S. Mill suggests that the greatest service rendered by the Reform Bill was not extending the suffrage, but showing that one could touch the constitution, and breaking the spell that seemed to numb England. It was Sydney forging the weapons and using them in the *Edinburgh Review* who demolished the Tory prejudices.

Sydney was an écrivan engagé in much of his writing, arguing his case with his readers in mind. 'Take care to make the justice of your cause so clear that it cannot be mistaken by the most illiterate gentleman who rides the earth,' he advised. And he used humour to sweeten the medicine, he who, in Hayward's words, 'could make the most irresistible wit and pleasantry the vehicle of the soundest and most unanswerable arguments'. Many of the liberal causes he championed were won long ago, but we can still enjoy the verve with which he writes and delight in the drollery that runs through all his work.

Even today so much remains relevant. Sydney can still speak to confirm our own late twentieth century enlightenment, as in his theories of education and the treatment of women; or to question it. He did not want England to intervene in the disputes of other nations; and we may well question whether the United Nations might have been more profitably engaged in these post-war years using its authority to control and diminish the arms trade rather than sending troops to troubled parts of the world. His fight against all forms of oppression, and his especial abhorrence of slavery, remind us that the fight must still continue, as the charities Anti-slavery and Survival International bear witness. His philippics against all that makes religion appear ridiculous, and his campaigning for religious toleration, put us on our guard against the growth of fundamentalism and fanaticism evident in the major religions. His many articles on the sufferings of the Irish people help us to understand the difficulty of finding a solution to the Irish problem today. His

1. Par un travail intérieur, l'âme anglaise s'est transformé, un vent de pitié s'est mis à souffler, le coeur de la nation s'est élargi. Par ses écrits, en plein régime de terreur, au moment où la foule honnit comme jacobin tout homme qui lève la voix en faveur d'une misère, par ses articles Sydney Smith inaugure le grand mouvement humanitaire de L'Angleterre au XIX siècle. . . . Comme Sydney Smith à Foston et à Combe Florey la bourgeoisie anglaise a conçu une notion sérieuse de son devoir envers les humbles. En effet, au XIX siècle, et au XIX siècle seulement, parait ce noble type du gentleman. L'idée Whig que conçoit Sydney Smith s'applique sans trop déformer dans la réalité, et cette période est une des beaux moments d'Angleterre où les gentlemen gouvernent pour le peuple.

criticism of bishops and their usurpation of more power causes us to reflect on the danger now of so much private patronage falling into their hands. His last battle through the columns of the *Morning Post* against the Great Western Railway raises a cheer from one who, helping a friend on to a train with his luggage at a small Devonshire station, found himself locked in, so brief was its halt there, and carried unwillingly to the next stop.

Some of the words he spoke or wrote deserve to be included in the perennial wisdom of aphorisms. For example of the Americans,

They are devout without being unjust: the great problem in religion.

Suspect all governments, for it is the constant tendency of those entrusted with power to conceive that they enjoy it through their own merits, and for their own use, and not by delegation, for the benefit of others.

What is the object of all government? The object of all government is roast mutton, potatoes, claret, a stout constable, an honest justice, a clear highway, a free chapel.

You must give me, not the best medicine in your shop, but the best medicine you can get me to take.'

We are convinced we have stated the greatest quantum of *attainable* good; which of course will not be attained, by the customary error of attending to what is desirable to be done, rather than what it is practicable to do.

On the more personal level, he can teach us much about how to live the good, sane, loving and happy life. He thought we were on earth to be as happy as we could and to keep each other as cheerful as we could.

Sir Edward Lytton-Bulmer once appended a note to a letter he had received from Sydney: 'His conversation was still more racy than his writing. His spirit was as joyous as Nature on a sunny day.' And to come to know someone with such a spirit, even at the remove of the printed page, is a singular privilege and pleasure.

Index

The Sydney Smith Association

The Sydney Smith Association was formed in 1996 in order

1. To perpetuate the memory and achievements of Sydney Smith.
2. To cultivate appreciation of the principles for which he stood.
3. To support the churches connected with his career.
4. To help in the preservation of mansucrits and memorabilia relating to him and his family.
5. To arrange periodic events, receptions and services in keeping with his inclinations.

Further information about the Association can be obtained from

The Membership Secretary
Sydney Smith Association
English Department
University of York
Heslington
YORK
Y01 5DD

Bronze statuette of Sydney Smith in Foston church.